SPREADING INK BLOTS

FROM DA NANG TO THE DMZ

The Origins and Implementation of US Marine Corps
Counterinsurgency Strategy in Vietnam
March 1965 to November 1968

David Strachan-Morris

Helion & Company Limited

For Karen and Grace

Helion & Company Limited
Unit 8 Amherst Business Centre
Budbrooke Road
Warwick
CV34 5WE
England
Tel. 01926 499619
Email: info@helion.co.uk
Website: www.helion.co.uk
X (formerly Twitter): @Helionbooks
Facebook: @HelionBooks
Visit our blog at https://helionbooks.wordpress.com/

Published by Helion & Company 2020. This paperback edition 2025
Designed and typeset by Battlefield Design (www.battlefield-design.co.uk)
Cover designed by Paul Hewitt, Battlefield Design (www.battlefield-design.co.uk)

ISBN 978-1-804517-79-6

British Library Cataloguing-in-Publication Data.
A catalogue record for this book is available from the British Library.

Contents

Acknowledgements iv
Acronyms v
Introduction 8

1 The State of the Art: Communist Revolutionary Warfare and Counterinsurgency in the Early 1960s 15
2 Development of USMC Counterinsurgency Doctrine in the 1960s and Preparations for Deployment to Vietnam 39
3 1965: USMC Deployment to Vietnam and the Evolving Mission 59
4 1966 – 1967: Developing the Strategy and Measuring Progress 86
5 1968: The Start of the General Offensive – General Uprising 116

Conclusion 138
Bibliography 143
Index 155

Acknowledgements

The first person I need to thank is my wife Karen, who has encouraged and supported this project for the entire time it took to research and write it (and put up with all the books around the house). She has accompanied me on my research trips, which often replaced holidays, and endured countless conferences and seminars, some of them in fairly remote and uncivilised parts of the world. Without her by my side to inspire me and keep me going this work would never have been completed.

I would like to thank my supervisory team for their advice and guidance during the PhD on which this book is based. Professor Mark Phythian helped me to start the project and mentored me through to the first complete draft before the move to Leicester, where he helped me find my feet in the academic world. Professor John Buckley provided an excellent second perspective on my work and guided me through the difficult final stretch. The insight and depth of knowledge provided by Professor Stephen Badsey, as well as his incredible attention to detail, were invaluable in the final run up to the viva.

The process of turning a PhD thesis into a book has been a long one and I would like to thank Dr Jacqueline Hazelton and Dr Andrew Mumford for their comments, encouragement, and support during that time. This would also not have been possible without the great team at Helion, Duncan Rogers and Dr Michael LoCicero.

Finally, there aren't enough words for me to express how grateful I am to the United States Marine Corps, which as an institution was unstinting in its support for this project. They provided most of the primary source material from their archives, encouraged my efforts and never displayed anything other than a positive attitude towards this examination from outside. At the History and Museums Division, when it was still in Washington DC, Colonel Jon Hoffman, Dr Jack Shulimson and Charles Melsom all spent a considerable amount of time talking to me about the Marines in Vietnam and helped me find the right sources – even allowing me to be the first foreign researcher to see General Greene's notes from the Joint Chiefs of Staff meetings. The staff at the Marine Corps Heritage Foundation and the Alfred M. Gray Research Center at the Marine Corps University in Quantico also provided considerable support during my research visits. I would also like to thank all the Marines, current and former, who took an interest in my research and talked to me about their experiences in Vietnam – particularly Dr Donald Bittner, at the Marine Corps Command and Staff College, and Robert 'Bud' McFarlane, a former Marine and National Security Advisor to President Ronald Reagan, who both helped correct some of my perceptions and provided some very useful information.

Acronyms

ARVN	Army of the Republic of Vietnam/South Vietnamese Army.
CAP	Combined Action Platoon.
CINCPAC	Commander in Chief Pacific.
CG	Commanding General (as in CG FMFPac).
COMUSMACV	Commander, US Military Assistance Command Vietnam
CORDS	Civil Operations and Revolutionary Development Support.
DRV	Democratic Republic of Vietnam. Also referred to as North Vietnam. See NVN.
FMFPac	Fleet Marine Force Pacific.
GVN	Government of Vietnam. Used in Marine Corps documents frequently to refer to the government of South Vietnam.
HES	Hamlet Evaluation System.
ICTZ	I Corps Tactical Zone. The military designation for the northern provinces of Vietnam to which the Marines were assigned,
JCS	Joint Chiefs of Staff.
MACV	Military Assistance Command Vietnam.
MAF	Marine Amphibious Force.
NVA	Common term for North Vietnamese Army. See PAVN.
NVN	North Vietnam. Often used in American official military or political documents. See DRV.
PAVN	People's Army of Vietnam. Correct term for North Vietnamese Army. See NVA.
RVN	Republic of Vietnam. Also referred to as South Vietnam. See SVN.
SVN	South Vietnam. Often used in American official military or political documents. See RVN.
VC	Viet Cong.

Map 1: Corps Areas of Responsibility in Vietnam.

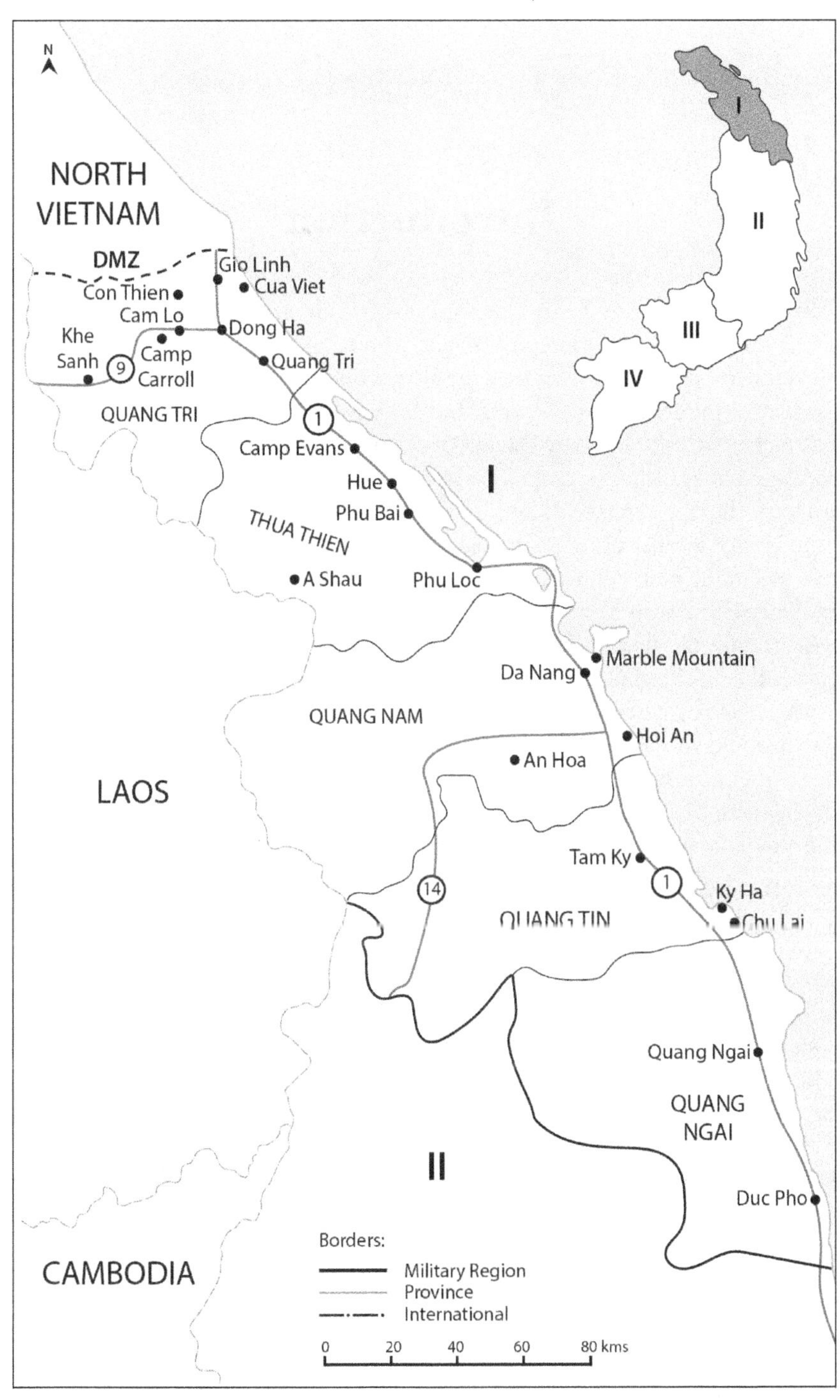

Map 2: Northern Provinces – I Corps Tactical Zone. (George Anderson)

Introduction

This volume takes its title from an approach to counterinsurgency first conceived by two French officers; General Joseph Gallieni, who talked of 'progressive occupation', and General Hubert Lyautey, who first used the phrase 'oil spots' to describe his strategy. During their service in Indochina, Madagascar, and Morocco they pioneered the techniques that would later be expanded upon by David Galula, another French officer, in Algeria and used by the United States Marine Corps (USMC) in Vietnam. The idea was to unite the civil and military effort, partner with local indigenous forces, and use economic and political means to 'pacify' local areas, then gradually expand outwards until the areas linked up and a whole region, or even country, was brought back under government control.[1] Unified civil-military effort with economic and political action being as important as the use of force is the core of what is now known as 'counterinsurgency'. The title of this book epitomises the US Marine Corps approach to counterinsurgency in Vietnam, in that the three bases it was assigned to defend on the coast were to be the centre of three large 'ink blots' that would spread until the entire coastal region within their area of operations was pacified from its southern boundary to the Demilitarised Zone (DMZ) at the border with North Vietnam.

The Vietnam War, also known as the Second Indochina War, was the result of the unsatisfactory end of the First Indochina War. This war, which last from 1946 until 1954, had ended with the French withdrawal from Vietnam and the temporary division of Vietnam along the 17th Parallel into two independent states, the Democratic Republic of Vietnam (DRV) in the north and the Republic of Vietnam (RVN) in the south.[2] One of the key elements of the Geneva Accords that had ended the Indochina War was that elections should be held in 1956 to settle the matter of Vietnamese reunification. These elections were never held as the newly elected President of South Vietnam, Ngo Dinh Diem, with the support and co-operation of the United States, managed to continually delay them. This refusal, and the subsequent operations against the VC by the South Vietnamese government, precipitated the insurgency that grew into the Vietnam War.

1 See Michael P.M. Finch, *A Progressive Occupation? The Gallieni-Lyautey Method and Colonial Pacification in Tonkin and Madagascar, 1885-1900* (Oxford: Oxford University Press, 2013) for analysis of the Gallieni-Lyautey Method.

2 The acronyms used for both entities vary, with American official sources using RVN and SVN (South Vietnam) interchangeably for the Republic of Vietnam and DRV or NVN (North Vietnam) for the Democratic Republic of Vietnam. In order to keep the acronyms to a minimum, this work will use the terms North and South Vietnam to refer to the entities.

In 1959, in the latter stages of the Eisenhower Administration, the United States began to commit advisors to assist the Army of the Republic of Vietnam (ARVN) under the proviso that they did not participate in combat operations.

Three years later, under the Kennedy Administration, the United States sent helicopter units and allowed advisors to take part in combat. In early August 1964 two US Navy warships reported that they had been fired on while conducting patrols close to the North Vietnamese coast in the Gulf of Tonkin. These attacks led to the passing of Congressional Joint Resolution 1145 (more commonly known as the Tonkin Resolution), giving the President the authority to 'take all necessary measures to repel any armed attack against the forces of the United States and to prevent further aggression' and, furthermore, 'to take all necessary steps, including the use of armed force, to assist any member or protocol state of the Southeast Asia Collective Defense Treaty requesting assistance in defense of its freedom'.[3] The facts surrounding the attacks have since been called into question, with many believing the Johnson Administration deliberately provoked them to provide a pretext for more direct action by the United States, although Secretary of Defense Robert McNamara believed the Tonkin Resolution would probably have passed even if the incident hadn't occurred, albeit with a more extensive debate.[4]

Little further major action was taken by the US until early February 1965, when the NVA attacked US Special Forces bases in Pleiku and Qui Nhon. The US response was Operation Rolling Thunder, a series of graduating bombing missions against North Vietnam. It was in this context and in order to defend three American bases on the coast in the northern provinces of South Vietnam from ground attacks that the 9th Marine Expeditionary Brigade landed at Da Nang on 8 March 1965.

This book examines one aspect of the Marines' war in Vietnam; the operational level decisions and rationale behind the use of counterinsurgency methods in the populated coastal areas in which the bases at Da Nang, Phu Bai, and Chu Lai were located. This focus on the operational level – specifically the III Marine Amphibious Force (III MAF), consisting of the 1st and 3rd Marine Divisions – is deliberate. This is the level at which strategy meets the 'art of the possible' as commanders have to implement their assigned tasks within the overall strategy. It is the level at which commanders have to decide how best to use the often limited resources available to them in conducting those tasks. The Marines were very tightly constrained when they first arrived in Vietnam, both by the task they were given and the forces at their disposal, which, even at their peak, consisted of two light infantry divisions heavily reliant on the US Navy for logistic support as well as crucial air cover and naval gunfire to fill the heavy artillery gap.

The Marines and the US Army approached the war in Vietnam from two different perspectives. To a certain extent this was inevitable, given their different histories, roles

3 US Congress, House, *Joint Resolution to Promote the Maintenance of International Peace and Security in Southeast Asia*, HR 1145, 88th Congress, 2nd Session, introduced in House August 10, 1964.

4 Robert McNamara, *In Retrospect* (New York, NY: Times Books, 1995), pp. 127-129.

and composition. Following the Korean War, the Marines had developed into a 'Force in Readiness', a rapidly deployable force that could take action in the world's littoral areas. The Corps was lightly equipped, relying on naval gunfire support and its own integral air capability to provide the firepower it lacked. It did not have a large logistic component and thus, did not have the 'staying power' of the Army. It was envisaged that in any future conflict the Marines' role would be to conduct relatively short small to medium scale operations or, if required, establish a beachhead from which the Army would conduct major offensive operations further inland.[5] In contrast the US Army, which had much larger divisions in terms of manpower with heavier organic artillery, was designed primarily for positional and attritional warfare.

This disparity in approach led to tensions between the senior officers of both services in the early years of the Vietnam War, because not only did they have different operational outlooks and resources they also disagreed to a large extent over the manner in which the war as a whole should be conducted. General Victor Krulak, who as Commanding General Fleet Marine Force Pacific (CG FMFPac) had administrative but not operational control over the Marines in Vietnam, had previously been Special Advisor on Counterinsurgency to the Joint Chiefs of Staff and had determined that pacification, or a war for the 'hearts and minds', of the people was a more appropriate countermeasure to the Viet Cong insurgency. In addition to winning the support of the people, this approach also involved the creation of local security forces as a 'force multiplier'. The Marines had come to appreciate the importance of this in the first half of the 20th Century in counterguerrilla warfare when this had allowed their small and lightly armed forces in the Caribbean to make use of these techniques to mitigate the lack of resources.[6] General William Westmoreland, Commander US Military Assistance Command Vietnam (COMUSMACV), and in overall command of all US forces in-country, was a former artillery officer and airborne divisional commander, who is often characterised as being wedded to positional and attritional warfare in Vietnam.[7] General Lewis Walt, commander of III Marine Amphibious Force (III MAF) between 1965 and 1967, admitted that he had no real preconceptions about the war because he did not come to understand it until his arrival. He wrote that in his view counterinsurgency was more appropriate to achieve his initial mission of defending the air bases in the coastal region and was based on the principles he had been taught as a junior officer by the veterans of the Caribbean guerrilla wars.[8]

5 General Victor Krulak, *First to Fight* (Annapolis, MD: Naval Institute Press, 1984), pp. 18-38 and Alan R. Millett *Semper Fidelis: A History of the United States Marine Corps*, (New York, NY: The Free Press, 1991), pp. 524-527.

6 Keith Bickel, *Mars Learning: The Marine Corps Development of Small Wars Doctrine, 1915-1940* (Boulder, CO: Westview Press, 2001), pp. 75-76.

7 General William C. Westmoreland, *A Soldier Reports* (New York: Da Capo, 1989), p. 153.

8 Colin Leinster, "The Two Wars of General Walt", *Life Magazine*, 26 May 1967, p. 83; General Lewis Walt, *Strange War, Strange Strategy* (New York, NY: Funk & Wagnall's, 1970), p. 29.

The argument being made here about counterinsurgency is still an important one. The Vietnam War cast its shadow on later wars and the tensions between the apparent positions of Krulak and Westmoreland still exist within current debates on counterinsurgency. The wars in Iraq and Afghanistan in the early 21st Century led to a new wave of thinking and writing on counterinsurgency, reaching its apex with the publication of Field Manual 3-24 *Counterinsurgency* in the United States at the end of 2006, which drew heavily upon work from the so-called 'classical era' of counterinsurgency (1940s to the late 1960s) as well as contemporary expertise.[9] The writing team was led by Lieutenant General David Petraeus, who had written his PhD thesis on the US Army in Vietnam, and consisted of some of the most influential counterinsurgency experts at the time such as John Nagl, author of *Learning to Eat Soup with a Knife: Counterinsurgency Lessons from Malaya and Vietnam*,[10] and David Kilcullen, later to become the author of *The Accidental Guerrilla: Fighting Small Wars in the Midst of a Big One*,[11] whose influential *Twenty-Eight Articles; Fundamentals of Company Level Counterinsurgency* was incorporated into FM3-24 as Appendix A.[12] Taking the term from *FM3-24* counterinsurgency became known as 'the graduate level of warfare' with the leading military experts, most of whom held PhDs, hailed as a new generation of warrior-scholars. Their ultimate vindication seemed to come during 'the surge' in Iraq in 2007 when a significant increase in the numbers of American troops and the appointment of General Petraeus as commander provided the opportunity to test the new manual. By the end of the year violence had indeed decreased and General Petraeus reported to Congress that 'the military objectives' of the surge were 'in large part, being met'.[13] But *FM 3-24* was an incredibly complex document in which counterinsurgency became a multi-dimensional, multi-agency effort with instructions that ranged from national level coordination with a host nation government down to vignettes on how to defuse a tense situation with a potentially hostile crowd. Counterinsurgency became conflated with nation-building and claims for its effectiveness overreached themselves.

Counterinsurgency, and the ideas behind it, very quickly came under scrutiny from sceptical military officers and critical academics, leading to acrimonious exchanges in the

9 HQ Department of the Army, *Field Manual 3-24: Counterinsurgency* (Washington DC: HQ Department of the Army, 2006). Simultaneously published by the US Marine Corps as *Marine Corps Warfighting Publication 3-33.5: Counterinsurgency.*

10 John Nagl, *Learning to Eat Soup with a Knife: Counterinsurgency Lessons from Malaya and Vietnam* (Chicago, IL: University of Chicago Press, 2005).

11 David Kilcullen, *The Accidental Guerrilla: Fighting Small Wars in the Midst of a Big One* (London: Charles Hurst & Co (Publishers(Ltd), 2009).

12 David Kilcullen, 'Twenty Eight Articles: Fundamentals of Company Level Counterinsurgency', *Military Review*83:3, (May-June 2006), pp. 103-108; HQ Dept of the Army, *FM 3-24*, Appendix A.

13 General David Petraeus, 'Report to the US House of Representatives on the Situation in Iraq', *Testimony to the US House of Representatives Committee on Foreign Affairs and Armed Services Committee*, 10 September 2007 <https://2001-2009.state.gov/p/nea/rls/rm/2007/91966.htm> (Last accessed July 2019).

press and academic journals. At one point the two schools of thought became divided into 'COINdinistas' and 'COINtras'; a play on words from the conflict in Nicaragua in which pro-government 'Sandinistas' fought anti-government 'Contras'.[14] The most vociferous critic of the complex counterinsurgency approach advocated in *FM 3-24* was Colonel Gian Gentile of the US Army. He argued that far from vindicating the manual, the surge in Iraq was largely successful because of external factors; the Shia militias stood down and many Sunni leaders not aligned to al-Qaeda were being paid off.[15] But interest in counterinsurgency moved outside the military and military history realm as more academics started to take an interest. Jacqueline Hazelton took a social sciences approach to counterinsurgency and surveyed Malaya, Oman, and El Salvador. Her subsequent article *The 'Hearts and Minds' Fallacy: Violence, Coercion, and Success in Counterinsurgency* argued that the so-called 'good governance' solution proposed by most of the counterinsurgency literature didn't explain the successes because few of the governments involved carried out any significant reforms and that most of the literature played down or ignored the extent to which violence (against the insurgents) and coercion (against the civilian population) played a part in the successes.[16] Andrew Mumford argued, after analysing the British experiences in counterinsurgency since the Second World War, that counterinsurgency remains relevant but there is no template that can be applied because each campaign is different, particularly in the modern globalised world, and when template solutions have been applied they have often been based on only selected elements of previous campaigns. Studying previous campaigns is important, however, to help speed up the learning process that takes place at the start of every new campaign; although there is no template for counterinsurgency this does not mean that there are no lessons that can be learned from previous experiences.[17]

This last point is where the US Marine Corps experience in Vietnam becomes significant. General Walt's approach to the war and his application of counterinsurgency triangulates between the positions on counterinsurgency, and has relevance for today. He had no illusions about counterinsurgency as a war-winning strategy, nor did he have a ready-made template. He had lessons learned from previous campaigns upon which he could draw and he allowed the Marines under his command to develop other solutions

14 David E. Johnston, *Doing What You Know: The United States and 250 Years of Irregular Warfare* (Washington, DC: Centre for Strategic and Budgetary Analysis, 2017), p. 4. The terms appear formally in articles and informally throughout online discussions on counterinsurgency.

15 Gian Gentile, 'Misreading the Surge Threatens US Army's Conventional Capabilities', *World Politics Review*, 4 March 2009 <https://www.worldpoliticsreview.com/articles/1715/misreading-the-surge-threatens-u-s-armys-conventional-capabilities> (Last accessed July 2019). See also Gian Gentile, *Wrong Turn: America's Deadly Embrace of Counterinsurgency* (New York: The New Press, 2013).

16 Jacqueline L. Hazelton, 'The "Hearts and Minds" Fallacy: Violence, Coercion, and Success in Counterinsurgency', *International Security*, 42:1 (Summer 2017), pp. 80-113.

17 Andrew Mumford, *The Counterinsurgency Myth: The British Experience of Irregular Warfare* (Abingdon, Oxon: Routledge, 2012), pp. 148-150.

to unique problems. Counterinsurgency was one item from an operational toolkit that he used to achieve one of the missions he was given.

This book focuses on the period between March 1965 and November 1968 because it is covers both the first landing of the Marines in Vietnam and the end of the Tet Offensive and the election of Richard Nixon on a platform of 'peace with honour' and gradual 'Vietnamisation' that signalled the start of the withdrawal of US ground forces and the beginning of the end of the American involvement in Vietnam. The Marines' efforts at pacification had also peaked by November 1968; the effects of the Tet Offensive, the battle for Khe Sanh and the construction of the barrier along the Demilitarized Zone had depleted resources in the coastal areas. General Cushman, III MAF Commander in November 1968, explained the threat from the north...drained the resources from pacification. I would say it prevented us from doing more pacification'.[18] Much of the responsibility for pacification had been handed over to the Civil Operations and Revolutionary Development Support (CORDS) programme under Robert Komer by late 1968, and therefore was less of an integral part of Marine operations than it had been up to that time. The period chosen, therefore, allows the best opportunity to study the evolution of counterinsurgency at the operational level and gauge its success by the time the United States began to contemplate withdrawal from Vietnam.

Most of the research for this book is based upon documents produced by the Marines during the Vietnam War. These include field manuals; command chronologies written at Command, Force, and Divisional level; statistical data gathered by the Marines; and, importantly, declassified private communications between Marine commanders that reveal their attitudes and opinions. Official letters and reports written by senior Marine officers have also been used, as well as transcripts of interviews conducted by the Oral History Department of the US Marine Corps History and Museums Division. Perhaps the most significant source was the private papers of General Wallace Greene, Commandant of the US Marine Corps between January 1964 and December 1967. In defiance of the convention that members of the Joint Chiefs of Staff (JCS) would not keep private records of their meetings, Greene did in fact write a series of Memoranda for the Record. These memoranda give detailed insight into the manner in which the Marines thought the war should be fought and the advice given by Greene to President Johnson. The memoranda also detail the animosity between the Marines and the US Army; a key element in the later operational tensions between senior commanders of both services in Vietnam. Other Marine sources include the books written after the war by the two senior commanders in Vietnam between 1965 and 1968, *First to Fight* by General Victor Krulak and *Strange War, Strange* Strategy by General Walt. Contemporaneous documents produced by both officers and media interviews with them have also contributed to the primary research. Although no formal interviews were conducted, several research visits

18 Jack Shulimson, Lt Col Leonard Blaisol, Charles Smith and Capt David Dawson, *US Marines in Vietnam: The Defining Year 1968* (Washington, DC: History and Museums Division, US Marine Corps, 1997), p. 608.

to the US Marine Corps History and Museums Division provided the opportunity to talk with many officers who served in Vietnam including Robert 'Bud' McFarlane, who later served as National Security Advisor under President Ronald Reagan.

This work consists of five chapters. The first two examine the intellectual antecedents of the Marines' strategy and development of their counterinsurgency doctrine and the last three chapters contain analysis of the implementation and effectiveness of the strategy. Chapter 1 provides an examination of the 'state of the art' in counterinsurgency thinking in the early 1960s, starting with Mao Zedong and his concept of protracted war and moving on to General Vo Nguyen Giap and the Vietnamese three stage strategy. It will also outline the work of the major counterinsurgency theorists of the time in order to help situate many of the actions taken by the Marines as their counterinsurgency strategy evolved in Vietnam. Chapter 2 analyses the development of Marine doctrine in the early 1960s, and their preparations for deployment to Vietnam. Chapter 3 covers the first year of the Marines' deployment, 1965 and explains the evolution of their strategy into one that relied on pacification as their area of responsibility expanded. It will introduce the concept of counterinsurgency as 'defence in depth', as the Marines used pacification to control the areas around the airfields they were sent to defend rather than as a means to actively defeat the enemy. Chapter 4 covers the period of the build-up of Marine units to their final total strength in Vietnam during 1966 and 1967, looking at the transition from a defensive role to one that combined defence in the coastal areas with offence in the highlands and border areas. Chapter 5 chronicles the Tet Offensive and examines the effectiveness of the defence in depth the Marines had created around the coastal bases by means of counterinsurgency. The concluding chapter will argue that a number of factors caused the Marine Corps to be pre-disposed to fight in the way they did in Vietnam. The infrastructure of the Corps, its intellectual background in 'small wars' and initial posture in Vietnam all called for a population-centric strategy based around the coastal airfields, which were in relatively densely populated areas. It will summarise the argument that counterinsurgency is a useful operational level tool but is not to be conflated with nation building, nor is it enough by itself to win wars.

1

The State of the Art: Communist Revolutionary Warfare and Counterinsurgency in the Early 1960s

The Vietnam War followed on from the partially successful guerrilla war fought by Ho Chi Minh and his military commander, General Vo Nguyen Giap, against the French during the First Indochina War. They had managed to create an independent state in the northern part of French Indochina, but the southern part remained under control of the regime left in place after the French withdrawal in 1954. The strategy used by Ho Chi Minh and General Giap during the First Indochina War was a refinement of Mao Tse Tung's principles of communist revolutionary warfare, which had been used to great effect in China between 1928 and 1949. During this time the Chinese communists managed to evolve from a relatively small movement to a force strong enough to assist in the defeat of the Japanese and then conduct a successful civil war against the Chinese nationalist forces. In the immediate aftermath of this victory, Southeast Asian communists embarked on two further overlapping insurgencies; an ultimately successful one against the French in Vietnam and an unsuccessful one against the British in Malaya. By the time the Marines became involved in Vietnam these two wars, along with the ongoing insurgency in Algeria, generated a considerable body of insurgency and counterinsurgency expertise. Mao Tse Tung's works on revolutionary war were much in circulation and General Giap published a book that described his campaign against the French.[1] Both were extensively covered in professional military literature at the time; an electronic search of the *Marine Corps Gazette* archives revealed 90 articles mentioning Mao and 19 mentioning Giap between January 1950 and March 1965. British counterinsurgency experts wrote about what they did in Malaya to defeat the communist guerrillas there and French counterinsurgency experts wrote about what they thought they should have done to defeat the insurgents in Vietnam and Algeria.[2]

1 General Vo Nguyen Giap, *People's War, People's Army: The Viet Cong Insurrection Manual for Underdeveloped Countries* (Honolulu, HI: University Press of the Pacific, 2001) reprinted from 1961 edition.

2 Key examples include: Sir Robert Thompson's *Defeating Communist Insurgency*, (St Petersburg,

Marine methods in Vietnam were based on their understanding of communist revolutionary war, as previously practised by their opponents and the expertise of the prevailing counterinsurgency theorists of the time, most of whom lectured extensively at American military training establishments, published numerous books on the subject, and conducted research at American institutions such as the RAND Corporation. Although the Marines had extensive experience fighting guerrillas, gained in the early 20th Century this had been overshadowed by the Second World War and the Korean War, during which these skills had been pushed to the background. By the time the Marines entered the Vietnam War, the veterans of the earlier guerrilla wars had left the Corps and military schools in the United States were teaching the more recent lessons learned by the British and the French in Malaya and Vietnam.[3]

What follows is a summary of what was understood by counterinsurgency experts at the time – the 'state of the art' when the US Marines were deployed in Vietnam. While the literature of the time contained much useful material for operational level counterinsurgency, an excessive focus on the political nature of the insurgency in Vietnam and overstated claims for what counterinsurgency could achieve contributed to a lack of understanding of the true utility of counterinsurgency and what its limitations were.

Communist Revolutionary Warfare

An early member of the Chinese Communist Party, Mao Tse Tung had manoeuvred his way to command of the Red Army (the armed wing of the party) by 1930 through a combination of political manoeuvring and terror.[4] He then led the army in an almost continual war for the next 20 years against the invading Japanese Army and the Chinese Nationalists until, eventually, the whole of China was brought under Communist rule. Mao's strategy rested on three elements: the need to fight a protracted war against a stronger enemy; reliance on the support of the people; and a phased campaign of political activity, guerrilla warfare and an all-out 'conventional' positional warfare. Mao's thoughts on communist revolutionary warfare were promulgated in a series of lengthy speeches at the Communist Party Plenum in Yenan in 1938 that were later collected in two volumes entitled *On Protracted War* and *Problems of Strategy in Guerrilla War against Japan*. In these speeches Mao explained how a peasant army could defeat a modern well-resourced

FL: Hailer Publishing, 2005) first published in 1966; David Galula's *Counterinsurgency Warfare: Theory and Practice* (Westport, CT: Praeger Security International, 2006), first published in 1964: and Roger Trinquier's *Modern Warfare: A French View of Counterinsurgency* (Westport, CT: Praeger Security International, 2006), first published in 1964.

3 Colonel John F. Greenwood, comments on draft manuscript of Jack Shulimson and Major Charles Johnson, *US Marines in Vietnam: The Landing and the Buildup: 1965* (Washington, DC: US Marine Corps History and Museums Division, 1978), p. 133.

4 See Jung Chang and Jon Halliday, *Mao: The Unknown Story* (London: Vintage, 2006) for a detailed account of Mao's rise to power and subsequent rule of China.

army and why a lengthy campaign was preferable to attempting a quick defeat of the Japanese.[5]

Mao's point was that the apparent weaknesses of the Chinese – their relative poverty and lack of advanced military forces – were more than compensated for by their superior numbers and growing industrial base, which would be able to eventually defeat the Japanese in a lengthy campaign that would sap their strength. He recognised that the Japanese military was hampered by its logistical demands, which drained resources and placed a considerable strain on the Japanese economy – a strain that would eventually become unbearable and force a Japanese withdrawal. Importantly, Mao also recognised that over time Japan would lose international support and the Chinese would be able to capitalise on worldwide sympathy, a key factor that the North Vietnamese capitalised on in dealing with the United States some 30 years later.[6]

Mao's strategy boiled down to a three-stage war against the Japanese and the Nationalists. He said that '[t]he first stage covers the period of the enemy's strategic offensive and our strategic defensive. The second stage will be the period of the enemy's strategic consolidation and our preparation for the counter-offensive. The third stage will be the period of our strategic counter-offensive and the enemy's strategic retreat'.[7] He conducted his war as a linear progression, moving from one stage to the other over the course of 20 years.

When the Vietnamese communists commenced their guerrilla war against the French they followed much the same strategy, although it should be pointed out that this was not their first choice. Ho Chi Minh generated sufficient support to fill the power vacuum left by the Japanese after their surrender in August 1945. During the so-called 'August Revolution' the Viet Minh gained control of Hanoi as well as much of the rest of Vietnam and Ho Chi Minh declared an independent 'Democratic Republic of Vietnam' on 2nd September 1945. By November 1946, however, the Viet Minh were ousted from Hanoi when the French retook the city, following almost a year of inconclusive negotiations, and they retreated to pre-prepared positions in the rural areas of the north. It was at this point that Ho Chi Minh and his military commanders decided to adopt Mao's three stage protracted war strategy, adding the lessons they had learned during the Second World War and the August Revolution.[8]

After their initial defeat in 1947, the Viet Minh turned to guerrilla war but instead of a linear progression, General Giap chose a more pragmatic approach in which the Viet Minh strategy would move up and down the scale of revolutionary war depending on the situation. Their strategy depended on two key elements; a military campaign and a

5 Mao Tse Tung, *On Protracted War*, from the *Selected Works of Mao Tse-tung*, Foreign Languages Press, Peking 1967 Vol. II <http://www.marx2mao.com/Mao/PW38.html#s1> (Accessed July 2019), pp. 119-120.

6 Mao Tse Tung, *On Protracted War*, pp. 122-123

7 Mao Tse Tung, *On Protracted War*, pp. 136-137.

8 David Marr, *Vietnam 1945: The Quest for Power* (Berkley, CA: University of California Press, 1997),

social/political campaign. Although both will be dealt with separately here, the two were inseparable in the Vietnamese communist notion of war, encapsulated in the phrase *dau tranh* or 'struggle'. *Dau tranh* consisted of the armed struggle (*dau tranh vu trang*) and political struggle (*dau tranh chinh tri*). The concept of both is ingrained in every recruit to the People's Army of Vietnam (PAVN) and is 'all important to the revolutionary. It shapes his thinking, fixes his attitudes, dictates his behaviour. His life, his revolutionary work, his whole world is *dau tranh* '.[9] The two elements of the struggle were mutually supporting, in that whichever one was emphasised would always be underpinned by the other in a delicate balancing act dictated by the situation. It was important to the Vietnamese communists to know 'how to give to the struggle [the] forms appropriate to the political situation at each stage…At the beginning, the political struggle was the main task, the armed struggle a secondary one. Gradually both the political struggle and the armed struggle became equally important. Later, we went forward to the stage where the armed struggle occupied the key role'.[10] The three phases in the Vietnamese strategy were:

> *Phase One*: Guerrilla warfare, also referred to as the defensive phase where the enemy has the strategic advantage. This relied on the political mobilisation of the people in order to 'unremittingly strengthen national solidarity and endeavour to smash all the enemies schemes to divide and deceive our people'.[11]
>
> *Phase Two*: Mobile Warfare, also referred to as the 'equilibrium phase' in which the forces begin to balance but the insurgents still do not have the strength to tip the strategic balance in their favour. In this phase the insurgents conduct larger operations designed to bleed the enemy's strength while at the same time continuing the guerrilla war and their efforts to secure the support of the general population. Giap was careful to stress that this was not a sudden change from one to the other, but a gradual shift to larger operations over time. In the war against the French, Giap 'had to hold firm the co-ordination between the two forms, the chief one being guerrilla warfare; mobile warfare was of lesser importance but was on the upgrade. Then came a new and higher stage, mobile warfare moved on to the main position, at first, only on one battlefield…then on an ever wider scope. During this time, guerrilla warfare extended but…moved back from the main position to a lesser but still important one …'.[12]

9 Douglas Pike, *PAVN: People's Army of Vietnam* (New York, NY: Da Capo, 1986), p. 217. Although PAVN is the more correct name, the form North Vietnamese Army (NVA) will be used in this work to maintain consistency with normal usage in the vast majority of primary sources.

10 Giap, *People's War, People's Army*, p. 76.

11 Giap, *People's War, People's Army*, p. 97.

12 Giap, *People's War, People's Army*, p.109.

> *Phase Three*: General Counteroffensive. By this phase the insurgents have built up sufficient conventional forces to gain numerical superiority and at least parity in equipment, while at the same time having worn down the enemy's morale and 'will to win' to such an extent that victory is virtually assured. The forces necessary to carry out this phase were generated during the first two phases, which required that they be fairly protracted as in the Maoist model of revolutionary war. The Vietnamese needed to keep the war going to buy time to create a first rate army, while at the same time wearing down the French forces and undermining their morale. This is an almost entirely conventional campaign, but again the transition is gradual. In this phase attacks become larger in scale and the targets are now fortified locations rather than mobile columns. In the war against the French, Giap launched a series of offensives before the final assault on Dien Bien Phu rather like a boxer delivers a flurry of punches to disorient his opponent before delivering the knockout punch.[13]

After the defeat of the French in 1954 and the failure to hold the elections agreed on at the Geneva Accords, a debate opened up within the ranks of the northern leadership about the strategy to be used to 'liberate' the south. General Giap favoured building up the North Vietnamese economy while conducting a similar protracted war in the south to that which had been fought in the north. Another faction, which included the eventual commander of the Viet Cong, General Nguyen Chi Tanh, favoured an almost immediate armed insurrection. The first faction held sway until 1960, when the apparently effective methods used against the communists by South Vietnamese Prime Minister Diem convinced the Politburo to act swiftly. In 1959 the first 4,000 cadres moved south to augment the nascent Viet Cong organisation that had been formed by the Communists in the south – the successor organisation to the Viet Minh. In 1960, the first battalion-sized operations were carried out by the Viet Cong and by 1961 the Diem regime was in serious difficulties under the combined weight of the insurrection and the general lawlessness that existed outside the main urban areas.[14]

Even though the North Vietnamese made the decision to accelerate the campaign in the south and begin the guerrilla war almost immediately, they still needed to conduct a parallel political struggle to gain the support of the population. The Viet Cong established an efficient supply system along the Ho Chi Minh Trail, through Laos and Cambodia, parallel to the Vietnamese border, but they were still heavily reliant on the local population in the coastal areas for supplies, transport, intelligence, safe havens and recruits to replace battle casualties. In order to secure food supplies to the VC Main Force and NVA units in South Vietnam, for example, the VC needed to control the population in the rice-growing areas, or at least be in a position to intimidate them into parting with a proportion of their crop. The VC needed to establish 'base areas' in the south to

13 Giap, *People's War, People's Army*, pp. 163-165.

14 Philip Davidson, *Vietnam at War* (Oxford: Oxford University Press, 1991), pp. 287-29.

support the guerrillas. These base areas were needed to have 'a closely integrated complex of villages prepared for defence; a politically indoctrinated population in which even children have their specific intelligence task; a network of food and weapons dumps; an administrative machine parallel to that of the legal authority, to which may be added any regular unit assigned to operations in the area'.[15]

The VC was also structured in the same way as the Viet Minh, although there was no intention of building a regular army in the south; that role would be filled by the NVA. The VC consisted of two elements; the paramilitary force and the Main Force.[16] The paramilitary force was itself broken down into two elements; the 'village guerrillas', who were essentially local defence volunteers, and the 'combat guerrillas', who would serve in a support role to the Main Force. These elements can be equated to the Popular Forces and Regional Forces in the Viet Minh. The VC Main Force, which equated to the Regular Forces in the Viet Minh, was made up of self-sufficient guerrilla units organised as independent companies, operating at a regional level, and battalions, which could either operate alone or come together as regiments for large-scale operations. The Main Force was expected to be self-sufficient, relying on the local population for food and clothing and stealing weapons and ammunition from government forces. As with the Viet Minh, each level of guerrilla force acted as a pool of recruits for the next level up.[17]

The fact that the North Vietnamese politburo took the decision to accelerate the pace of the armed struggle did not reduce the importance of the political struggle, since that too had to be accelerated in order to support the guerrillas and create the conditions necessary for the General Counteroffensive. The total integration of the local population into the fight meant that the political struggle had to keep pace, or even be ahead of, the armed struggle to ensure the necessary support structure was in place. While the armed struggle was engaged in wearing down the South Vietnamese and American military forces, the political struggle was engaged in securing the support of the people of South Vietnam.

In December 1965 Ho Chi Minh, realising that the war would take much longer following the introduction of US ground forces, announced a three-point strategy: first, the government and the army would ensure that they were able to protect themselves in the North, but would also support war activities in the South; second, in South Vietnam priority would be given to guerrilla warfare rather than 'conventional' big-unit warfare; third, more effort and resources would be put into the political education of the people of the whole of Vietnam, so as to convince them that they would win in the end.[18] This is entirely in keeping with Maoist guerrilla strategy; to play the long game in the face of a conventionally superior enemy.

15 George Tanham, *Communist Revolutionary Warfare: The Vietminh in Indochina* (London: Methuen, 1962), p. 25.

16 'Main Force' capitalized here as this was common usage at the time; The US military referred to VC Main Force units as such.

17 Douglas Pike, *Viet Cong*, pp. 233-240.

18 Peter MacDonald, *Giap: The Victor in Vietnam* (London: Warner Books, 1993), p. 199.

The political struggle to gain the support of, and control over, the population in the south was more than a means to an end for the Vietnamese communists. It was in fact also a vital war aim. The politburo would almost certainly have learned the lessons of the First Indochina War, during which it had failed to gain a meaningful foothold amongst the more politically and religiously diverse population of the south. The Vietnamese communists needed to ensure that by the end of the war they had not only gained sufficient support to win, but that they would be in a position to crush the potential opposition to their rule from Catholics, Buddhists, nationalists, *Cao Dai*, *Hoa Hao* and *Binh Xhuyen.*[19] When the war ended in May 1975 the importance placed on post-war control of the population rapidly became apparent as the North Vietnamese capitalised on their network of political cadre members and military presence to dominate the south. The members of the South Vietnamese Provisional Revolutionary Government (PRG), who had expected to govern an autonomous (if not independent) South Vietnam, realised that the North Vietnamese had expended a great deal of time and energy preparing for the eventual reunification of the entire country under the Hanoi government. Although the North Vietnamese were caught out by the speed of their offensive, having planned to fight until at least 1976, they were able to exploit the 'shock effect' and people in the south, including the *Hoa Hao* sect, flocked to the communist banner rather than take the risk of forming an opposition.[20]

Counterinsurgency, Pacification and 'Hearts and Minds'

By the late 1950s it was becoming clear that insurgencies were proliferating, and they became the subject of serious and sustained study by military experts in the west. Prompted by Nikita Khrushchev's declaration of Soviet support for 'wars of national liberation' in 1961, western armies responded by bringing counterinsurgency more into the mainstream of military doctrine. Most of the work of that time was written by British and French veterans of their wars in Malaya, Indochina and Algeria. Although the US Army had learned some useful lessons during its advisory role during the 'Huk' rebellion in the Philippines in the 1950s, dissemination of this experience appears to have been quite limited in the 1950s and 1960s.[21] Whilst derived from very different experiences,

19 Although Sir Robert Thompson, who was with the British Military Mission as an advisor in Vietnam at the time, was of the opinion that the Viet Cong had already reached an agreement with the *Hoa Hoa* as early as 1966 or 1967. Thompson, *No Exit From Vietnam*, pp. 151-152.

20 Gabriel Kolko, *Anatomy of a War* (New York: New Press, 1994), pp. 535-538.

21 Only one major work appears to have been written about the Philippine Insurrection of the 1950s. This was Napolean D. Valeriano and Charles T.R. Bohannan's *Counter-Guerrilla Operations: The Philippine Experience* (New York, NY: Praeger Security International Paperback, 2006), first published in 1962. Edward Lansdale, an advisor to the Philippine government during the insurrection was a prominent counterinsurgency expert in the 1960s who worked extensively in Southeast Asia and held senior positions in the Department of Defense but did not write of his experiences until his autobiography in 1972 – *In the Midst of Wars* (New York, NY:

the counterinsurgency methods put forward by these experts all put the war for and among the people at their core. Among those who particularly influenced contemporary counterinsurgency thinking were Sir Robert Thompson, David Galula and Roger Trinquier – all veterans of the campaigns in Malaya, Indochina and Algeria. Between them they articulated strategies that they believed would counter the full-spectrum armed and political *dau tranh* campaign that had proved so successful in Southeast Asia.

Thompson had been the Permanent Secretary for Defence during the Malayan Emergency between 1948 and 1960, when British forces were fighting Chinese Communist insurgents, and was one of the principal advisors to General Gerald Templer, British High Commissioner of Malaya between 1952 and 1954, whose ideas regarding the importance of winning hearts and minds turned the tide against the insurgents. Although Thompson's first book on counterinsurgency, *Defeating Communist Insurgency*,[22] was not published until 1966, his influence on the Marines counterinsurgency strategy was the result of his work with the British Advisory Mission to Vietnam, which led to regular visits to the White House in the early 1960s. His advice to the South Vietnamese and US Governments eventually led to the 'Strategic Hamlets Program', which was an attempt to replicate the programme the British had used to resettle and improve the lives of Chinese squatters who were living in or near guerrilla safe havens in Malaya during the Emergency.[23] During these visits he met with President Kennedy and the Special Assistant to the Joint Chiefs of Staff for Counterinsurgency Activities, Major General Victor Krulak USMC.[24] Thompson's ideas had a significant effect on Krulak who, as Commanding General Fleet Marine Force Pacific at the time the Marines first deployed to Vietnam, was able to exert considerable influence upon Marine Corps strategy and ensure that it developed along the lines advocated by Thompson.[25]

David Galula served as a company-level officer in Algeria and Indochina and later worked at the RAND Corporation, while Roger Trinquier was a renowned leader of indigenous forces in Vietnam and commander of a parachute regiment in Algeria. Although the French experience had been different to that of the British, officers at battalion and company level, such as Galula and Trinquier, had seen limited success when they applied

Fordham University Press, 1991), Thus the Philippine lessons were more than likely to have been disseminated by virtue of an individual's influence than through publication.

22 Sir Robert Thompson. *Defeating Communist Insurgency* (St Petersburg, FL: Hailer Publishing, Florida, 2005), Reprint of 1966 edition.

23 A description of how Thompson's advice was merged with that of the US Military Assistance Advisory Group can be found in the *Pentagon Papers, Gravel Edition*, Vol. 2, Chapter 2 <http://www.mtholyoke.edu/acad/intrel/pentagon2/pent4.htm> (Accessed July 2019)

24 Although Krulak makes frequent references to Thompson it is not clear how many times the two men actually met. Thompson makes no mention of Krulak in any of his writings but Krulak refers to 'several meetings' in *First to Fight*. It is highly probable, however, that due to his position Krulak would have attended meetings where Thompson was present and been familiar with Thompson's ideas through reading documents produced by, or relating to, Thompson and his counterinsurgency advice to the US and South Vietnamese governments.

25 Lt. Gen. Victor Krulak, *First to Fight* (Annapolis: Naval Institute Press, 1984), p. 180.

a combination of military action (in particular small unit tactics) and civil affairs in their respective areas of operation. In *Pacification in Algeria 1956 – 1958* Galula describes how he achieved some limited success in his twin goals of 'destroying or expelling the large rebel bands' and eventually 'winning [the population] over' by providing security for the local population, conducting civil affairs projects and attempting to replace rebel control over the villages in his area of operations with local leadership.[26] While Trinquier's ideas on the use of small units and self-defence forces were adopted by the US Army's Special Forces in Vietnam, particularly with the successful use of Montagnard tribesmen in the jungle highlands, his advocacy of the use of torture, albeit briefly and for a specific purpose, is considered counter-productive to say the least in modern counterinsurgency warfare.[27]

The ideas put forward by Thompson, Galula, and Trinquier (and, in fact, most of their contemporary colleagues) were intended to counter both the armed *and* political campaigns fought by the insurgents, particularly the Viet Cong operating in South Vietnam. They believed that the support of the local population was of paramount importance and that, therefore, counterinsurgency operations should concentrate upon providing protection from the insurgents and persuading the population to choose to support the government rather than supporting, or even joining, the insurgency. This was the 'battle for the hearts and minds' of the people, to use the phrase that first gained currency during the British campaign in Malaya. The basis of a hearts and minds campaign was more than simply providing welfare to the population to buy their support or gratitude, which had been a mistake made by some French troops in Algeria, who assumed that it was enough to 'be kind' in order to pacify an area.[28] A hearts and minds campaign should give the population a clear choice between supporting the insurgency or the government through 'an adroit and judicious mixture of ruthlessness and sympathy'.[29] Although there was some disagreement over specific methods, such as whether security operations should target guerrilla leaders specifically or the concentration of troops in particular areas versus a more widespread approach, there was general agreement that the support of the population was a key element and that this co-operation should be gained by encouragement rather than through coercion; the people should think of the government forces as 'essentially good'.[30]

The British idea of hearts and minds included a certain element of carrot and stick, with considerable sanctions imposed upon villages that were thought to be supporting

26 David Galula, *Pacification in Algeria 1956 – 1958* (Santa Monica: RAND Corporation, 2006), Reprint of 1963 edition, pp. 258-259.

27 Roger Trinquier, *Modern Warfare: a French View of Counterinsurgency* (New York: Praeger Security International Paperback, 2006), Reprint of 1964 edition, pp. 21-25.

28 RAND Corporation, *Counterinsurgency: A Symposium, April 16-20, 1962* (Santa Monica, CA: RAND Corporation, 1962), p. 57. The point was made by David Galula.

29 Thompson, *Defeating Communist Insurgency*, p. 146.

30 RAND Corporation, *Counterinsurgency: A Symposium, April 16-20, 1962*, p21. The point was made by Brigadier Powell-Jones of the British Army.

the insurgents. These included curfews, food restrictions and collective fines. General Templer, for example, would often visit leaders of villages he suspected of knowing about terrorist attacks and personally harangue them before imposing sanctions and providing the means to pass information secretly to the government[31]. Paul Dixon was one of the first scholars to look at the role coercion played in counterinsurgency and argued that the British hearts and minds campaign in Malaya was far more coercive in nature than is generally recognised, with widespread use of force and allegations of human rights abuses.[32] Thompson argued that a similar coercive attitude was also necessary in Vietnam, but not to the extent of abusing human rights, in order to show the population that the government had the will to win; one of several lines of operation designed to counter the political *dich van* propaganda campaign being waged by the Vietnamese communists. He believed that, '[p]eople will stand very harsh measures indeed, provided that they are strictly enforced and fairly applied to all, are effective in their purpose and are seen to be so'.[33]

Analysis of the counterinsurgency literature that existed in the early 1960s reveals four basic lines of operation for an effective campaign: security; information operations; civil affairs, including assistance with economic recovery; and regeneration of the local political infrastructure (or the introduction of a local political system if one had not existed before). The counterinsurgency campaign was to use these lines of operation to win the support of the population and deny their support to the enemy, defeating the insurgents by causing them to wither away rather than the almost impossible task of completely destroying the insurgent forces. As well as countering the armed and political struggles, this strategy was also intended to undercut the parallel governance and welfare structures that the insurgents built in the absence of strong local and national government.

Breaking the contemporary theories down in this way provides a structure for analysis of the Marines' strategy as it was described in July 1966, when their mission was in the process of expanding beyond defence of air bases on the northern coast of Vietnam to offensive operations against the Viet Cong and NVA. These four lines of operation can clearly be seen in the III MAF strategy (Table 1) and the means devised by the Marines for measuring progress (Table 2). Although the development of both will be analysed in more detail in later chapters, they are shown here so that they can be directly compared with the prevailing theories of the time:

31 Harry Miller, *The Communist Menace in Malaya* (New York, NY: Frederick A Praeger, 1954), pp. 206-210.

32 Dixon, Paul, ''Hearts and Minds'? British Counter-Insurgency from Malaya to Iraq', *Journal of Strategic Studies*, 32: 3, (2009), pp. 353- 381.

33 Thompson, *Defeating Communist Insurgency*, p. 146.

Table 1: III MAF Campaign Plan, February 1966[34]

MAJOR FUNCTIONAL AREAS	SUPPORTING PROGRAMS	SUBPROGRAMS
Counterguerrilla: Aim – Destroy Guerrilla Forces	1. Kill VC Guerrillas And 2. Destroy VC Infrastructure	Ambush
		Snipe
		Patrol
		Search and Destroy
		Collect Intell (sic) from Civilians
		Conduct County Fairs
	Phase-in VN Local Security Forces	Demonstrate Proper Security
		Train Local Security Forces
Large Unit Operations: Aim – Destroy VC and NVA Main Forces	Watch	Man Deep Recon Posts
		Reconnoitre By Air
		Execute Stay Behind Recon
	Strike	Conduct Large Unit Search and Destroy Operations
Pacification: Aim – Assist in Nation Building	Establish Village Security	Train Village Local Defense Forces
		Complete Village Defense Plans
		Establish Village Intel Networks
		Establish Village Psy-War Public Information Programs
	Establish Village Governments	Encourage Village Census
		Assist in Installing Government Officials
		Restore Security for Village Officials
		Maintain Close Contact with Village Officials
	Improve Local Economy	Assist in Establishing Local Markets
		Protect Rice Harvest
		Improve Communications
		Assist in Local Construction Projects
	Improve Public Health	Give Medical Treatment
		Evacuate Critically Ill
		Give Medical Training
		Feed Hungry Vietnamese
	Improve Public Education	Support Students
		Teach English Language
		Help Build Schools
		Give Vocational Training

34 FMFPac, *Operations of US Marine Forces Vietnam, July 1966*, p. 6.

Table 2: Revolutionary Development Indices, October 1966[35]

GOAL	MEASURABLE INDICATOR	POINTS	TOTAL
Destruction of Enemy Units	VC Units Destroyed or Expelled	15	
	Local Defensive Force Established	5	20
Destruction of Enemy Infrastructure	Village Census Completed	2	
	VC Infrastructure Destroyed	8	
	Local Intelligence Network Established	5	
	Census, Grievance Interviews Completed	2	
	Action Completed on Grievances	3	20
Vietnamese Establishment of Security	Defensive Plan Completed	2	
	Defensive Installations Completed	3	
	Security Forces Trained and in Place	12	
	Communications Net Established	3	20
Establishment of Local Government	Village Chief and Council in Office	4	
	Village Chief Residing in Village	3	
	Hamlet Chiefs and Councils in Office	4	
	Hamlet Chiefs Residing in Village	4	
	Psy-Ops and Information Program Established	3	
	Minimum Social and Administrative Organisation	2	20
Degree of New Life Development	Adequate Public Health Program	4	
	Adequate Education Facilities	4	
	Adequate Agricultural Development	4	
	Adequate Transportation Facilities	4	
	Necessary Markets Established	4	20

These tables demonstrate that the Marines had chosen to adopt a population centric approach to counterinsurgency that was intended to provide a cognitive choice by taking action to improve the political, social and economic infrastructure. This was characterised by General Krulak as a 'treat the whole patient' approach to counterinsurgency.[36] The

35 FMFPac, *Operations of US Marine Forces Vietnam, October 1966*, p. 8.

36 General Krulak, letter to Secretary of Defense Robert McNamara, dated 9 May 1966. Krulak Papers, Alfred M Gray Research Center, US Marine Corps University, Quantico, VA.

measures used to assess progress in Table 2 show that although the Marines intended to conduct the full spectrum of operations in their area of responsibility, the emphasis was on reconstruction and drawing support away from the insurgency. Of the 22 criteria used in scoring only two were related to destruction of enemy forces – the remaining 20 indicators were all intended to show the extent to which the population had made its 'cognitive choice'. The problem is that indicators measured the effort being put into the campaign rather than its effectiveness and thus were misleading.

The operational concepts put forward by Thompson and Galula in particular can clearly be seen in these Marine documents. In *Defeating Communist Insurgency* Thompson proposed four stages for military operations in counterinsurgency; clearing, holding, winning, and won.[37] He defined the four stages as:

> *Stage One*: Clearing operations in a carefully selected area (ideally adjacent to an already 'cleared' area with good natural boundaries and communications), which would be saturated with 'joint military and police forces' to 'force the insurgent units either to disperse within the area or possibly to withdraw to neighbouring areas still under their control or disputed'. But, Thompson pointed out, clearing operations would be a 'waste of time' unless they were followed up with operations to hold the area. Without this, the clearing operation would simply be 'a general sweep through the area, which, when the government forces withdraw, will revert to its original state'[38].

> *Stage Two*: Holding operations to 'restore government authority in the area and to establish a firm security network'. These would include 'the creation of strategic hamlets, the formation of hamlet militia and the imposition of various control measures...designed to isolate the guerrilla forces from the population, to provide protection for the people themselves and eliminate the insurgent underground subversive element in the villages'.[39] This stage was intended to continue throughout the insurgency and overlap with the third stage. Strategic hamlets were thought to have contributed to the success in Malaya, where the resettled population consisted of squatters living on the edges of the jungle and movement to the new villages had represented a significant improvement in their lives. The squatters were relocated to specially-built villages where they were given farmland and integrated into the mainstream Malay society. Relocation combined with food control measures, such as only permitting the sale of cooked rice, which meant that it had to be eaten quickly since it could not be stored once cooked. The purpose of

37 Stages that pertained to counterinsurgency operations in Iraq – the 'Clear, hold and build' concept of operations promulgated under General Petraeus during the period 2006-07. See HQ Department of the Army, *Field Manual 3-24: Counterinsurgency* (Washington DC: HQ Department of the Army, 2006),

38 Robert Thompson, *Defeating Communist Insurgency*, p. 112.

39 Robert Thompson, *Defeating Communist Insurgency*, p. 112.

this was to prevent the insurgents from being able to stockpile food in their base areas in the jungle and thus sustain themselves for long periods. This achieved two things; first, the villagers were removed from the area where the Chinese insurgents operated and thus could not provide support to them and second, it gave them a stake in the newly independent Malaya, since they were afforded citizenship and an improved standard of living. In 1961 Thompson recommended the adoption of similar measures by the South Vietnamese government to secure the area around Saigon.[40] In Vietnam, however, the programme largely failed. Thompson ascribed this to mismanagement of the programme itself by the Vietnamese government and their underestimation of the extent of the infiltration of the Viet Cong.[41] The American view was that the programme was inappropriate for the Vietnam theatre of operations. The Joint Chiefs of Staff pointed out in a memo to General Maxwell Taylor, who at the time was serving in the specially-created post of Military Representative to the President, that these measures were easier to implement in Malaya because, 'the racial characteristics of the Chinese insurgents in Malaya made identification and segregation a relatively simple matter ' and '[t]he scarcity of food in Malaya versus the relative plenty in South Vietnam made the denial of food to the Communist guerrillas a far more important and readily useable weapon in Malaya'.[42]

Stage Three: This stage was described as 'winning the population' or 'good government in all its aspects'. This stage would include measures to improve health, education, communications and the local economy using local resources where possible rather than 'outright gifts'.[43] Although Thompson does not mention local government in relation to this stage, elsewhere he highlighted the importance of effective local government at village level, so it can be assumed that he would have considered establishment of local authorities at this stage as an implied task. This stage is intended to be the turning point of the hearts and minds campaign, wherein the government demonstrates that it is not only acting in the best interests of the people but also that it intends to maintain a permanent presence. Its success would be determined by the extent to which the local population begin to resist the insurgent presence and provide information to government forces about the insurgents.

Stage Four: This is the stage at which the government determines that 'the people have demonstrated by their positive action that they are on the side of

40 Robert Thompson, Memorandum Attachment to Letter to President Diem, 11 November 1961.

41 Robert Thompson, *Defeating Communist Insurgency*, p. 126

42 General Lyman Lemnitzer, *Counterinsurgency Operations in South Vietnam* , Memorandum for General Taylor, 18 October 1961. *The Pentagon Papers, Gravel Edition*, Vol. 2, pp. 650-651 <http://www.mtholyoke.edu/acad/intrel/pentagon2/doc102.htm> (Accessed 30 August 2008).

43 Robert Thompson, *Defeating Communist Insurgency*, pp. 112-113.

the government' and, therefore the government has won. Rather than conducting operations against the insurgents, restrictions imposed during the previous stages are lifted and the government begins to concentrate on 'creating a politically and economically stable and viable community'.[44] This stage is not obvious in the Marines' campaign plan and this is most likely because one of the aims of the Marines was pass control of pacified areas to the Vietnamese as soon as possible.[45]

David Galula had a similar campaign plan, but in eight stages rather than four. Although the security operations he advocated were similar to Thompson's and occurred in the same order, his later stages were more concerned with strengthening local government and developing local leadership. In his view, based on his success in his area of operations in Algeria, community leaders were the key to turning the tide of local opinion, especially those chosen by the local community itself rather than by the government or counterinsurgent forces.[46] Galula's eight stage campaign plan was as follows:

Stage One: Destruction or expulsion of the insurgent forces by reinforcing existing units and then conducting a sweep from the boundary to the centre in order to destroy the insurgent forces, followed by a sweep from the centre outwards to expel the remaining insurgents. In order for this stage to be successful Galula did not consider it necessary to completely destroy the insurgents, just disperse them and prevent them from regrouping.[47]

Stage Two: Deployment of static forces to protect the population and prevent the return of the insurgents. Forces should be deployed according to population density and not necessarily at strategic points. Galula stated that although the communications infrastructure was to be protected, 'counterinsurgent forces should not be wasted in traditionally commanding positions, for in revolutionary warfare, these positions generally command nothing'. This point is probably a result of the frustration and anger many French officers felt about the strategy in Indochina that had brought about the De Lattre Line and Dien Bien Phu and led to ultimate defeat. Galula also took issue with Thompson (although not mentioning him by name) by dismissing the idea of moving the population into 'strategic hamlets'. He had two principal objections. The first was that these strategic hamlets were defensive in nature and ceded the countryside to the insurgents. Therefore, they should be seen as a 'last resort measure, borne out of the counterinsurgent's weakness'. Galula's second objection to resettlement was that it would unduly antagonise the population at a sensitive time and would be

44 Robert Thompson, *Defeating Communist Insurgency*, p. 113.
45 General Krulak, letter to Secretary of Defense Robert McNamara, 9 May 1966.
46 David Galula, *Pacification in Algeria 1956 – 1958*, pp. 157 – 164, p. 294 and David Galula *Counterinsurgency Warfare*, p. 90.
47 Galula, David, *Counterinsurgency Warfare: Theory and Practice*, pp. 75-76.

counterproductive despite the long-term benefits it might bring.[48]. Thompson's counter was that resettling the population into strategic hamlets was only the start. These hamlets would be used as bases for offensive operations against the insurgency.[49]

Step Three: Galula's third step was to establish contact with, and control over, the local population. The purpose of this stage was to remove whatever vestigial secret control the insurgents still had over the population and replace that with control by the counterinsurgents. Galula advised that this be done carefully by means of small but enforceable orders to the population, ideally things that are to the benefit of the population such as cleaning the streets or repairing village infrastructure. This would be followed up with a census and movement restrictions, to disrupt the operations of any remaining insurgents, along with projects to improve health, education and the local economy. Galula considered this the most important step because it represented the transition of emphasis from military to political operations, but still required considerable effort on both fronts.[50] It is at this point that the local population begin to make their conscious decision to support the government and the security forces; the insurgent threat has been removed and the government has started to demonstrate an interest in the welfare of the population and is showing signs of a permanent presence.

Steps Four to Seven: These steps in Galula's strategy can be combined as tasks within a fourth 'political consolidation' step. Having removed the insurgent threat and begun the process of winning over the population, these next steps were designed to encourage the local population to coalesce around leaders opposed to the insurgency that they themselves have selected, with the intention that this local movement then becomes part of a national movement that supports the government. Before this can happen, Galula advised the complete excision of the insurgent political organisation, which may still be in place even though the armed members have been killed, captured or driven away during the earlier stages. It is debateable whether this is necessary or desirable in a democratic context. Although Galula cautions care in handling the political supporters of the insurgency (releasing them as soon as they have seen the error of their ways) arresting political opponents sends the wrong message, potentially giving the insurgent campaign greater legitimacy as they can claim that the government is a totalitarian one that does not allow peaceful dissent, thus leaving armed insurrection as the only option. Rather than removing the political elements of the insurgency, counterinsurgents should be at pains to explain that it is not the dissent itself that they are fighting – it is the use

48 Galula, David, *Counterinsurgency Warfare: Theory and Practice*, p. 78.
49 Thompson, Robert, *Defeating Communist Insurgency*, p. 126.
50 David Galula, *Counterinsurgency Warfare: Theory and Practice*, pp. 81-85.

of force that is unacceptable. Since most insurgencies are politically motivated, a certain amount of political interaction at all levels is likely to be part of the eventual solution. The next two steps in Galula's plan were to hold local elections, without interference from the counterinsurgents, and then to test (and train) the leaders by giving them tasks connected with running the local government and improving the local economy. This was intended to gain the support of the population, which in turn improves security since the population now has a stake in their own future. The final part of the political process that Galula suggests is the formation of a local political party containing all the newly elected leaders that will enable the local population to solidify their resistance to the insurgents on a larger scale and provide a counter to the insurgent political platform. Given his statement that his third step was the point at which the emphasis would move from military to political operations, it is unlikely that Galula intended that military forces do more than just provide security for this process and facilitate where necessary. As can be seen in the section entitled 'Establish Village Governments' in Table 1, this is the approach the Marines appear to have adopted in Vietnam.

Stage Eight: Galula's final stage was to win over or suppress the last remaining guerrillas with a series of large-scale operations designed to kill or capture the last remaining cells, with a carefully controlled amnesty programme for suitable candidates. His intention was twofold; first to eliminate the last of the hard core element of the insurgency and, second, was to demonstrate the government's continued determination to stamp out armed dissent and provide security for the population. This stage could last for many years and Galula gives the contemporary example of Malaya where, 'in September 1962, fourteen years after the start of the insurgency…20 to 30 Communist guerrillas are still holding out in the deep jungle inside Malaya, not counting 300 more operating on the Malaya-Thailand border'.[51]

Although there are some differences with regard to methods, Galula and Thompson's approaches are broadly similar population-centric strategies intended to persuade the people to make an active choice to support the government. Galula's approach, though, probably comes closer to being an effective counter to the doctrine of Vietnamese Communist political struggle in that at each stage he provides guidance on a three-pronged propaganda campaign directed towards the counterinsurgent forces, the local population, and the insurgents. Generally speaking, the propaganda directed towards the counterinsurgent forces is aimed at explaining to the troops why they are doing what they are doing and making sure that they understand that the support of the population is the key to their success. Propaganda directed towards the population is aimed at explaining why the counterinsurgents are taking certain measures, telling them that the government

51 David Galula, *Counterinsurgency Warfare: Theory and Practice*, p. 94.

intends to maintain a permanent presence in the area, and explaining why it is in the best interests of the population to co-operate with the government rather than the insurgents. The propaganda directed against the insurgents is, as one would expect, intended to undermine their fighting spirit and morale. Many French officers had seen what effective propaganda could do in Indochina. Some had been subjected to it in prison camps after the fall of Dien Bien Phu.[52]

Psychological warfare and propaganda both found their place in the Marines' campaign, but not until late in 1966 when the Psychological Warfare Section was established in III MAF HQ, with four tasks: To reduce the combat efficiency of the Viet Cong and North Vietnamese Army forces; To further the effort of the Government of Vietnam in re-establishing its effective control over the population by modifying or manipulating attitudes and behaviour of special audiences; To facilitate the rural construction efforts of the Government of Vietnam by coordinating this command's psychological operations with its civic action program; To obtain the cooperation and assistance of villagers in the Government of Vietnam's effort to quell the Viet Cong insurgency.[53]

Counterinsurgency theorists in the 1950s and 1960s also largely agreed upon the need for small unit operations to take primacy in the 'war amongst the people', but again differed with regard to the specifics. Thompson, Galula and Trinquier had seen the failure of campaigns where large unit operations had achieved little. In Malaya the British had started by conducting large-scale sweeps of the jungle that had been so ponderous that the insurgents were able to escape long before government forces could reach them. At the same time, captured documents showed that 'surprise raids and ambushes by small parties were greatly feared'.[54] In Indochina, the French had seen how effective insurgent forces could disrupt the lines of communication necessary for such operations, such as during the attempt to take Hoa Binh in the winter of 1951, and had a significant proportion of their forces tied down in static defence positions like the controversial (but nonetheless temporarily effective) 'De Lattre' Line built to defend the Red River Delta and ports on the Gulf of Tonkin.

Thompson described counterinsurgency as a 'junior commander's war' with Division Commanders effectively becoming administrators, and quoted one senior British officer as saying that all he really had to do was see that his troops had enough beer.[55] Thompson believed that the main effort should be 'clear and hold' operations designed to force the insurgents out of populated areas, and that 'search and clear' operations were not effective because they did not 'achieve the dual purpose of killing insurgents and destroying their infrastructure' as '[t]he ratio of contacts and number of insurgents killed are very limited

52 David Galula, *Counterinsurgency Warfare: Theory and Practice*, pp. 65-67.

53 III MAF Force Order 5401.1 dated 5 September 1966, *Establishment of the Psychological Operations Section*, attached to Annex E, Part II, Section IX, III MAF *Command Chronology, February 1967.*

54 Riley Sunderland, *Army Operations in Malaya, 1947 – 1960* in John Nagl, *Learning to Eat Soup with a Knife: Counterinsurgency Lessons from Malaya and Vietnam* (Chicago: University of Chicago Press, 2005), p. 67.

55 Robert Thompson, *Defeating Communist Insurgency*, p. 61.

and depend greatly on chance'.[56] Of course, the enemy also gets a vote – insurgent units may disperse into the general population in the immediate area or surrounding areas in the face of overwhelming opposition and wait until the situation becomes more favourable. Thompson argued that in order to be successful in the unpopulated areas, used as base areas by the insurgents, the counterinsurgent forces should fight according to his 'same element ' principle. That is, they should conduct long term deep penetration small-unit operations in these areas against the insurgent's main lines of communication, disrupting their rear area in the same way that the insurgents disrupt that of the government forces.[57] These units also become reliant on the same resources as the insurgents – water, shelter, lines of communication, etc – as they are operating in the same element. Thus, their chances of encountering insurgent forces increase, and Thompson quoted a casualty ratio of 200:1 in favour of the Australian Special Air Service, which used this technique (acknowledging that the real measure of success is the disruption caused to the VC in the area and not the casualties themselves).[58] The French experts, however, remained supportive of 'sweep and clear' operations. Roger Trinquier suggested methods of dividing an area into 'grids' in which units no larger than a battalion would operate in conjunction with the police, once the towns and villages had been cordoned off to deny their use to the insurgents. He did not envisage large unit offensives, but a series of cordon and search operations that would eventually drive the insurgents out.[59] Galula emphasised the need for mobility, in a three-phase initial campaign, in which forces would first surround an area and work inwards to capture the guerrillas, then sweep back outwards to expel those that were left (since the aim of the counterinsurgency campaign, in his view, was to expel and isolate the insurgents rather than kill them) and, finally, disperse into smaller elements to operate in roughly the same manner as Trinquier's grid system.[60]

Counterinsurgency military operations were discussed at a counterinsurgency symposium organised by the RAND Corporation in April 1962. Among those present were David Galula, Frank Kitson (a British counterinsurgency expert with experience in Kenya and Malaya who later commanded a brigade in Northern Ireland), Edward Lansdale (an American counterinsurgency expert with experience in Indochina and the Philippines) and George Tanham (a leading expert in the Viet Minh and communist insurgency). This symposium is significant in that its participants were considered to be the leading experts from their respective nations, many of whom had a role to play in counterinsurgency policy either at that time or later in their careers, and the discussions allowed for a direct comparison of contemporary experiences and theories. It therefore represented the 'state of the art' of counterinsurgency at the time that the Marines were preparing for deployment to Vietnam.

56 Robert Thompson, *Defeating Communist Insurgency*, p. 117.
57 Robert Thompson, *Defeating Communist Insurgency*, p. 117.
58 Robert Thompson, *No Exit from Vietnam*, p. 173.
59 Roger Trinquier, *Modern Warfare*, pp. 60-74.
60 David Galula, *Counterinsurgency Warfare: Theory and Practice*, pp. 75-77,

Although there appeared to be general agreement that the aim of military operations should be to separate the insurgents from the population by killing them, driving them away or otherwise making it impossible for them to continue their activities, there was considerable disagreement on some of the specifics such as the desirability of deliberately targeting insurgent leaders and whether intelligence should be the responsibility of one agency or many. The British and French view on targeting leadership, derived from experience in Malaya, Indochina and Algeria, was that this had had little or no effect as Communists in particular placed little value on individual leaders at the lower levels, emphasising group effort. Leaders in those campaigns had been quickly replaced, often with more capable leaders, with little noticeable effect. The American view, based on experience in the Philippines, was that insurgent groups had been significantly affected by the death of a leader with the result that it would be some weeks or even months before the group returned to action.[61]

These discussions on military operations highlight the fact that, by the early 1960s, although there was agreement on some guiding principles for counterinsurgency warfare, such as the necessity for a population-centric approach, the need for unity of command, a primary focus on intelligence-led operations, and the primacy of the rule of law, there remained considerable differences of opinion on how these principles should be translated into action. There was a similar debate regarding the use of intelligence in counterinsurgency. It was generally agreed that intelligence was of paramount importance in counterinsurgency, but the British had found that giving intelligence primacy to the police had worked effectively in Malaya whereas the American experience was that no single agency should be entrusted with the task. In their view, it was better to have multiple agencies that could provide a check on each other and prevent any one of them becoming too powerful; an important factor in many South American countries and in Vietnam. Galula struck the balance here, having seen the benefits of both systems in Algeria; in the cities the police and *Surété* had responsibility for intelligence, whereas in the more rural areas, where the *Surété* did not operate and the police could not operate, the task was left entirely to the military.[62] It was clear that no two insurgencies were the same and therefore the counterinsurgency campaign had to be tailored to fit the situation, sometimes as a result of trial and error. While the nature of the insurgency, the terrain and the political landscape differ in each situation so too do the counterinsurgents. Armies have different approaches to counterinsurgency based on institutional culture, experience, structure and resources. Their approach also has to be tailored according to their relationship with the host government, depending on whether the military force is present to support its own government in internal security or is there by invitation in an advisory or support role.

When the subject of measuring success was discussed at the RAND symposium, Galula suggested a number of military and non-military indicators that could be used. The main military indicators were those that gave an idea of the insurgents' capabilities; their

61 RAND Corporation, *Counterinsurgency: A Symposium, April 16-20, 1962*, pp. 13-15.
62 RAND Corporation, *Counterinsurgency: A Symposium, April 16-20, 1962*, pp. 105-108.

ability to move up to a higher stage of warfare, the number of insurgents that could be massed for a single engagement, estimates of weapon stocks and activity levels. The non-military indicators showed the level of support the government had gained, measured by the number of volunteers joining the counterinsurgent forces, the amount of information spontaneously offered and the willingness of the local population to break the rules imposed by the insurgents (here he quoted strictures from Algeria against smoking and making contact with the counterinsurgent forces). The other participants agreed that the military indicators could be useful, but could equally be explained by other factors (again the principle that the enemy has a vote rears its ugly head) but that the non-military indicators were more important and more telling, particularly those that involved some positive act by the population such as offering information or refusing to comply with insurgent demands.[63] The conversation then moved on without elaborating on techniques to measure success. Thompson, unfortunately not present at the symposium, is equally lacking in specifics in his writing. He agreed with the symposium's participants that:

> The two best guides ... are an improvement in intelligence voluntarily given by the population and a decrease in the insurgents' recruitment rate. Much can be learnt merely from the faces of the population in villages that are subject to clear-and-hold operations, if these are visited at regular intervals. Faces which at first are resigned and apathetic, or even sullen, six months or a year later are full of cheerful welcoming smiles. The people know who is winning.[64]

He did not elaborate with specific metrics for measuring progress. Later, in *No Exit From Vietnam*, Thompson described an incident in which he was asked how he could tell if the counterinsurgents were winning. His response was; 'If you are in the business you know whether you are winning or not. If you don't know, you are not in the business'.[65]

The contemporary experts established general principles, but it is apparent that they meant the specific methodology to be determined by the situation. The means for measuring success will depend upon government's desired end state or victory conditions. In Vietnam it was the inability to find a reliable means to measure progress that undermined public confidence in the military claims of success. Although a range of indicators was used, including 'enemy killed, weapons captured, miles of waterways and roads opened, villages pacified, percentage of population under government control, logistical installations completed, proficiency ratings of ARVN units', it was the notorious 'body count' that came to dominate media reporting.[66] The Revolutionary Development Index at Table 2 was an attempt to use more meaningful indicators but show input rather than output. That is, they demonstrate the amount of effort the Marines were putting into their campaign in terms of creating infrastructure, but not the effect that it had. For example, a village

63 RAND Corporation, *Counterinsurgency: A Symposium, April 16-20, 1962*, pp. 141-142.
64 Robert Thompson, *Defeating Communist Insurgency*, pp. 169-170.
65 RobertThompson, *No Exit from Vietnam*, p. 143.
66 General William Westmoreland, *A Soldier Reports*, p. 273.

that had its own local government, defence force, school, market and public health facility would be rated as 'pacified', but there is no indication of how good any of these things actually were. There was no system to judge the effectiveness of the local leaders in the manner that Galula suggested, by giving them tasks and measuring how well they are performed. There is no indicator as to whether the school or market is used, or how the health of the local population has changed. There are points awarded for the establishment of a system for reporting local intelligence but no points for the number of actionable intelligence reports submitted – a key indicator of support for the government. Although the fact that these elements have been put in place is an indication that some progress is being made, their effect may not become apparent for some months (or even a year or two) and therefore one has to look at different indicators to gauge the effect.

Galula argued that if the enemy can be prevented from moving on to a higher form of warfare, for example moving from the guerrilla phase to mobile warfare with formed units, then this is a sign that government forces are winning. Equally, it can be argued that if the insurgents are prevented from achieving their aims (assuming these have been correctly assessed) then the government forces can also take this as a sign of progress.

This dependence on the government's aims as a means to determine success makes victory a difficult concept to define in a counterinsurgency context. Some governments may aim for total eradication of the insurgency and its political infrastructure while others may just want to stop the violence while being prepared to accept the political activity (the point effectively reached in the Good Friday Agreement in Northern Ireland in 1998). David Galula defined victory as the, 'destruction in a given area of the insurgent's forces and political organization...plus the permanent isolation of the insurgent from the population, isolation not enforced upon the population but maintained by and with the population'.[67] Although Thompson did not go as far as to define victory, he did write about the end state of a counterinsurgency campaign in which the insurgents have lost the support of the people and have withdrawn to the 'jungles, mountains and swamps' where the 'dreary process of mopping up' eradicates the last of them.[68] This can take place over an extended period of time, as long as the government does not become complacent and allow the insurgency to regain strength. The Malayan Emergency is a case in point. After the emergency was declared over in 1960 there were still up to 500 guerrillas in the border area between Malaya and Thailand, but they posed almost no threat to the government even though they later formed the nucleus of a second short-lived insurgency in 1969. Despite this, the Malayan Emergency is still considered a victory for counterinsurgents.

The idea of victory is different, however, for foreign forces rendering assistance to the government. This makes sense in the context of Communist revolutionary war in which the insurgents are prepared to wait for a more strategically impatient enemy to withdraw. At the RAND symposium in 1962, Rufus Phillips, a psychological warfare and counterinsurgency expert who had worked in Vietnam and Laos, argued that once

67 David Galula, *Counterinsurgency Warfare*, p. 54.

68 Robert Thompson, *Defeating Communist Insurgency*, p. 149.

the situation had been sufficiently stabilised under a strong government the foreign forces would be asked to leave anyway. Colonel Bohannan, a retired US Army officer with experience in the Philippines, made the prescient response that American troops were 'almost invariably withdrawn prematurely in response to political and economic pressures at home'.[69] Although Bohannan did not give examples to support his comment, David Galula offered up that this had been the case in Indochina with the French.[70] Although the eventual withdrawal of US armed forces from Vietnam is beyond the scope of this study, it will provide a snapshot of the conditions in late 1968, when Richard Nixon won the presidential election on a platform of 'peace with honour' and a promise to withdraw American forces.

The Problem With Counterinsurgency Doctrine

The increase in attention given to counterinsurgency in the late 1950s and 1960s helped build an intellectual framework in which the Marines could construct a counterinsurgency strategy for Vietnam. Many of the principles and techniques used can be clearly traced back to the prevailing theories of the time contained within the works of Thompson, Galula and Trinquier. As will be seen, however, the Marines had to compose a strategy 'on the fly' as their initial mission was not to conduct operations against the insurgents or pacify the area but simply to defend a number of coastal air bases. Offensive operations and pacification only began as a local initiative to provide defence in depth to these installations, and then expanded as the US increased its commitment to the war. Although these principles and techniques were considered an effective means of countering the revolutionary warfare doctrine of the North Vietnamese, the lack of clarity regarding the means to measure progress or define victory was to have a significant negative impact on the Marines in later years, as the Corps' claims of progress, based on its Revolutionary Development Indices, were undermined by continuing VC activity in its area of operations.

But the contemporary doctrine was problematic for a number of reasons. The experiences upon which it was based was gained in fighting limited insurgencies that were largely confined to the borders of the countries in which they occurred. Obviously in the case of the Philippines geography played a large part in that the operational areas were islands. But in the cases of Malaya, Algeria, and even the First Indochina War, external support was extremely limited and largely consisted of providing safe havens across the border. Vietnam, by the late 1950s was a very different prospect. The *dau tranh* campaign was a major element of the North Vietnamese strategy because control of the population was one of their key war aims. But North Vietnam could rely on considerable material support from its allies. Soviet Russia and Communist China. But following the defeat of the French, the North Vietnamese began to slowly build their army, overcoming

69 RAND Corporation, *Counterinsurgency: A Symposium, April 16-20, 1962*, p. 147.
70 RAND Corporation, *Counterinsurgency: A Symposium, April 16-20, 1962*, p. 147.

considerable logistical and administrative problems.[71] By 1964, the year before the US Marines deployed to Vietnam, there were already regular North Vietnamese Army (NVA) units operating in the south. At this point, and until the war was well established some years later, the cheerleaders for counterinsurgency were not entirely wrong; there was a hybrid war going on as the regular NVA units were operating in a guerrilla manner. Counterinsurgency could solve some of the problems but not all of them and it was not the answer to what was happening outside the borders of South Vietnam.

This leads on to the next problem with the counterinsurgency thinking of the time. It made claims for counterinsurgency that could not be supported. Robert Thompson's experience had been gained in Malaya, where conditions were far more conducive to a British victory than they were in Vietnam for the Americans. In fact, as Andrew Mumford points out, there is no surprise that the British won in Malaya, but what is surprising is it took them so long to do it.[72] David Galula had achieved success in somewhat more trying circumstances, but this was as a company commander in a relatively small area. Examining their campaign plans in the context of their experience it become clear they can only really provide support for counterinsurgency in the early stages. Thompson had seen Stages 1, 2, and 4 of his plan implemented in Malaya but these ignored the extent to which coercion and violence had contributed to the success. But crucially Stage 3, when the government tips the balance of support its way, was never really a factor in Malaya. Arguably even Stage 4 was not a Stage in itself in Malaya, but a return to the *status quo ante*. David Galula had only really tested the first three stages of his eight stage plan as a company commander in Algeria. The remaining five stages were a theoretical approach based on his understanding of the nature of insurgency. What they had was the intellectual underpinnings for counterinsurgency at an operational level, but not a strategy that could win in Vietnam. A far more realistic approach is the one contained in the 1962 RAND Symposium, at which officers with considerable operational level experience had pooled their knowledge and proposed a set of principles for counterinsurgency at that level, acknowledging that the exact techniques and approaches would almost certainly differ from one situation to another.

71 Phillip Davidson, *Vietnam at War*, pp. 284-286.
72 Andrew Mumford, *The Counterinsurgency Myth*, p. 25.

2

Development of USMC Counterinsurgency Doctrine in the 1960s and Preparations for Deployment to Vietnam

Against the backdrop of the small wars and insurgencies of the 1950s and 1960s the US military, the Army in particular, continued its preparations to fight a large, and potentially nuclear, war in Europe against an invading Soviet Army. The US Army and the US Marine Corps were allocated different roles in the event that the Cold War became a 'Hot' War. The US Army became a heavyweight organisation relying on tanks and artillery; weapons that could defeat another heavyweight army on the plains of central Europe. The US Army concentrated on building up its weight of firepower by the American 'way of war'; responding to unambiguous aggression with overwhelming force with the aim of total victory. This had developed during the 1950s as a means of responding to mainly Soviet aggression but, as the case of Korea had proved, it did not deter limited (or ambiguous) aggression, nor did it allow for 'total victory' against limited aggression. In Korea this would have meant complete destruction of the North Korean state, which the United States feared would provoke a military response from the Soviet Union and China a risk the Americans were not prepared to take. In addition, developing the means to fight a range of wars was costly and the Eisenhower administration of the mid-1950s was committed to defence cuts as part of its New Look policy, which tied defence spending to the state of the economy in order to prevent an undue burden. As part of the New Look, the overall military establishment was reduced, offset by spending on strategic-level technology, particularly nuclear weapons and air power.[1] As Andrew Krepinevich points out in *The Army and Vietnam*, the US military was keenly aware of the political consequences of casualties and therefore technology was used wherever possible as a means of limiting casualties. As Krepinevich goes on to say, the US Army had never lost a war until Vietnam and saw no need to change its attitude.[2] Although the US

1 Russell Weigley, *The American Way of War* (Bloomington, IN: Indiana University Press, 1977), pp. 410-416.

2 Andrew Krepinevich, *The Army and Vietnam* (Baltimore: Johns Hopkins University Press). pp. 5-6.

Army had some counterinsurgency experience, primarily in the Philippines, this type of warfare was seen as an aberration and as such no special attention was paid to it. In Kalev Sepp's introduction to the 2006 edition of Valeriano and Bohannan's *Counter-Guerrilla Operations: The Philippine Experience*, he makes the point that the 1954 campaign was 'eclipsed' by the war in Korea and the publication of *Counter-Guerrilla Operations* eight years later was itself lost amid the works on the British campaign in Malaya and the growing insurgency in Vietnam, by which time it 'seemed dated and less relevant'.[3]

The Marines developed slightly differently, but still had a mainly conventional role as a Force in Readiness. The Marines were affected by the manpower reductions of the New Look policy, with overall strength reduced from 248,000 in fiscal year (FY) 1954 to around 200,000 by the end of FY 1956. Earlier, in 1952 the Douglas-Mansfield Act structured the Marine Corps into three divisions and three air wings and provided it with a level of legislative protection it had not enjoyed in the past as it now became a service in its own right and, as a consequence, the Commandant of the Marine Corps gained the status of a full member of the Joint Chiefs of Staff. While the US Army was oriented towards Europe, the Marine Corps oriented itself towards the Pacific; a division of labour that seemed to linger from the Second World War, although Korea remained mainly an Army task after the 1st Marine Division redeployed to California. The 1st and 3rd Marine Divisions were based in California and Japan respectively, while the 2nd Marine Division was based in South Carolina, each with an air wing.[4] In addition to the restructuring that resulted from the Douglas-Mansfield Act and the New Look policy, the Marines conducted internal reforms, in an attempt to adjust to the manpower and budget restrictions but also to meet the requirements of its role as a Force in Readiness, able to respond at short notice to crises around the world. The Fleet Marine Force Composition and Organisation Board, known as the Hogaboom Board, after its chairman Major General Robert Hogaboom, met in late 1956 to consider the shape of the Marine Corps. Its report, delivered in 1957, essentially trimmed the fat off the divisions in the Corps and emphasised mobility and flexibility as the most desirable qualities. The report established five criteria that a Marine division should be able to meet. These included the ability to conduct amphibious assaults against 'the most modern defences…in accordance with…modern concepts for amphibious operations and atomic warfare'.[5] Other criteria included shedding 'maintenance and support functions to the greatest degree', creation and organisation of temporary task groups, and the capability to make 'rapid strategic movements by limited air, sea or land transportation means'. The board was at pains to point out that the division should also be prepared to adopt new techniques or equipment rapidly without requiring major changes; a concept the board

3 Napolean D. Valeriano and Charles T.R. Bohannan, *Counter-Guerrilla Operations: The Philippine Experience* (New York, NY: Greenwood, 2006), pp. ix-x.

4 Allan R. Millett, *Semper Fidelis: The History of the United States Marine Corps* (New York, NY: Free Press, 1991), pp. 518-522.

5 United States Marine Corps, 'FMF Organization and Composition Report: The Division', *Marine Corps Gazette*, April 1957, p. 26.

called 'change potential'. The board expected the division to be able to fight in a nuclear environment, so dispersal of assets and speed of manoeuvre were considered essential in a potentially fluid battlefield.[6]

In order to facilitate dispersal and speed, the logistic and support elements were cut dramatically, partly by removing those units specifically, but also by reducing the heavy equipment assigned to the division. The tank battalion was removed, and the artillery was reduced by replacing the 105mm howitzers used by the division's Close Support Battalions and replacing them with mortars. As well as reducing the number of heavy guns, this also cut the vehicle establishment with jeeps and light trucks replacing the larger vehicles. The 105mm howitzers were given to the Intermediate Support Battalion, which lost its 155mm howitzers. The heavy artillery units, including rocket batteries, and the tank battalions were cut in number and retained as force level troops, assigned to divisions according to need rather than on a permanent basis. The reduction in divisional-level heavy artillery was to be offset by increased capabilities in close air support (in terms of control and communications rather than new or more aircraft) and naval gunfire, although there was less emphasis on the latter because the board felt that the need to disperse the ships in case of nuclear attack and the likelihood of deeper inland penetration by Marine units would reduce the effectiveness of naval gunfire.[7] If one keeps in mind the old adage that 'amateurs talk about tactics but professionals talk about logistics', the key to the ethos of the Force in Readiness can be found in the changes that the Hogaboom Board made to the support elements. The divisional logistic tail was cut to the bare minimum. The Divisional Service Regiment became a battalion with sufficient resources to sustain the division in combat for 15-20 days.[8] The Force Service Regiment was given the task of providing 'the supply link between the depot and fleet logistic agencies and the landing force elements deployed in the objective area'.[9]

The implications of this for operations in Vietnam are clear; the Marine Corps was intended to be a light, mobile force capable of short duration operations in littoral areas but with the ability to adapt to changes in mission, techniques and equipment. What they lacked was the ability to fight an extended large scale war deep in the hinterland. Thus the Marines were ideally suited for their original task in Vietnam; defence of three coastal air bases, where they would have the advantage of short supply lines and the umbrella of close air support and naval gunfire.

6 United States Marine Corps, 'FMF Organization and Composition Report: The Division', *Marine Corps Gazette*, April 1957, p. 26.

7 United States Marine Corps, 'FMF Organization and Composition Report: Fire Support', *Marine Corps Gazette*, June 1957, p. 10.

8 United States Marine Corps, 'FMF Organization and Composition Report: Service Elements', *Marine Corps Gazette*, July 1957, p. 22.

9 *Marine Corps Gazette*, July 1957, p. 23.

Marine Corps Response to President Kennedy's Counterinsurgency Initiative

Nikita Khrushchev's explicit statement that the Soviet Union would support 'wars of national liberation' in January 1961, precipitated President Kennedy's order for the US military to develop a counterinsurgency capability later that same year.[10] The doctrine of 'massive retaliation' to unambiguous aggression gave way to a new doctrine of 'flexible response'; the ability to not only deter Soviet aggression but also react to lesser acts of aggression around the world, sponsored by the Soviet Union. The nature of the Soviet Union's support for these small wars of national liberation, in the context of the overall Cold War, was interpreted by many in the US foreign policy establishment as part of a top down strategy in which these wars were co-ordinated by Moscow and/or Peking in order to extend communism globally.[11] Robert McNamara summed up the prevailing view within the Kennedy Administration in 1961 when he observed:

> Like most Americans I saw Communism as monolithic. I believed the Soviets and the Chinese were cooperating in trying to extend their hegemony...At the time, Communism still seemed on the march. Mao Tse Tung and his followers had controlled China since 1949 and had fought with North Korea against the West; Nikita Khrushchev had predicted Communist Victory through 'wars of national liberation' in the Third World and had told the West, 'We will bury you'...[In 1958] Khrushchev started turning up the heat on West Berlin. And now Castro had transformed Cuba into a Communist beachhead in our hemisphere. We felt beset and at risk. This fear underlay our involvement in Vietnam.[12]

Pushed to the top of Kennedy's agenda by Walt Rostow, the Deputy National Security Advisor, Vietnam was seen in terms of an overall Sino-Soviet drive to expand communism. In the context of other insurgencies in Southeast Asia during the 1950s, the insurgency in Vietnam did appear to part of 'a unified Communist drive for hegemony in Asia'.[13]

During his time in Congress Kennedy had made many anti-Communist speeches, but these were almost *de rigeur* for any politician at the time, but on assuming the Presidency in 1961 he ordered that the US military develop the means to fight non-traditional and non-conventional military conflicts. Not satisfied with General Maxwell Taylor's response that Kennedy needn't worry about 'special situations' because the Army had soldiers 'trained for all sorts of things', Kennedy doubled the size of the US Army's

10 Andrew Krepinevich, *The Army and Vietnam*, pp. 29-31.

11 Although the capital of China is now referred to as Beijing, this book will retain usage that was common in contemporary official and personal documents for the sake of consistency. For the same reason Ho Chi Minh City will be referred to as Saigon and Mao Zedong is referred to as Mao Tse Tung.

12 Robert S. McNamara, *In Retrospect* (New York, NY: Times Books, 1995) p. 30.

13 Robert S. McNamara, *In Retrospect,* p. 31.

Special Forces from three groups to six and, in an effort to raise their profile and prestige, authorised the previously unofficial green beret. [14] On 30 November 1961 he called the Army's senior commanders to the White House to address the issue of counterinsurgency and he continued to apply pressure over the next few months by continually asking what progress was being made. The Army's reaction was largely negative, believing that counterinsurgency was simply a smaller version of conventional war or largely unnecessary in the context of Vietnam.[15]

On the face of it, the Marine Corps' response appeared as negative as that of the US Army. The Corps, already going through a period of change from the large Corps of the Second World War and Korean War into a smaller and more streamlined 'Force in Readiness', adopted the position that counterinsurgency was nothing new, but did acknowledge that it was a unique form of warfare in its own right. The Marine Corps therefore felt that no change was needed to its existing doctrine or force composition. General David Shoup, Commandant of the Marine Corps between 1962 and 1964, was particularly sceptical of the modern theories of counterinsurgency and was confident that the existing body of knowledge within the Corps, plus its own ethos of small unit leadership and flexibility, would suffice:

> Counterinsurgency is an attention-getting word these days and you may properly ask what the Marine Corps is doing in the field. We do not claim to be experts in the entire scope of actions required in counterinsurgency operations... The Marine Corps has long recognised that fighting guerrillas is an inherent part of landing force operations. Counterguerrilla warfare is essentially one of small units and we have traditionally emphasized individual leadership and small unit operations.[16]

General Krulak put it more bluntly:

> The Marines knew [counterinsurgency] was going to go away. Of all the services, the Navy and the Marines were the most obtuse, and the Marines most obtuse of all. 'Hell, we've been to Nicaragua, we know about all that jazz. We don't need any special individual in our outfit – and they never had one'. [sic] They paid the President of the United States lip service, assigning Bill Buse the job but it was really lip service. The poor guy already had ten times as much to do as he could handle. Anyhow, he was their point of contact. I believe that was Shoup's solution.[17]

14 Andrew Krepinevich, *The Army and Vietnam*, p. 30.

15 Andrew Krepinevich, *The Army and Vietnam*, pp. 36 – 38.

16 General Shoup's testimony to the House Armed Services Committee Hearings on Defense Appropriations for FY 1964, quoted in Alan Millett, *Semper Fidelis*, p. 548.

17 Frank Benis, transcript of interview with General Victor Krulak, Washington, DC: US Marine Corps Historical Division, Oral History Section, Interview conducted on 23 June 1970, p. 188.

This attitude is fairly typical of the US Marine Corps, which maintained its position that this was a task that any well-trained rifleman could carry out. In fact, when the Marines did create a special unit to carry out counterinsurgency, the Combined Action Platoons (CAP), these were recruited from units already in-country and trained locally. On completion of their task, the individuals were returned to their units. The Marines did, however, begin to address the issue of counterinsurgency doctrine and began to produce its own manuals.

Gaining Counterinsurgency Experience – The 'Banana Wars' and the Small Wars Manual

In three major campaigns the Marines had fought guerrillas in Haiti (1915-34), the Dominican Republic (1916-24) and Nicaragua (1926-33). These campaigns were collectively known as the Banana Wars. All three campaigns were conducted in a similar manner. After an initial landing, followed by operations against the guerrillas, the Marines settled into a wider role of providing a stable security environment, which in all three cases included the establishment of a local National Guard or *gendarmerie* that was trained, and initially led, by Marine officers and NCOs. The Marines also made extensive use of civil affairs during these interventions, even to the extent of establishing a military government in the Dominican Republic. In Haiti the Marines became agents of the civilian government established by the US Navy and the State Department. In Nicaragua their political role was largely concerned with management of the elections in 1924 and 1928. Specific lessons learned from these campaigns were the basis for the last three chapters of the *Small Wars Manual;* 'Chapter XII – Armed Native Organizations', 'Chapter XIII – Military Government' and 'Chapter XIV- Supervising Elections'.[18] The *Small Wars Manual*, published in 1940, was an attempt to capture the lessons learned in the Caribbean and Latin America and establish doctrine for what was becoming a core task for the Marine Corps, until the Second World War broke out and the Marines found a new role as seaborne shock troops. It should be noted however, that these roles were not considered as being as essential to success in counter-guerrilla warfare in the 1920s and 1930s as they were in the 1960s. Instead, these tasks were a necessity as a means to restore order before the civil authorities could resume their responsibilities.

The importance of the 'Banana Wars' to the Marine Corps experience in Vietnam is that many senior officers in the Corps claimed that this experience provided the basis of their strategy in Vietnam. Generals Krulak and Walt both later wrote that the lessons learned in the Caribbean were a key element in developing their strategy in Vietnam.[19] Neither officer had actually participated in the Banana Wars, but had served

18 Ronald Schaffer (ed.), *Small Wars Manual.* (Manhattan, NY: Sunflower Univ. Press, 1996 reprint of the 1940 edition).

19 Victor Krulak, in *First to Fight* and Lewis Walt, in *Strange War, Strange Strategy*, both made numerous references to the utility of the Marine Corp's previous experience in the Caribbean and

under (or been taught by) veterans of those campaigns and said that what they learned from these officers, together with the corporate knowledge within the Marine Corps regarding these earlier campaigns, was invaluable in Vietnam. General Lew Walt, the first Marine commander in Vietnam, was especially influenced by Lt. General Lewis 'Chesty' Puller and Maj. General Merrill 'Red Mike' Edson. General Puller had served with the *Gendarmerie d'Haiti* and the Nicaraguan National Guard, later becoming one of Walt's instructors when he was undergoing initial officer training at the Marine Corps Basic School. General Edson served for a year in Nicaragua and was chair of the 'Edson Board' that was responsible for updating the Marine Corps' first attempt at a manual, *Small Wars Operations* which was published in 1935. General Walt later observed:

> I was reminded of my early days as a young officer, learning the fundamentals of my profession from men who had fought Sandino in Nicaragua or Charlemagne in Haiti. The Caribbean campaigns had many lessons applicable to Vietnam forty or fifty years later. I could recall the instruction of veterans of those campaigns and their lessons on tempering the fight with an understanding of the people, compassion toward them, and the exercise of good works, even in the midst of war. These lessons were spelled out in the US Marine Corps Small Wars Manual.[20]

Major Ben Connable USMC, writing on Marine Corps organisational culture in the *Small Wars Journal*, argued that both Puller and Edson, by virtue of their positions at The Basic School, together with Majors Utley (author of the 1935 manual) and Harrington, who both wrote extensively on counter-guerrilla warfare, were able to have a 'disproportionately significant effect on doctrine in a small Marine Corps'.[21] This was because of their larger than life personae, the greater latitude afforded to Marine officers to write on professional matters and the fact that this seemingly new role appeared to give the Marine Corps the direction it was looking for.[22] Connable also argues that the Marine Corps in the 1930s and 1940s conformed to the criteria of a 'learning organisation' as defined in Lieutenant Colonel John Nagl's *Learning to Eat Soup with a Knife*, in that it promoted suggestions from the field, encouraged subordinates to question policies, institutionally questioned its basic assumptions, generated local standard operating procedures (SOP), and had senior officers who were in close touch with their men in the field.[23] The first part of Connable's argument that, the Marine Corps was a learning organisation is supported by the Corps' extensive use of the *Marine Corps Gazette* as a means of disseminating ideas, questioning existing practices and promoting debate within the officer ranks of the Marine Corps. In

its relevance to Vietnam.

20 Lewis Walt, *Strange War, Strange Strategy*, p. 29.

21 Major Ben Connable USMC, 'Culture Warriors: Marine Corps Organisational Culture and Adaptation to Cultural Terrain', *Small Wars Journal* website, 7 Feb 2008, p. 3 <http://smallwarsjournal.com/mag/docs-temp/4-connable.pdf> (Accessed July 2019).

22 Ben Connable, *Culture Warriors*, p. 3.

23 Ben Connable, *Culture Warriors*, p. 4.

Mars Learning: The Marine Corps' Development of Small Wars Doctrine 1915-1940, Keith Bickel points out that the *Marine Corps Gazette* and *Naval Institute Proceedings* were used as informal means of passing on lessons learned and debating doctrine, although most articles concentrated on the military aspects of small wars rather than civil affairs or pacification.[24] The pace of publication of articles relating to small wars accelerated between 1927 and 1941, with at least half of the articles being either solicited by HQ USMC or were official after action reports, printed in order that the lessons learned could be passed on to Marines still in the field.[25]

The ability to create local standard operating procedures is also borne out in Bickel's work; despite the lack of formal counterinsurgency or 'small wars' doctrine and the fact that the Dominican and Haitian campaigns were being fought on the same island almost concurrently, there was little or no cross-pollination of ideas; the commanders in both campaigns appear to have settled on the same strategy independently. The situation should have changed by the time the Marines became involved in Nicaragua, but it appears that the Corps went through the same learning curve as it did in Haiti and the Dominican Republic.[26] Bickel puts this down to the lack of a formal mechanism for passing on lessons learned, the absence of training in counterinsurgency at Marine Corps schools and the deployment of new officers who had not served in either of the previous campaigns.[27] Following the Nicaragua intervention there was a concerted effort to produce a manual on small wars and the subject was taught at Company and Field level schools, with teaching hours peaking between 1934 and 1939. After that, the number of hours devoted to small wars began to drop off again.[28] The situation was much the same in the years immediately prior to the Marines' deployment to Vietnam, although the means of informal dissemination of small wars/counterinsurgency doctrine had improved and there were senior officers who had learned from the generation who trained them; the generation that had served in the 'Banana Wars'.

Despite the existence of the *Small Wars Manual*, it is often argued that the Marines' strategy in Vietnam was based more on contemporary counterinsurgency thinking than its own pre-war experience. Some scholars have argued that the Marine Corps lost the expertise it had gained in earlier counterinsurgency during the middle part of the 20th Century, when small wars were overshadowed by the Second World War and Korea, and that the doctrine developed in the 1960s was mainly based upon the US Army and British doctrines derived from their experiences in the Philippines and Malaya.[29] Senior Marine officers even acknowledged this loss of counterinsurgency skills in their writings. In April 1950, for example, Lt. Col. Robert Heinl submitted an article to the *Marine*

24 Keith Bickel, *Mars Learning: The Marine Corps Development of Small Wars Doctrine 1915-1940* (Boulder: Westview Press, 2001), p. 184, Table 5.2.

25 Keith Bickel, *Mars Learning*, p. 179

26 Keith Bickel, *Mars Learning*, Tables 2.1, 3.1 and 4.1.

27 Keith Bickel, *Mars Learning*, p. 161.

28 Keith Bickel, *Mars Learning*, Figure 6.1.

29 Ronald Schaffer, introduction to *Small Wars Manual.*

Corps Gazette, in which he lamented the loss of expertise in small-unit operations and urged the Corps to address this issue as a matter of urgency because '...the next war, if any, may find a very large volume of [small unit operations] going begging...'.[30] Although Lt Col Heinl was mainly referring to small unit commando or partisan-type operations in the context of a wider Eurasian war, he included 'small wars' in the list of specialisations the Corps should consider developing. With particular respect to the *Small Wars Manual*, Ronald Schaffer wrote in the introduction to the Sunflower University Press edition:

> What was the fate of this prophetic work, product of historical investigation and personal experience of veteran officers? To all intents and purposes, the *Small Wars Manual* of 1940 was forgotten...When a Marine officer prepared a study of guerrilla and counter-guerrilla tactics in 1960 for the training manual *Anti-Guerrilla Warfare*, he was unaware that the 1940 *Small Wars Manual* existed.[31]

The official history of the Marines in Vietnam, however, puts this in context by explaining that the younger generation of officers were learning new skills vicariously from contemporary experience while senior officers still retained the knowledge gained from their early days in the Corps:

> A former III MAF Staff officer in 1965 and, later, a battalion and combined action group commander, Colonel John E. Greenwood, cautioned that the relationship between Marine Corps counterinsurgency theory and earlier Marine experience in the Caribbean era can be overdrawn. Colonel Greenwood remarked that during the Kennedy era 'guerrilla warfare expertise' was one of the 'popular 'in' topics' and the 'hundreds of Marine officers,' including himself 'attended the Army schools and studied the doctrine developed and articulated by the British and by the US Army'. He made the point that for officers of his generation, as opposed to the senior commanders such as General Walt, 'our insights in war of this kind came from this nearly contemporaneous effort, not from Marine Corps experience 30 years previous'.[32]

The Corps' first manual on counterinsurgency after President Kennedy's initiative (and in fact its first counterinsurgency manual since the *Small Wars Manual*) was Fleet Marine Force Manual (FMFM) 21 *Operations against Guerrilla Forces*, produced in 1962.[33] This

30 Lieutenant Colonel Robert D. Heinl, 'Small Wars – Vanishing Art?', *Marine Corps Gazette*, April 1950, pp. 22-25.

31 Ronald Schaffer, *Small Wars Manual*, p xii. Unfortunately, Schaffer does not name the officer or elaborate on this particular manual.

32 Colonel John E. Greenwood, comments on draft manuscript, in Jack Shulimson and Charles Johnson, *US Marines in Vietnam: The Landing and the Buildup: 1965* (Washington, DC: History and Museums Division, US Marine Corps, 1978), p. 133.

33 United States Marine Corps, *Operations Against Guerrilla Forces, FMFM 21* (Washington, DC:

manual does have clear links with the *Small Wars Manual*, blended with expertise gained from the US Army and the British. In the Foreword, General Wallace M. Greene (then Chief of Staff of the USMC, later to be Commandant of the Marine Corps) wrote that the manual '...takes its departure from the US Marine Corps publication *The Small Wars Manual, 1940...*'.[34] According to the bibliographies in the Marines' Field Manuals published in 1962 and 1964, the *Small Wars Manual* is annotated as being out of print.

Although *FMFM 21 (1962)* was a much shorter book than the *Small Wars Manual*, the links between the two are clear. For example, the sections on the relationship between the Marine Corps and the US State Department appear early in both manuals and give similar instructions. *FMFM 21 (1962)* clearly indicates the chain of command, the role of the State Department, the need for liaison between the military and diplomatic agencies and urges close contact and co-operation between US forces and the local government. Both documents also emphasise the fact that most insurgencies are based on political, economic or social issues and that military force alone will not solve the problem. *FMFM 21 (1962)* and the *Small Wars Manual* both contain chapters on the role of the military when acting as the government, although *FMFM 21 (1962)* has more to say on civil action and reconstruction, whereas the *Small Wars Manual* is more concerned with the administrative considerations in setting up a military government. Both, however, emphasise the need to work through existing local authorities wherever possible and caution against being over-strict with the local population as this may be counter-productive. Both also highlight the need to hand authority back to the local government as soon as is practicable.[35]

The next edition of *FMFM 21*, published in 1964, enhanced the 1962 edition and was designated *FMFM 8-2*. The introduction was expanded to refer to the communist exploitation of nations emerging from colonial rule as one cause of insurgency and the need to improve the political climate and 'firm up the civic status' was included in the list of general tasks within a counterinsurgency campaign, the others being improvement of the education services and economy and assisting the armed forces to stabilise the nation.[36] *FMFM 8-2* also included more detail in the section on intelligence on the staff requirements. The need for specialists such as imagery analysts, surveillance specialists and technical intelligence personnel was added in *FMFM 8-2* (1964).[37] Although this was only a small change, it showed an increasing reliance by the Marines on remote sensors and listening devices as a means of conserving resources and reducing casualties. This was apparent when, in 1967 and 1968, the Marines were engaged in a debate with General Westmoreland regarding the establishment of a major combat base in a remote inland location. Among the reasons given by the Marines for not wanting to deploy a large force

HQ USMC, 1962).

34 General Wallace Greene, foreword to *FMFM 21* (1962).

35 FMFM 21 (1962) Section 10 and *Small Wars Manual*, Chapter XIII.

36 United States Marine Corps, *Operations against Guerrilla Forces, FMFM 8-2*, (Washington, DC: HQ USMC, 1964), p 1. Hereafter referred to as *FMFM 8-2* (1964).

37 FMFM 8-2 (1964), pp. 19-20.

to the base to monitor the area for NVA activity was their view that the job could be done more effectively through the increased use of electronic surveillance in addition to the already effective use of the local population to provide information.[38]

A significant feature of the Vietnam War was the use of artillery, and in particular the use of artillery to harass and interdict insurgent operations. This use of artillery, known as H&I, led to indiscriminate and random artillery barrages on locations and routes that the enemy was thought likely to use, such as jungle clearings and road junctions. H&I was also used as a means of reducing enemy morale because it was thought that the random nature of the barrages would keep the enemy off balance and deny enemy forces the chance to rest. In the 1962 edition of *FMFM 21*, H&I was defined as 'planned to deny use of communications routes, selected areas and terrain features, and to disrupt guerrilla operations'.[39] In the 1964 edition of the manual, H&I was split into two parts. Harassing fire was intended to 'disturb the rest of the guerrilla, to curtail his movement, and by threat of loss, to lower his morale', while interdiction fires were 'placed on an area or point to prevent the enemy from using the area or point'.[40] Although this change may have been simply to clarify the terminology, it was foreshadowed the reliance placed on artillery in Vietnam.

The doctrine on the use of local defence units was strengthened in the 1964 edition. As well as 'being capable of repelling terrorist attacks and preventing loss of supplies and equipment', the Marines now expected to train them to a sufficient standard to 'hold an attacking guerrilla force until the arrival of mobile military reaction forces'.[41] This change may well have been a result of the successful VC attacks against American advisory and Special Forces compounds during 1964. The Special Forces at that time were engaged in training the tribes in the mountainous inland area and one of their compounds, at Kontum, was overrun in July 1964. Fifty South Vietnamese and two Americans were killed in the attack.[42] It was therefore apparent that local militias needed a high standard of training. This does reflect the two stage development of local forces in the *Small Wars Manual*. The first stage is that Marine and local forces work together to provide security and the second stage, described in *FMFM 8-2* (1964), is that local forces provide their own protection while Marines act as a quick response force if required.[43] The use of local defence forces had always been a key element of Marine counterguerrilla strategy partly, as Bickel argues, as a force multiplier to make up for lack of resources but also as part of the process of withdrawal and handing the responsibility for security back to the local authorities. It is not clear, though, why this element of counterinsurgency was de-emphasised in contemporary manuals unless it had become a lost art until this point.

38 General Victor Krulak, Top Secret exclusive SPECAT message for General Chapman, dated 13 Jan 1968, III MAF Incoming Message file, Jan 1968, pp. 32-37.

39 *FMFM 21* (1962), p. 60.

40 *FMFM 8-2* (1964), p. 60.

41 *FMFM 8-2* (1964), p. 74.

42 Phillip Davidson, *Vietnam at War*, p. 316.

43 *Small Wars Manual*, Chapter 12, p. 19.

The counterinsurgency forces in Malaya, Indochina and Algeria had not made great use of locally raised militias, although there were regular army and police units consisting of local nationals. Since much of the doctrine in the Marines' manuals was based upon contemporary experience, this may explain the deficiency. The Marine Corps does appear to have re-discovered the value of local militias in late 1965 with the advent of the CAPs and other initiatives, including extra training and improved pay and conditions, to enhance the local militias already in place.

A third edition of the manual was produced in 1967, this time named *Counterinsurgency Operations* but with the same serial number – *FMFM 8-2*.[44] This edition appears to have been updated with lessons learned by the Marines in the field in Vietnam. For example, a section was added to address command relationships between a landing force and the forces already ashore.[45]

The biggest difference between the two manuals was the expansion of the chapter on Civic Action. In previous versions of the manual, civic action was covered in less than half a page and provided a fairly short list of likely areas for civic action: transport and communication infrastructure; schools; hospitals; churches, agriculture; and provision of emergency supplies. A fairly short introductory paragraph explained the utility of civic action as a means of restoring support for the government rather than being used as a gift or charity.[46] In *FMFM 8-2* (1967), this section was considerably expanded to cover three pages, with deeper explanation of the role of civic action as a means of improving the 'standing of the military forces with the population'.[47]

By the time that *FMFM 8-2* was written, the Marines had been in Vietnam for two years and during this time pacification, including civic action, had been a key element of their operations. Many of the items listed in the manual as examples of civic action projects directly relate to the 1966 campaign plan (see Table 1 in Chapter 1) and the Hamlet Evaluation System (See Table 2 in Chapter 1). The manual specifically listed protection of harvested crops as a worthwhile civic action project and this almost certainly resulted from the success of the Golden Fleece operations, which were intended for that purpose. What is clear from this is that the Marines had learned that civic action was more than an almost random selection of projects in the hoping of gaining popular support for the government; civic action needed to be focused with specific activities carried out at the appropriate time and place to achieve a specific result. What was still lacking, however, was the means to report on the effects of civic action. Although a paragraph was added to cover reporting on civic action, it was vague and only referred to reporting 'events concerning civic action', including 'apparent or actual attempts by insurgent elements to inhibit the civic action program through intimidation, terror, or other means'.[48] The

44 United States Marine Corps, *Counterinsurgency Operations, FMFM 8-2* (Washington, DC: HQ USMC, 1967).

45 FMFM 8-2 (1967), p24.

46 *FMFM 8-2* (1964), p. 73.

47 *FMFM 8-2* (1967), p. 173.

48 *FMFM 8-2* (1967), p. 174.

expansion of this section was still a step forward in developing a doctrine that combined civic action with military operations.

Dissemination of Doctrine and Training for Vietnam

As with the Caribbean small wars, the Marine Corps' schools and the *Marine Corps Gazette* were the main ways in which counterinsurgency doctrine was disseminated prior to and during the Marines' involvement in Vietnam. The essential difference is that, with regard to Vietnam, this process began before the war and not toward the end or afterward, as was the case in the Caribbean wars. In the early 1960s there was an increase in counterinsurgency training at USMC schools and in unit tactical training, but this remained focused at the level of small unit operations against guerrilla forces rather than any in-depth practice in deep operations such as civil affairs or population control.[49] Counterinsurgency at that time was only a small part of the range of missions that the Marines were expected to perform. The Corps was developing as a Force in Readiness – a quick reaction force that could project power from the sea in response in amphibious assaults and 'aerial envelopment', fighting wars that ranged in scale from minor interventions to just below nuclear conflicts. Training could not, therefore concentrate too much on any one aspect, but had to ensure that units could perform well at a range of core functions such as amphibious warfare, air-ground co-operation and heliborne assault.

One major exercise to practise the techniques of counterinsurgency was held in 1964. General Krulak, who had taken over as Commanding General Fleet Marine Force Pacific (CG FMFPac) after a tour of duty as special advisor on counterinsurgency to the Joint Chiefs of Staff, wanted to ensure that the units most likely to deploy to Vietnam were trained in current counterinsurgency techniques. As a consequence, Exercise Silver Lance simulated a small but weak nation (Lancelot) that was undergoing an insurgent campaign sponsored by a stronger neighbour (Merlin), which was itself supported by a third even stronger nation (Mordred). All three nations notionally shared a border with a fourth, neutral neighbour (named Neutrala, somewhat unimaginatively compared to the others). The exercise began at the point where the northern province of Lancelot had been virtually taken over by the insurgents. Marines were drafted in to play the inhabitants, some of whom were villagers by day and guerrillas by night. A wide range of roles was created including local defence forces, village leaders, agitators, refugees and politicians. Other Marines were used to play the role of US government officials. Those who were to interact with the landing force were all Spanish speakers, to increase the level of realism as landing force members were forced to rely on linguists to communicate. The guerrilla forces consisted of a field force and local part-time guerrillas. The initial force was a single brigade which rapidly became overwhelmed by the task at hand, so a full corps (minus some elements) was landed. The Marines managed to achieve the military goals

49 Alan Millett, *Semper Fidelis*, p. 548.

of the task within a week and then moved on to the reconstruction or 'nation-building' (although this term was not coined until many years later) phase.[50]

The exercise actually ended early when the Marine commander managed to carry out a pincer movement, combined with a vertical envelopment, which destroyed the guerrilla field force fairly rapidly.[51] Due to the short nature of the exercise, it is difficult to assess exactly how much was learned by the majority of the troops, especially as success was achieved by mainly traditional military means, but it did give all the units a taste of what was to come in Vietnam; all of the participating units eventually deployed in the war. It is not clear from the literature available whether the Marine landing force won the battle by superior tactics or whether the opposing force were too conventional as guerrillas, thus becoming more susceptible to conventional military tactics.

The *Marine Corps Gazette* played a similar role in disseminating doctrine, theory and lessons learned as it had in the 1920s and 1930s during the Caribbean wars. *FMFM 21 (1962)* was serialised in the *Marine Corps Gazette* between June 1962 and February 1963. The January 1962 edition was a 'Guerrilla Warfare Special', with an article by Bernard Fall and another by Peter Paret and John Shy, as well as a condensed version of Mao Tse Tung's primer on guerrilla warfare.[52] Articles on guerrilla warfare by world experts on strategy were published regularly between 1960 and 1965, including pieces by: Bernard Fall;[53] Basil Liddel Hart;[54] Richard Clutterbuck;[55] and General Vo Nguyen Giap's book on guerrilla warfare was serialised between April 1962 and August 1962. Between January 1960 and December 1968 there were 525 items in the *Marine Corps Gazette* that mentioned insurgency or guerrilla warfare and 73 main articles that directly addressed the subject.[56]

Role and Influence of Senior Officers in Applying Doctrine in Vietnam

General Krulak had taken a great interest in counterinsurgency from the 1960s, partly because his duties demanded it, but also because he was an innovator. During his career

50 Colonel Clifford Robichaud, 'Silver Lance', *Marine Corps Gazette*, July 1965, pp. 44-47.

51 Anonymous, 'Silver Lance Ends; Mission Accomplished', *Marine Corps Gazette*, April 1965, p. 5.

52 Bernard Fall, 'Street Without Joy', *Marine Corps Gazette*, January 1962, pp. 33-42; Peter Paret & John Shy, 'Guerrilla War and US Military Policy', *Marine Corps Gazette*, January 1962, pp. 24-32.

53 Bernard Fall, 'Vo Nguyen Giap - Man and Myth', *Marine Corps Gazette*, August 1963, pp. 34-37.

54 Basil Liddell Hart, 'Guerrilla War: Factors and Reflections', *Marine Corps Gazette*, December 1962, pp. 22-27.

55 Richard Clutterbuck, 'Jungle Courier', *Marine Corps Gazette*, June 1964, pp. 32-36; 'Why Chi Keong Surrendered', *Marine Corps Gazette*, pp. 32-36; 'An Anti-Communist Agent in Malaya', *Marine Corps Gazette*, August 1964, pp. 32-35.

56 Based on word searches of the *Marine Corps Gazette* online archives. When the terms 'insurgent', 'guerrilla', 'counterinsurgency', 'counter-insurgency', 'counterguerrilla' and 'insurgency' were entered into a free text search of the entire magazine for the period there were 525 returns. There were 73 returns when these terms were entered into a search of headlines only during the same period.

he had worked on the introduction of front-ramp landing craft and helicopters to the Corps and had played a major role in the inter-service battles that took place in 1946 and 1947 when it appeared that the Marine Corps was to be abolished.[57] He was heavily influenced by the counterinsurgency principles promulgated by Sir Robert Thompson. Whilst serving as Special Assistant for Counterinsurgency to the Joint Chiefs of Staff, Krulak met with Thompson a number of times:

> Several meetings with Sir Robert Thompson, who contributed so much to the British victory over the guerrillas in Malaya, established a set of basic counterinsurgency principles in my mind. Thompson said, 'The peoples' trust is primary. It will come hard because they are fearful and suspicious. Protection is the most important thing you can bring them. After that comes health. And after that, many things – land, prosperity, education, and privacy to name a few'. The more I saw of the situation facing the Vietnamese Government and the Vietnamese Army, the more convinced I became – along with many other Americans – that our success in the counterinsurgency conflict would depend on a complete and intimate understanding by all ranks top to bottom of the principles Thompson had articulated.[58]

General Krulak was also influenced by earlier French experiences during the Indochina War. He cites two works in particular as being influential, Philippe Devillers' *Histoire du Vietnam, 1940 d' 1952* and General Henri Navarre's *Agonie de l'Indochinie, 1953-1954*.[59]

Following his posting to Washington, Krulak was appointed as Commanding General Fleet Marine Force Pacific (CG FMFPac). Although not in operational command of the Marine forces in Vietnam, he was responsible for their administration, training and equipment. He was also the senior Marine Corps advisor to the Commander-in-Chief Pacific (CinCPac), who was in command of all forces in the Southeast Asia theatre of operations. This put him in a position to influence Marine commanders in Vietnam and gave him sufficient seniority to approach the JCS, and even the President, with his views on counterinsurgency and its application to the war in Vietnam. He had the support of the Commandant of the Marine Corps and Admiral Sharp (CINCPAC) in presenting his ideas to the Secretary of Defense, Robert McNamara. He wrote a strategic appraisal, which recommended that the main effort of US forces should be to protect the civilian population, more effort should be put into destroying the infrastructure of North Vietnam and thereby reduce its ability to supply the insurgents, civic action programmes should be increased and the Government of South Vietnam should be persuaded to

57 Victor Krulak, *First to Fight*, pp. 28-50 and 90-91; Allan Millet, *Semper Fidelis*, pp. 340, 454-456 and 458-464.

58 Victor Krulak, *First to Fight*, p. 180.

59 Philippe Devillers, *Histoire du Vietnam, 1940 d' 1952* (Paris: Editions du Seuil, 1952); General Henri Navarre *Agonie de l'Indochinie, 1953 – 1954* (Paris: Plon, 1952), all quoted in Victor Krulak, *First to Fight*, p. 241.

embark on a major land reform programme.[60] Unfortunately his ideas were not well received in Washington and he was shunted from one senior official to another.[61] Krulak continued to press his views, however, and was eventually able to come to an agreement with Westmoreland on combining the Marines' approach with the Army's strategy of attrition.

It is not clear what direct influence Krulak had on operations in Vietnam. Clearly he and General Walt had a similar view of the utility of counterinsurgency in order to achieve the Marines' mission in the early part of the campaign but Walt recognised there had been a turning point in the war in mid-1966 as the Marines faced regular NVA units near the border and that the fight in the northern part of Vietnam, along the DMZ, was very different to that in the rest of the country at the time.[62]

Preparations for Deployment and Transition to War

The Marine Corps, as a force in readiness, was prepared for deployment throughout the Southeast Asia theatre of operations. Available forces in that area consisted of III Marine Expeditionary Force (MEF), which was comprised of the 3rd Marine Division and 1st Marine Air Wing (MAW), with their respective HQs in Japan. These were referred to as the Western Pacific Fleet Marine Force (WestPac FMF), which was under command of the Fleet Marine Force Pacific (FMFPac). The other element of FMFPAC, EastPac FMF, was based in Hawaii and California. Although the Commanding General FMFPac declared the WestPac FMF to be fully combat ready, the Commander's Readiness Report for 1965 noted the lack of amphibious transports in the Western Pacific region. The report stated that WestPac FMF only had assets to land a single brigade.[63]

After August 1964 it seemed likely that US Marines would be required in Vietnam following the Gulf of Tonkin incident. The 9th Marine Expeditionary Brigade (MEB) was activated with components from the 3rd Marine Division and 1st MAW. Although the 9th MEB embarked for landing in August 1964 it was not deployed. The brigade then remained on standby for contingencies in Vietnam and elsewhere in theatre. It was this deployment which highlighted the shortage of amphibious assets referred to in the Commander's Readiness Report. These same problems were to hinder Marine Corps deployment to Da Nang in March 1965.

The extent of Marine Corps preparations to deploy to Vietnam is apparent in the plans issued in 1964 for the landing of a Regimental Landing Team (RLT) and III MEF

60 General Victor Krulak, 'A Strategic Concept for the Republic of Vietnam', June 1965, US Marine Corps University Archives, Quantico, Virginia.

61 Victor Krulak, *First to Fight*, pp. 199-202.

62 Lewis Walt, *Strange War, Strange Strategy*, pp. 137-140, 156-157.

63 FMFPac, 'Commander's Readiness Report for Financial Year 1965', dated 25 Sep 1964, p. 2. The report gives the state of readiness for units under command at the beginning of the financial year, which runs from October to October. Thus FY 1965 is October 64 to October 65.

itself. Operational Plan (OPPLAN) 37-64 comprised of a set of orders for a Regimental Landing Team (the ground component of a Marine Expeditionary Brigade) to land in Da Nang in support of American and South Vietnamese operations in the northern provinces, in the I Corps Tactical Zone (ICTZ). South Vietnam was divided militarily into zones numbered sequentially from the border with North Vietnam, each of which conformed to a corps boundary. The most northerly zone was designated I Corps (corps are given Roman numerals and I Corps is spoken phonetically as 'Eye Corps'). This was the area in which the Marines were to operate in the event that a landing was carried out in 1964 and was the area to which Marines were in fact deployed in February 1965. The order gave three possible missions: 'Control or curtailment of VC activity on or through the RVN/LAOS and RVN/CAMBODIA borders'; 'Selective retaliatory actions by RVN forces against DRV'; 'Expanded military pressures by both US and RVN forces against DRV'.[64]

The Marines were therefore prepared for three possible scenarios, although the order itself was mainly geared towards the third, which involved a deployment to Da Nang as a base of operations.[65] On arrival at Da Nang, once the initial base areas were secured, the RLT mission was:

> [T]o conduct such operations during the deterrent stage of the deployment as required and as directed by CG 9th MEB. Possible operations include:
> 1. Reinforcement and support of RVN operations
> 2. Amphibious raids against targets in DRV
> 3. Counterinsurgency operations against VIET CONG.[66]

The 'deterrent stage' refers to an earlier paragraph in the order, which acknowledged the possibility of a retaliation against South Vietnam by either North Vietnam or the Chinese in the event of offensive action by the South Vietnamese. The Marines were tasked to act as a deterrent by having forces in place in South Vietnam prior to any such action.[67] The concern about retaliation by North Vietnam or the Chinese resulted from discussions held in early 1964 between President Johnson and the Joint Chiefs of Staff (JCS). While General Taylor, the chairman of the JCS, favoured gradual and selective attacks against North Vietnam, whereas General Greene (Commandant of the Marine Corps) and General LeMay (Chief of Staff of the Air Force) both believed that the only two real options were a complete withdrawal or a complete commitment to full scale war with North Vietnam, because gradual or selective attacks were highly likely to 'result in a major campaign, smaller perhaps, but similar to that which took place in KOREA and

64 3rd Marine Division, 'OPPLAN 37-64 for RLT CO', dated 18 Aug 1964, pp. 1–2, US Marine Corps Historical Division, Washington, DC.

65 3rd Marine Division, 'OPPLAN 37-64 for RLT CO', 18 Aug 1964, p. 2.

66 3rd Marine Division, 'OPPLAN 37-64 for RLT CO', 18 Aug 1964, Annex B, p. 2.

67 3rd Marine Division, 'OPPLAN 37-64 for RLT CO', 18 Aug 1964, Annex B, p. 1.

that there was a risk of a possible escalation into another world war'.[68] Greene and LeMay maintained that the conduct of a total war against North Vietnam, would prevent this. The prevailing view at the time, however, was that a graduated response would keep the threshold of conflict so low that neither Hanoi nor Peking would be presented with a cause to commit forces directly in South Vietnam.[69]

OPPLAN 37-64 reflected this belief in the possibility of large scale retaliation by North Vietnam and China, and also represented Marine Corps doctrine at the time. Both OPPLAN 37-64 and OPPLAN 32-65 (the plan for the deployment of the entire III MEF) were geared towards limited operations in the Da Nang area, with the defence of military assets and counterinsurgency against VC guerrilla forces as the main aims, although there is an acknowledgement that Marine Corps elements may end up engaging regular military units of the North Vietnamese or even Chinese armies. This emphasis on counterinsurgency operations in the littoral area would later be the catalyst for conflict between the Marines and the overall commander of US forces in Vietnam, General William Westmoreland.

Between 1961 and 1965 the Marines' presence in Vietnam slowly escalated in line with the overall American presence in-country. The Marines sent elements to support the operations of the US Military Assistance Advisory Group (MAAG) (which was transformed into the US Military Assistance Command Vietnam (MACV) in 1964), starting with advisors in 1959, followed by Operation Shufly in 1962, in which a helicopter squadron was sent to Vietnam in direct support of the ARVN. By the end of 1963 there were around 16,000 American military personnel in Vietnam, as the United States became more directly involved in the war and became more invested in the success of the regime in South Vietnam.[70] The situation in the country had deteriorated to a greater extent than the US government had realised after the coup that removed the South Vietnamese Prime Minister Diem in November 1963. The Johnson Administration became aware that, as a result of an 'undue dependence on Vietnamese reporting', it had been misled with regard to the situation and the VC now controlled 'very high proportions of the people in certain key provinces', as Robert McNamara put it in a memorandum to President Johnson in December 1963.[71]

In March 1964 the Commandant of the Marine Corps, General Wallace Greene, recorded that President Johnson was still wary of a direct US involvement in Vietnam, such as committing ground troops or bombing targets in the North, because 'he felt that

68 General Wallace M. Greene, notes from Joint Chiefs conference with the President, dated 4 March 1964. General Wallace M. Greene Personal Papers, US Marine Corps Historical Division, Washington, DC at the time of writing. Unless otherwise specified all references to General Greene's notes are from this collection.

69 H.R. McMaster, *Dereliction of Duty: Lyndon Johnson, Robert McNamara, the Joint Chiefs of Staff, and the Lies that led to Vietnam* (New York: Harper Perennial, 1998), pp. 73-75.

70 H.R. McMaster, *Dereliction of Duty*, p. 56.

71 Robert McNamara, Memorandum for the President, dated 21 December 1963. Reproduced in Gareth Porter, *Vietnam: A History in Documents* (New York, NY: Meridian, 1981), p. 258.

such action would almost certainly result in a war – that the Chinese Communists, and possibly the Russians, would actively enter the picture'. Greene proposed four possible courses of action to President Johnson at a meeting with the JCS. These were: continuing with advice and support, with the risk that this would result in a 'slow bleed of men and money' that would become so unpopular that the American electorate would demand some other course of action; complete withdrawal, with the accompanying loss of face to the US; a 'neutralisation' agreement of the type that had prevented war in Laos but had effectively handed the country over to the communists (something approaching a 'peace with honour' solution); and an immediate expansion of operations against North Vietnam, Laos and Cambodia. Greene's own position was that the US should either decide to fight and win in Vietnam, by taking the war to the North, or withdraw completely. President Johnson stated that either a complete withdrawal or total involvement were preferable to any half measures, but he did not want to become involved in a wider war before the presidential election, due in November 1964, as this might adversely affect the Democrats' chances of winning. After the election Johnson felt that the time would be right to introduce a joint resolution in Congress to support an expanded war in Vietnam and explain to the American people why it was necessary to risk another Southeast Asian war. Greene was of the opinion that the President was telling General Taylor, who was due to visit Vietnam on 8 March 1964, 'that [the President] did not want [Taylor] to return from SVN with a recommendation that the campaign there be expanded to include NVN to the extent that the risk might arise of a Korean-type war, or all-out war with the Communists'.[72]

The President's wish to delay a decision about further commitment to Vietnam until after the election was, however, overtaken by events. The Tonkin Incident in August 1964 created the environment in which Congress approved a Joint Resolution that gave the President the authority 'to take all necessary measures to repel any armed attack against the armed forces of the United States...to prevent further aggression…[and] to assist any member or protocol state of the Southeast Asia Collective Defense Treaty requesting assistance in defense of its freedom'.[73]

The actual flashpoint for the deployment of Marines to Vietnam, however, was a series of attacks by the VC against American military installations in Pleiku and Qui Nhon in early February 1965. After the first attack, against the US Army Special Forces at Pleiku in the central highlands, President Johnson ordered Operation Rolling Thunder, a series of punitive bombing attacks against North Vietnam. Fearing for the safety of the air bases around Da Nang, the USMC was ordered to deploy a light anti-aircraft missile battery to the area. No sooner had the battery arrived than a further attack took place at another US Army installation at Qui Nhon, on the coast, during which 23 US soldiers were killed

72 General Wallace M. Greene, notes from Joint Chiefs' conference with the President, 4 March 1964.

73 US Congress, House, 'Joint Resolution to Promote the Maintenance of International Peace and Security in Southeast Asia', HR 1145, 88th Congress, 2nd Session, introduced in House August 10, 1964.

and 21 wounded. On 22 February 1965 General Westmoreland, acting on the advice of his deputy, Lieutenant General Throckmorton, who had conducted a security survey of the air bases around Da Nang, asked for a Marine Expeditionary Brigade to be deployed to secure the bases due to the threat posed by the VC.[74]

Conclusion

In the decade preceding the Marines' deployment to Vietnam there were a number of factors put in place that almost pre-determined their strategy in Vietnam. First, the Hogaboom Board created an expeditionary Marine Corps that would be reliant on support from the sea, for logistics and supporting arms (naval gunfire and air support). The relative lack of transport within Marine units meant that they would not be able to establish robust supply lines deep inland. The allocation of a defensive mission that tied them to coastal bases, which further reinforced this littoral posture and made operations inland difficult. The Marines apparent reluctance to move away from the coastal enclaves they created would later be interpreted as a reluctance to engage the enemy, but in fact this attitude was almost forced upon them by circumstances.

Second, the Marines had not only developed a counterinsurgency doctrine based upon the most recent 'lessons learned' from contemporary campaigns fought by the French and British, but they also had a counterinsurgency legacy of their own. Experience from the Banana Wars had been passed down to the generation of officers who commanded Marine units in Vietnam, which was to stand them in good stead when they arrived in Vietnam and found themselves in the midst of a potentially hostile population.

The Marines did not have a prepared strategy for the war in Vietnam, even though the Commandant had some input at the grand strategic level in Washington DC. It is clear that the senior leadership of the Marine Corps, apart from Krulak, did not see counterinsurgency as the solution to the war, but favoured a conventional approach against North Vietnam, although this was not an option the Johnson Administration would countenance. At the operational level, however, they arrived equipped with a counterinsurgency 'toolset' which, coupled with their operational establishment and specific mission, did a great deal to determine their approach to the war.

74 Jack Shulimson & Charles Johnson, *US Marines in Vietnam*, p. 7.

3

1965: USMC Deployment to Vietnam and the Evolving Mission

The 9th Marine Expeditionary Brigade landed in Da Nang on 8 March 1965 and took up positions around the perimeter of Da Nang airfield. Its orders were to defend the airfield only and not to conduct offensive operations against the Viet Cong (VC).[1] General Westmoreland reinforced that order by stating 'Overall responsibility for the defense of the Danang [sic] area remains an [Republic of Vietnam Armed Forces (RVNAF)] responsibility'.[2] Within days of the first landing, however, strategic level thinking had changed. It was becoming apparent to the President and his senior advisors that bombing was having little or no effect upon North Vietnamese Army (NVA) and VC operations in the South. In fact, if anything, Communist activity had increased. On 6 March 1965 General Westmoreland informed the JCS that:

> [T]hroughout the RVN the Viet Cong hold the initiative. They have had continuing success in their efforts to consolidate political gains in the rural areas; to increase their military strength by a combination of infiltrated cadre and levies on available manpower; and to improve their organization, weaponry, and logistic capability. Through the use of military action, intimidation, and propaganda, they are implanting a sense of the inevitability of VC success. The VC have a propaganda advantage.[3]

General Greene recorded that President Johnson became increasingly frustrated at the apparent inability of the US armed forces to stem the flow of insurgents into South Vietnam, making it clear that he 'wanted more Viet Cong killed'.[4] On 6 April the

1 Joint Chiefs of Staff message to Commander in Chief, Pacific, 6 March 1965, in Jack Shulimson and Charles Johnson, *US Marines in Vietnam: The Landing and the Build-up: 1965* (Washington, DC: History and Museums Division, US Marine Corps, 1978), p. 16.

2 Fleet Marine Force Pacific, *Operations of the III MAF, Vietnam, Mar – Sep 1965*, p. 5.

3 General William Westmoreland, Telegram to the Joint Chiefs of Staff, Saigon, Vietnam, 6 Mar 1965. Foreign Relations of the United States, Vol. II, Vietnam.

4 General Wallace Greene, Memorandum for the Record: Conference with the President 081530 –

President approved National Security Action Memorandum 328, which authorised an additional 18-20,000 troops, plus two more Marine battalions with supporting troops, and gave the Marines a 'change of mission to permit their more active use under considerations to be established and approved by the Secretary of Defense in consultation with the Secretary of State'.[5] The President remained impatient and told a meeting of the JCS on 8 April 1965 that, 'I want you to come back here next Tuesday and tell me how we are going to kill more Viet Cong. At the present time we are limited as to what we can do in [North Vietnam], but we have almost free rein in [South Vietnam], and I want to kill more Viet Cong'. General Greene reminded the President that he had made similar comments at the previous meeting on 15 March and that, at the time of this meeting almost a month later, the Marines had only just been given permission to conduct offensive operations. He also reminded the President that initial operations would have to be small-scale to begin with 'due to the security mission for which they are also responsible' and took the opportunity to ask for more manpower, including the first elements of a Marine Air Wing, in order to expand operations. General Greene also recommended that the Vietnamese Marine Corps be moved to Da Nang in order to conduct joint operations with the Marines 'just as we have done many times with indigenous troops in Latin American countries'.[6]

A week later, at the next meeting of the JCS, General Greene outlined a plan for joint operations that would require fewer US troops, which met with some approval by President Johnson because it seemed to offer an alternative to the three extra divisions that General Wheeler, Chairman of the JCS, was recommending. H.R. McMaster, in *Dereliction of Duty*, characterised this exchange as Johnson 'pandering' to Greene in order to get the answer he wanted.[7] Johnson was still reluctant to ask Congress to approve committing large numbers of American troops to Vietnam, despite his previous assurances to the JCS that he would send whatever force they considered necessary and the consistent advice from the JCS, General Westmoreland and Ambassador Taylor that this is exactly what would be required. In fact Taylor went as far as to say that the combined forces in Vietnam compared to North Vietnamese forces needed to achieve a ratio of between 10:1 and 20:1 if they were to have any chance of success.[8] Although McMaster provides an excellent analysis of the dysfunctional nature of the relationship between the President and the Joint Chiefs, he is perhaps being a little over-cynical

1740April65, p. 3-4.

5 'National Security Action Memorandum (NSAM) 328', Washington DC: 6 April 1965 in George Herring (ed.), *The Pentagon Papers: Abridged Edition* (New York, NY: McGraw Hill, 1993), p121. The original document appears to indicate that the Marine units are in addition to the extra 18-20,00 troops.

6 General Wallace Greene, Memorandum for the Record: Conference with the President 081530 – 1740April65, p. 3.

7 H.R. McMaster, *Dereliction of Duty*, p. 271.

8 Ambassador Maxwell Taylor, Telegram From the Embassy in Vietnam to the State Department, Saigon, Vietnam, 7 Mar 1965, Foreign Relations of the United States (hereafter FRUS), Vol. II, Vietnam.

here. The President was almost certainly pleased that Greene was giving him the answer he wanted, but it was not due to Greene being taken in by Johnson's 'pandering', as McMaster implies, nor was it a deliberate attempt to 'spare the president the "cold hard facts" that he and the Marine Corps Staff had recorded in an estimate of the situation'.[9] Greene estimated that to clear just the coastal strip (50 miles wide and 150 miles long) the Marines would need at least two divisions, two air wings and a brigade of the Vietnamese Marine Corps, so it is clear that he was generally supportive of increasing the US force in Vietnam.[10] Greene's response was more likely to have been generated by three other factors. First, it would be almost natural to a Marine of Greene's generation to consider the use of indigenous forces to boost the Marine force. The senior officers in the Marine Corps had been trained by, and served with, veterans of the interventions in Latin America where the creation and use of indigenous forces had been a significant factor in the Marines' success and withdrawal strategy. Second, the Marines had invested a great deal of advisory time and effort in building up the Vietnamese Marine Corps and making it more combat effective after a disastrous defeat in December 1964, so there was a certain logic in choosing to request troops that were a known quantity, with similar methods of operation.[11] Finally, although Greene supported the Joint Chiefs' position that a further three US divisions should be committed to Vietnam he would almost certainly have been aware of the practical difficulties involved in doing this at that time. The Marines' logistic chain in the Pacific had almost collapsed within weeks of the deployment to Vietnam: the computerised stock system broke down when humidity made the punch cards swell so they couldn't fit into the computers making stock control extremely difficult; there were shortages of almost everything because units failed to accurately forecast the quantities of supplies they would need for combat operations; the poor roads caused more damage to vehicles than had been expected, putting greater strain on the logistic services to provide spare parts and maintenance; and the port facilities in the northern provinces were completely inadequate for the Marine Corps' needs in Vietnam.[12] The debate about troop levels aside, Greene and the rest of the Joint Chiefs were no closer to agreeing on a strategy for the ground war and still the only direction they had from the President were his continued exhortations to 'kill more Viet Cong'.

Meantime, the 9th MEB was settling into its positions in Vietnam and beginning to assess the situation. The brigade had only landed two of its battalions initially, but this was increased to four following the approval of NSAM 328 on 6 April. The Command

9 H.R. McMaster, *Dereliction of Duty* p. 272.

10 General Wallace Greene, Memorandum for the Record, 28 April 1965.

11 The 4th Battalion, Vietnamese Marine Corps (VNMC) was destroyed by a VC force during a battle at Binh Gia, near Saigon. Subsequent operations revealed significant weaknesses in the VNMC brigade level staff and, as a result, FMFPac increased the complement of Marine advisors to the VNMC. See Jack Shulimson & Charles Johnson, *US Marines in Vietnam: 1965*, pp. 204-205.

12 Jack Shulimson & Charles Johnson, *US Marines in Vietnam: 1965*, pp. 181-182.

History of MACV records that on 14 April, General Westmoreland promulgated a four-phase concept of operations to the brigade: establishment of defensive bases; deep reconnaissance patrols along possible enemy avenues of approach; offensive operations as a reaction force alongside the RVNAF; and offensive operations to destroy VC forces in the Da Nang area.[13] In order for the Marines to conduct more offensive operations, however, they had to gain permission from the Vietnamese Corps Commander, General Thi, in whose area they were operating. Thi granted limited authority to expand the Marines' tactical area of responsibility (TAOR) beyond the airfield at Da Nang, but only to the north and west. He told General Karch and General Krulak that 'this is enemy country. You are not ready to operate there'.[14] Thi, having been an army officer during the Indochina War was probably concerned that the Marines, like the French before them, lacked the understanding of Vietnamese culture and the nature of the war that would be necessary to conduct effective operations in populated areas.

Command & Control

This brief incident highlights one of the biggest problems the Marines faced in Vietnam. The command relationships within the US military infrastructure and between the US and their Vietnamese allies were extremely complex. These relationships created competition and lack of trust between the various elements that 'virtually assured disputes...between American military commanders' in the words of one historian of the Marine Corps.[15]

The US military infrastructure placed the Marine elements deployed to Vietnam in two different chains of command. The fact that they were operating in support of the Vietnamese military placed them loosely in a third. Unity of command is one of the United States Army's principles of war and in Vietnam it was largely ignored.[16] Figure 1, below, is an organisation chart showing the two US chains of command above III MAF, as the Marine Corps element in Vietnam was designated.

13 US Military Assistance Command Vietnam Command History, 1965, p. 40.

14 Victor Krulak, *First to Fight*, p. 182.

15 Allan R. Millett, *Semper Fidelis*, pp. 567-568.

16 Department of the Army, *Field Service Regulations–Operations, Field Manual 100-5* (Washington, DC: Department of the Army, 1954), pp. 25-27. The full definition is: 'The decisive application of full combat power requires unity of command. Unity of command results in unity of effort by coordinated action of all forces toward a common goal. Coordination may be achieved by direction or by cooperation. It is best achieved by vesting a single commander with requisite authority'.

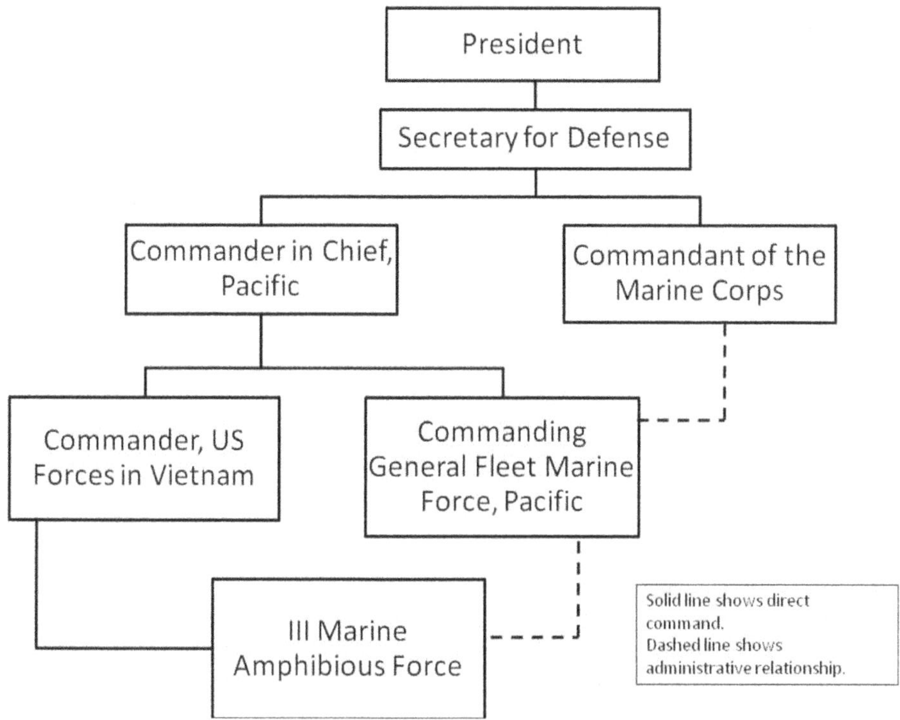

Figure 3.1: Chain of Command for III Marine Amphibious Force.

This diagram clearly shows that the chain of command ran from III MAF to the Commander US Military Assistance Command Vietnam (COMUSMACV), General Westmoreland, then up to the Commander in Chief Pacific (CINCPAC), Admiral Ulysses Sharp, and up to the Department of Defense. This fairly straightforward system was complicated by the fact that III MAF was from a different service to COMUSMACV and was also answerable to its own chain of command within the Marine Corps. III MAF was also under the logistic and administrative control of the Commanding General Fleet Marine Force Pacific (CG FMFPac), General Victor Krulak.[17]

An indication of the continued poor state of the relationship between the two services in the early stages of the American military involvement in Vietnam is contained in a memorandum written by General Greene in June 1965:

17 Although the chain of command is implied in the various instructions and orders given to III MAF, the clearest delineation of responsibilities is in Victor Krulak, *First to Fight*, p. 182.

> During conversations between Sharp [Admiral USG Sharp – CINCPAC] and the Commandant last evening and early this morning, Sharp made the following observations:
>
> General WESTMORELAND and Ambassador TAYLOR do not like Marines and will do everything they can 'to prevent the Marine Corps from getting credit for their accomplishments in South Vietnam. This includes press releases regarding Marine Corps actions and also assignment of Marine Corps units.[18]

Relations between the two services at the level of the JCS almost certainly took a turn for the worse when General Greene learned that Lieutenant General Goodpaster – a US Army officer who at the time was Assistant to the Chairman of the Joint Chiefs of Staff – had established a study group to consider strategy in Vietnam. This had been done under the Chairman's direction without consulting the JCS and, more irksome to Greene, without including a Navy or Marine Corps officer despite the fact that the Marine Corps had 'the most US combat troops in Vietnam thus far'.[19] This level of animosity did not bode well for the future, and the two services continued their institutional running battles over strategy and resources for the remainder of the war.

The third chain of command that the III MAF operated within was the Vietnamese military infrastructure. Although the commander of III MAF was also the senior US advisor to the Commanding General I Corps, the Vietnamese formation that was responsible for the northern provinces of Vietnam where the Marines were operating. The area of operations to which the Marines were assigned was the I Corps Tactical Zone (ICTZ), which consisted of the four northern provinces of South Vietnam. Although there was a formal relationship advisory between the III MAF commander and the Vietnamese commander of ICTZ there was no direct command relationship between the two. This issue was, however, addressed in a Letter of Instruction (LOI) from COMUSMACV to III MAF on 5 May 1965:

> As a matter of policy, US Forces will not be placed under command of allied commanders nor is the [Government of Vietnam] prepared to accept the operational control of US commanders. However, this restriction is not intended to preclude the temporary tactical direction of US Forces by [Republic of Vietnam Armed Forces (RVNAF)] commanders under particular circumstances so warranting or the temporary tactical direction of RVNAF by US commanders under similar circumstances when mutually agreed by the appropriate commanders. Matters

18 Greene, General Wallace, Memorandum for the Record, HQ USMC, Washington DC, 28 June 1965.

19 General Wallace Greene, handwritten additional notes dated 12 July 1965 on a Memorandum for the Record, 10 July 1965.

> of this nature which cannot be resolved by subordinate US commanders will be referred to COMUSMACV.[20]

The South Vietnamese were very sensitive to any perception that the United States was taking over, an attitude General Westmoreland attributed to their newly-won independence. Abandoning the idea of a unified command, Westmoreland came to the conclusion that establishing a relationship built on 'mutual confidence' to ensure that suggestions made by American officers carried sufficient weight to be turned into action by the Vietnamese was the best solution.[21] The spirit of the relationship can be seen early on, in the response of the Vietnamese I Corps commander's response to the III MAF request to expand their areas of operations in July 1965. Noting the 'lack of experience on the part of the 9th USMC Regt [sic] in distinguishing the civilian people from the VC', the I Corps Commander 'agree[d] entirely with the recommendation' but advised caution and recommended a carefully phased operation 'to avoid deplorable incidents'.[22] The Marines worked on this relationship throughout 1965, with General Walt advising at the highest level, Marine Corps officers assigned as military advisors at battalion to division-level and individual units providing training and assistance to village-level militia forces. That the Marines would put so much effort into building up the local forces is hardly surprising given their long established tradition of using indigenous troops. This effort at all levels became a mainstay of the USMC strategy in Vietnam for the entire war.

The rapid changes in command of the Marine forces in Vietnam during the first months of their deployment did nothing to alleviate the situation. The 9th MEB was under command of Brigadier General Karch between 8 March and 6 May. On 6 May, the 3rd Marine Division and the headquarters of III MAF arrived in Da Nang under command of Major General William Collins. The 3rd Marine Division was under command of III MAF, which in turn commanded the other major Marine command in-country – the 3rd Marine Air Wing. The III MAF commander, however, was also 'double-hatted' as the 3rd Marine Division commander at this time. The 9th MEB was dissolved as its component units returned to the 3rd Marine Division. General Karch resumed his position as deputy divisional commander of the 3rd Marine Division. Collins handed over command of III MAF to Major General Lewis Walt, just under a month after his arrival on 4 June. This was a planned change of command as Collins had completed his 13 month tour of duty overseas, having been stationed in Okinawa as commander of the 3rd Marine Division for 12 months prior to his arrival in Vietnam. General Walt remained in command of III MAF until the summer of 1967 and was therefore able to provide some continuity but

20 COMUSMACV, 'Letter of Instruction Governing Operations of the III Marine Expeditionary Force in the Republic of Vietnam' dated 5 May 1965 held as Enclosure 1 to III MAF Command Chronology, July 1965.

21 William Westmoreland, *A Soldier Reports*, pp. 133-134.

22 Brigadier General Nguyen Chanh Thi, 'Letter to CG III MAF authorizing expansion of Da Nang TAOR', 20 July 1965. Enclosure 4 to III MAF Command Chronology, July 1965.

realised that he had a difficult job to pull to co-ordinate the demands of all three chains of command. As he put it:

> My own circumstances, as commander of the Marines, were especially peculiar. We Marines were in the I Corps area of the Vietnamese Army. The Vietnamese commander was responsible to his own Army command in Saigon; I was responsible to Gen. William Westmoreland, who commanded all American forces in Vietnam. I was also designated as the American advisor to the Vietnamese commander of I Corps and as the senior officer of the US Naval Services in all of Vietnam. I commanded my own support facilities and also the Marine Division within my own force.[23]

This last point shows how anomalous the chain of command could be in Vietnam. General Walt was commander of III MAF and the 3rd Marine Division until March 1966, when the 1st Marine Division arrived to augment III MAF, at which time Walt retained command of III MAF (on promotion to Lieutenant General) while command of the 3rd Marine Division passed to Major General Wood Kyle. The complex command relationships within III MAF in the first year of the deployment 'caused some humorous and often confusing staff work. MAF staff and division staff working on [the] same project or MAF staff doing work division staff rightly should'.[24] In the end, General Walt found himself trying to compromise between the demands of his Marine Corps and COMUSMACV masters as a result of the dual chains of command he operated under and because of the very different approaches his seniors within those chains of command expected him to take in his strategy.

The command relationships were also complicated by the fact that the province chiefs were subordinate to the military divisional commander but also directly responsible to the Ministry of the Interior for law enforcement and the competing nature of the two agencies, coupled with the lack of initiative among junior commanders, made combined operations practically impossible[25]. As the JCS pointed out in a contemporary memo criticising Thompson's advice to the South Vietnamese Government, it was relatively easy for the British to achieve this unity of command because at the time Malaya was still a colonial power, therefore the British were able to keep control of both the government and military.[26] Vietnam was somewhat unique in terms of contemporary counterinsurgency

23 Lewis Walt, *Strange War, Strange Strategy*, p. 27.

24 Colonel Rex Denny, quoted in Jack Shulimson and Charles Johnson, *US Marines in Vietnam: 1965*, p. 44.

25 Robert Thompson, *Defeating Communist Insurgency*, pp. 59-62.

26 General Lyman Lemnitzer, 'Counterinsurgency Operations in South Vietnam , Memorandum for General Taylor, 18 October 1961. Quoted in The Pentagon Papers, Gravel edition, Volume Two, pp. 650-651. See *Pentagon Papers, Gravel Edition* <http://www.mtholyoke.edu/acad/intrel/pentagon2/doc102.htm> (Accessed 30 August 2008). The same would have been true for the French in their counterinsurgency campaigns in Indochina and Algeria, even though they were

campaigns in that almost all of the others – the Philippines, Malaya, Indochina and Algeria – were fought and won (or lost) by what were effectively government forces under a single command structure. There was no guidance in the work of the counterinsurgency experts of the 1960s regarding forces conducting combat operations in support of a counterinsurgency campaign in a foreign country. For the Marines, this deficiency was fortunately addressed in their own doctrine. As shown in the previous chapter, the *Small Wars Manual* and the USMC's counterinsurgency manuals stressed that the Marines were most likely to act in support of a host nation government and that authority should be retained by the host government or handed back as soon as possible.[27] The Marines applied this mind-set early in Vietnam, as shown in the first three recommendations in the 3rd Marine Division *Lessons Learned* report of June 1965:

> All civic actions be accomplished through established local officials. In an area where local leadership is weak or non-existent, efforts must first be directed toward the establishment of local government.
>
> Units must insist that the locals do their share in all civic action projects on all levels. Whenever possible, the initiative for conception of ideas and projects should be passed to local officials.
>
> Distribution of all gifts of farm implements, school supplies and other CARE and USOM-type goods be made only to local officials at their seats of government and without publicity.[28]

Given the emphasis on no publicity, these recommendations were probably as much intended to help the Vietnamese preserve 'face' as to promote good local governance. In terms of counterinsurgency theory they clearly fall within David Galula's concept of improving security by enhancing local government.[29] At first III MAF's efforts to work through the local government infrastructure were confounded by the problems Thompson described regarding the lack of quality amongst the Vietnamese personnel. In addition the Commanding General of I (ARVN) Corps was suspicious of the Marines' efforts, according to a study of pacification carried out by a Marine Corps officer at the time.[30] In order to overcome the problems of lack of information regarding all the various US and Vietnamese civic action programs, lack of good local governance and the absence of a central guiding hand, General Walt established a number of Joint Coordinating

less successful in defeating the insurgents.

27 *FMFM 21* (1962) Section 10 and *Small Wars Manual*, Chapter XIII.

28 3rd Marine Division, *Lessons Learned* (Da Nang, Vietnam: May 1965), p. 1, 3rd Marine Division Lessons Learned File 1965.

29 David Galula, *Counterinsurgency Warfare: Theory and Practice*, pp. 81-85.

30 Captain Russell Stolfi, *US Marine Corps Civic Action Effort in Vietnam, March 1965 to March 1966* (Washington, DC: Historical Branch, G-3 Division, HQ US Marine Corps, March 1968), p. 29.

Councils.[31] The presence of Vietnamese representatives on the councils would have provided transparency, to assuage the suspicions of General Thi, but also allowed the Vietnamese the opportunity to have some input into the American efforts to ensure they remained in line with Vietnamese goals. This was consistent with General Walt's Force Order 1750 entitled *Concepts of Civic Action in the Republic of Vietnam*, 7 June 1965:

> Civic action will be conducted as needed and/or requested in a guest-host relationship with the government of the Republic of Vietnam. Reliance will be placed on agreement and cooperation for the achievement of mutually advantageous objectives of the two governments.[32]

It was clear that the Marines understood the need for pacification in order to reduce support from the Viet Cong and, at the same time, ensure that support went to the host government rather than the Marines. The principle of enhancing local institutions in order to improve security later became a mainstay of the III MAF campaign plan, promulgated in mid-1966, and was based upon long established Marine doctrine of working with the local government as part of an eventual withdrawal strategy.[33] The Marines alone did not have the means to defeat the Communist forces in ICTZ; this could only be done by improving the capability of the South Vietnamese forces and persuading the local population to actively turn against the Communists. It would also require a lot more Marines.

Evolution of the Marine Corps Approach

Marine Corps strategy between 1965 and 1968 was largely determined by the events of 1965 and evolved from a defensive posture, with units tied to the coast, into a hybrid pacification/attrition campaign that tried to balance the need to defend the coastal installations and orders from higher command to destroy the NVA regular units in the border areas. During 1965 Marine Corps operational strategy went through three distinct phases. The first was a purely defensive posture with units positioned within or near the perimeter of three key coastal installations. The second phase can be described as defence in depth using pacification as a means to improve security in the area around the installations that III MAF had been ordered to protect. The third, and final phase, was a dual strategy in which the emphasis was on pacification in the coastal areas and on destruction of NVA/VC in the border areas and highlands. These three phases matched

31 III MAF, *Command Chronology, September 1965* p. 11.

32 III MAF, Force Order 1750: Concepts of Civic Action in the Republic of Vietnam, 7 June 1965, quoted in Russell Stolfi, *US Marine Corps Civic Action Effort in Vietnam*, p. 21.

33 FMFPac, *Operations of US Marine Forces Vietnam, July 1966*, p. 6. See also Section 15-2, Chapter XV, 'Withdrawal', *Small Wars Manual*, which advises that local government functions should be turned over to local authorities as soon as possible in the campaign.

the shift in the overall US strategy in Vietnam, analysed above, as the US moved from providing advice and support to the South Vietnamese and went on to combat troops with orders to conduct large scale offensive operations.

Phase One – Defence of the Installations (8 March-5 May)

Upon its arrival 9th MEB deployed to three installations on the coast of the northern provinces of the Republic of Vietnam, with a Tactical Area of Responsibility of about 8 square miles[34]. The first elements of the brigade, a Regimental Landing Team of two infantry battalions (increased to three on 10 April and four on 14 April), two helicopter squadrons and a fighter/attack squadron were based at the airfield near Da Nang, in Quang Nam province. Their area of operations included the airfield and an area to the west that 'was essentially uninhabited and was far too small to give assurance of any real security to the airfield'.[35] The Marines had been given an area with carefully drawn boundaries that excluded all but one village and three hamlets. The area immediately to the south of the airfield was quite densely populated but, as already mentioned, General Thi, CG I Corps, was reluctant to allow the Marines into that area because he considered that they were not ready to operate in enemy country. Generals Krulak and Karch were able to persuade him otherwise and III MAF's TAOR around Da Nang was increased to include another small area to the northwest of the airfield. This area too was fairly uninhabited but included another two villages and 12 hamlets, with a total population of 11,441 people. On 14 April III MAF deployed a battalion to defend a second airfield at Phu Bai, in Thua Thien province, approximately 50 miles northwest of Da Nang. Their TAOR was an area of two square miles around the airfield that held a population of 2,406 people.[36]

The Marines' operations were extremely limited in the first eight weeks of their deployment. 9th MEB was hampered by lack of supplies, restrictive rules of engagement and almost complete ignorance of the enemy's strength and disposition.[37] The supply situation, already discussed above, was eased slightly when General Westmoreland ordered that the Marines be supplied by MACV rather than relying on what they had brought with them. The supply chain, however, continued to be strained by the demands placed upon it by combat units and garrison units demanding large quantities of very different types of materiel as they established themselves in country. By May many units had to restrict the number of patrols they conducted due to a shortage of batteries.[38]

The rules of engagement also hindered the Marines' operations by restricting their ability to react to attacks on the installations they were guarding. 9th MEB was not

34 FMFPac, *Operations of III MAF, Vietnam, May to September 1965*, p. 1.
35 FMFPac, *Operations of III MAF, Vietnam, May to September 1965*, p. 17.
36 FMFPac, *Operations of III MAF, Vietnam, May to September 1965*, p. 23.
37 Jack Shulimson and Charles Johnson, *US Marines in Vietnam: 1965*, p. 20.
38 Jack Shulimson and Charles Johnson, *US Marines in Vietnam: 1965*, pp. 28-29, 181-182.

permitted to move outside its areas of responsibility in Da Nang and Phu Bai, nor were they permitted to return fire if the incoming fire originated from outside their perimeters. In a presentation to the Marine Corps Command and Staff College on 27 May 1965, General Karch explained that he had come to an agreement with General Thi that the Marines within the perimeter of Da Nang airbase were not allowed to fire on anyone outside the wire, but had to report them to a joint US-Vietnamese Command Coordination Center. General Thi was concerned that the Marines might not be able to distinguish readily between VC guerrillas and non-combatant civilians, which could lead to avoidable civilian casualties. Rules of engagement in counterinsurgency straddle a fine line between force protection and avoiding civilian casualties; no easy task when the insurgents are intermixed with the civilian population and do not wear uniforms or carry distinguishing marks to identify them. The epitome of a later over-emphasis on force protection and destruction of the enemy were the 'free fire zones' and use of H&I artillery fire that became a controversial feature of the war in Vietnam. Free fire zones were areas that were declared hostile and free of civilians, into which American and Vietnamese units could fire without asking permission or giving warning. Although there is no specific mention of when III MAF was first allocated its free fire zones, the III MAF Command Chronology of October 1965 mentions 'additional free fire areas' being granted in Quang Nam province, so it is clear that these were established early in the Marines' deployment.[39] H&I fire was advocated in the counterguerrilla manuals of the time for its proposed utility in disrupting the insurgents' lines of communication, being directed against likely staging areas or key points such as road junctions. As the war progressed such methods became necessary in the unpopulated border areas, where the Marines faced large conventional units in battle. In March and April 1965, however, the Marines were in their bases surrounded by densely populated villages that came almost up to the perimeters and it was unlikely that keeping the enemy at a distance through the use of artillery was an option, especially under the extant rules of engagement. In this case, therefore, the Marines understood that the best option for their security, and that of the local population, was to patrol beyond their perimeters. Not only would this enable them to keep the VC at arm's length, but they would be able to get to know the local people and therefore be able to distinguish friend from foe more readily. The risk would also transfer back to the Marines, who would actively seek out insurgents rather than simply using force to keep everyone away from their perimeter.

In order for the Marines to seek out and engage the enemy, though, they needed to know where they were and in what numbers. The official III MAF reports indicate a build-up of VC forces in the areas around their enclaves in March and April, with the number of enemy troops within 50 miles of the airbase at Da Nang increasing from 1480

39 III MAF Command Chronology, October 1965, p. 16.

to 3410.[40] Contact with the enemy was restricted to a few minor engagements, resulting in a total of 13 VC killed and two captured.[41]

Fortunately for the Marines this situation did not last. The President had already authorised more troops and an expansion of the rules of engagement in NSAM 328 on 6 April. Permission was also given for a third Marine enclave at Chu Lai, to the south of Da Nang, where a new airfield was to be constructed.[42]

Phase Two – Pacification as 'Defence in Depth' (May to November 1965)

The decision in Washington, DC to commit more American troops and permit them to engage in offensive operations took effect in ICTZ on 5 May 1965. The 3rd Marine Division received the following orders in a new Letter of Instruction from COMUSMACV:

> In general render combat support to RVNAF. In co-ordination with CG, I Corps, participate in or provide for the defense of the HUE, PHU BAI, DA NANG and CHU LAI airfields and ancillary facilities. Maintain the capability to conduct, on order, deep patrolling and offensive operations and reserve/reaction operations in coordination with CG, I Corps. Be prepared to execute US contingency plans as directed by COMUSMACV.[43]

One of the first major operations by III MAF established civic action and pacification as a central part of their operations in the coastal enclaves. On 11 May, the 2nd Battalion of the 3rd Marine Regiment conducted a search and destroy operation in the area of Le My village to the northwest of Da Nang. The command diary of the 3rd Marine Division simply records that after clearing the village of VC it was handed over to the South Vietnamese Army, although a company remained in the area and provided medical treatment to the local population.[44] The Division's G3 Journal (a log of all activity maintained by the division's operations staff) records that the returning Vietnamese forces were warmly welcomed by the villagers.[45] The general view of the Marines regarding their strategy in Vietnam is, however, still reflected in the following comments made in the 3rd Marine Division's command diary:

> This was the first such operation conducted by Marine Corps Forces in Vietnam, and the results are being closely monitored. The villagers have welcomed the

40 FMFPac, *Operations of III MAF, Vietnam, May to September 1965*, pp. 20, 24.

41 FMFPac, *Operations of III MAF, Vietnam, May to September 1965*, p. 24.

42 FMFPac, *Operations of III MAF, Vietnam, May to September 1965*, p. 25. The name *Chu Lai* is not Vietnamese – it is the phonetic pronunciation of the two Chinese characters that make up General Krulak's surname.

43 3rd Marine Division (Forward), Command Diary, May 1965, Part 2, Section 1, para 6.

44 3rd Marine Division (Forward), Command Diary, May 1965, Part 2, Section 2.

45 3rd Marine Division (Forward), *G-3 Journal*, Serial J-17, DTG 111045H.

> medical treatment afforded them and have thus far appeared to be cooperative with the newly constituted civil and military authority established by the Republic of Vietnam. General COLLINS defined the actual military objective of this Division as being the people of Vietnam and stated that if they can be won over to the side of their own government by such tactics, the LE MY operation may well be the pattern for future employment of Marine Corps forces in this area.[46]

III MAF described the operation as, 'the first real attempt at pursuing the full pacification cycle ... the village chief was told that we were there to stay as long as required, his wants were solicited and civic action really initiated'. The Marines had, at this early stage, decided that pacification was an essential aspect of their task despite General Westmoreland's order to the 9th MEB on their arrival in Vietnam that they were 'not responsible for pacification of their areas, though civic actions are encouraged'.[47]

In addition to civic action projects, the Marine unit in Le My also assisted the local population to prepare its own defence by providing training, carrying out weapons maintenance and preparing defensive positions.[48] This operation set the tone for the Marines throughout the rest of the period 1965–68, largely as a result that its success had upon General Walt when he assumed command of III MAF on 5 June. General Walt was keen to increase security around the Da Nang, Phu Bai and Chu Lai bases and to formalise the Marines' civic action programme in Vietnam, which, until that time, had been conducted by each of the units on an *ad hoc* basis. The command diary for the 3rd Marine Division for June stated:

> During this period, primary emphasis was placed on obtaining permission for expansion of all TAORs and the conduct of deeper and more aggressive patrolling by all infantry units. Concurrently, and as a result of the liberation of the LE MY village complex from Communist control, the Division embarked on a civic action program in that area which has thus far been an unqualified success.[49]

Describing his first few months in-country in an interview with *Life Magazine* in 1967 General Walt said that 'for two weeks I just fooled and floundered around', but that after visiting Le My, 'Walt theorized that if the 18,000 Vietnamese living within mortar range around Da Nang could be turned into friends, they not only wouldn't help blast the airfield but they might also provide useful information about the enemy'.[50]

June and July 1965 marked the point at which the tensions between the US Marines and General Westmoreland really began. As General Walt was widening the III MAF spectrum of operations around the coastal enclaves, General Westmoreland started to

46 3rd Marine Division (Forward), *Command Diary, May 1965*, Part 2, Section 2.
47 FMFPac, *Operations of III MAF, Vietnam, Mar-Sep 1965*, p25.
48 Victor Krulak, *First to Fight*, pp. 183 – 185.
49 3rd Marine Division (Forward), Command Diary, June 1965, Part 2, Section 2.
50 Life Magazine, *General Lewis Walt on Vietnam's Hottest Spot*, 26 May 1967.

concentrate on the threat of NVA infiltration across the borders into South Vietnam from Laos and Cambodia using the so-called 'Ho Chi Minh Trail'. He believed that the NVA/VC was in the 'third phase of revolutionary warfare, committing regiments and divisions to seize and retain territory and to destroy the government's troops and eliminate all vestiges of government control'.[51] Westmoreland's concept of operations, which led to his request for 44 additional battalions in the summer of 1965, was that American forces should move inland and counter the threat from the regular NVA units while the ARVN was left 'free to protect the people'.[52]

Walt, however, saw the situation differently and believed that the incursions across the border by the NVA were intended to draw resources away from the main battle, which would come in the coastal areas. He later wrote:

> I've seen captured documents; I've talked to prisoners and I've talked to defectors and they all tell me the same thing. The primary mission of the NVA is to pull the American and South Vietnamese troops away from the populated areas in order to 'get them off the back of the guerrilla'. Their secondary mission is to inflict as many casualties as possible on the US Forces so as to 'make headlines in the United States'.[53]

General Walt would also certainly have been mindful of the need to provide security for the coastal bases, a task that took up all of the resources available to him at the time. Although the Marines were beginning to conduct increasingly larger scale operations, up to battalion size, in the coastal areas against VC units that threatened the bases they still had not completely secured their area of operations. This became apparent when the airbase at Da Nang was attacked on 1 July. The VC carried out a combined arms attack on the airfield, consisting of mortar and small arms fire, and managed to penetrate the perimeter and destroy six American aircraft.[54] Following the attack, the Marine area of responsibility around the airfield was expanded to include the heavily populated area to the south, which entailed an increased pacification effort, which included relocating people living within 400 metres of the airfield perimeter, including their family graves, 'to allow unrestricted fields of fire'.[55] At the same time, the South Vietnamese pacification programme had ground to a halt in the rural areas surrounding the coastal bases. Captain Russell Stolfi's study of Marine Corps civil affairs between March 1965 and March 1966 (written in 1968) stated that by August 1965:

51 William Westmoreland, *A Soldier Reports*, p. 145.

52 William Westmoreland, *A Soldier Reports*, p. 140.

53 General Lewis Walt, *Marine Corps Bulletin 5700* dated 31 March 1969.

54 III MAF, *Command Chronology, July 1965*, p. 2.

55 III MAF, *Command Chronology, July 1965*, pp. 6-7. Although no full details are given regarding the operations, the report states that the move 'progressed smoothly from a civil affairs standpoint'.

> HQ, III MAF and the infantry battalions realised had learned that successful engagements against main force enemy units and interference with the movements of guerrillas were of little importance if the GVN was unable to fill the resulting political and military vacuum. In the area to the south of the Da Nang air base, the GVN was unable either to execute an effective program of rural reconstruction or to re-construct Republican government and the 9th Marines was obliged to carry out operations behind its frontline positions because of the Viet Cong dominated peasantry in Cam Ne village.[56]

At this point the Marines' pacification efforts became more formalised, with the implementation of three programmes that laid the foundations for their future pacification strategy. These were the establishment of the Joint Co-Ordinating Council, the Combined Action Platoons and the Golden Fleece operations. All of these programmes began in August 1965, within six months of the Marines' arrival in Vietnam. This is a small but important point because it demonstrates that the US Marine Corps must have had counterinsurgency almost 'hardwired' into their warfighting methodology, vindicating the comments put to Congress by General Shoup that fighting guerrillas is an inherent part of landing force operations.

According to Russell Stolfi's contemporary study of the III MAF civic action programme, General Walt realised that 'the diffuse idea of winning the people was simply not enough to direct a useful program of civic action'.[57] Walt's view was that although the government of South Vietnam, US aid agencies and the Marines were all beginning to win the population over, the lack of co-ordination meant that the South Vietnamese government was not securing the areas that had been cleared by the Marines. As already described, the lack of a unified command structure exacerbated the problem. Stolfi went on to say:

> But the complexities of fighting in a foreign, sovereign state presented problems. Neither the United Stated nor South Vietnamese would accept a single military commander and staff. Yet the Republican Government required the efficient use of all of the resources available for the struggle if it were ever to re-establish control over its Northern Region. The situation called for great tact; both the United States and Vietnam required a coordinating body to ensure the use of available resources in support of an effective plan for the survival of the Vietnamese Government.[58]

The solution was the Joint Co-Ordinating Council (JCC), which first met on 30 August 1965, originally consisted of representatives from III MAF (originally a Colonel but later

56 Russell Stolfi, *US Marine Corps Civic Action Effort in Vietnam*, p. 34. The information is taken from an interview with Colonel Don Wyckoff, 3rd Marine Division Assistant Chief of Staff, G3, by Stolfi in 1967.

57 Russell Stolfi, *US Marine Corps Civic Action Effort in Vietnam*, p. 34.

58 Russell Stolfi, *US Marine Corps Civic Action Effort in Vietnam*, p. 35.

the Assistant Division Commander of 3rd Marine Division and the Air Wing Commander, both one-star generals, attended the meetings), MACV, the United States Overseas Mission (USOM) and the Joint United States Public Affairs Office (JUSPAO). The plan was that representatives from the Government of Vietnam and South Vietnamese Army would also attend when the committee was more fully operational. Various sub-committees covering logistics, finance, public health, agriculture, public works and security (with the latter including responsibility for the local village militias) were formed 'to canvass completely the problems in its respective field; determine the assets, capabilities and limitations of each agency working in said field, and recommend a coordinated plan of operations to the senior committee for approval and execution'.[59] The meeting appears to have been more substantial than this short paragraph indicates, however. The III MAF Command Chronology for 31 August to 2 September records a three day seminar involving all of the agencies listed above as well as the US Embassy and the US Special Forces. The first two days comprised a series of briefings on the current situation in the III MAF area of operations and the respective roles and capabilities of the various agencies attending the seminar. The final day consisted of a series of workshops to discuss the problems identified and the approaches to be adopted in order to solve them.[60] This three day planning session was a considerable investment in time and effort by III MAF, demonstrating that the effort was more than merely cosmetic. In October 1965 the civil affairs section was 'promoted' to the status of a full department within III MAF headquarters, alongside operations, intelligence and logistics.[61] This is an important development as it placed civil affairs at the planning top table and increased its allocation of resources. That same month the Vietnamese I Corps commander appointed his Rural Construction Staff officer to the Joint Co-Ordinating Council and the Public Health Committee started to integrate the American and Vietnamese health workers in the 25 rural medical centres that were being operated by III MAF.[62] By the end of the year the JCC was meeting weekly and most of the sub-committees were operational.[63] Of particular significance, though, was the fact that the 1966 Vietnamese Pacification Budget for I Corps Tactical Zone and the accompanying plan were both reviewed and accepted by the JCC, which would take responsibility for both.[64] By implementing the Joint Co-Ordinating Council to merge the military and civil aspects of the plan, including budgetary management, the US Marines had achieved something that the Johnson Administration and US representatives in Vietnam could not. In Washington, 'the Americans bifurcated the war effort into civil and military components: splitting military responsibility for the war from civilian responsibility for pacification and segregating military and civil programs under separate

59 3rd Marine Division, *Command Chronology, August 1965*, p. 9.

60 Civic Action Seminar Schedule, Enclosure 7 to III MAF, *Command Chronology August 1965*.

61 III MAF, *Command Chronology October 1965*, p. 10.

62 III MAF, *Command Chronology October 1965*, p11.

63 III MAF, *Command Chronology December 1965*, p. 14.

64 FMFPac, *Operations of the III MAF, December 1965*, p. 35.

chains of command'.[65] In Vietnam, Ambassador Lodge, although a supporter of the need for pacification as well as purely military effort, did not make any attempt to co-ordinate the various civilian agencies or link the civil and military efforts in a meaningful way – largely because he did not want to undermine the autonomy of the various agencies involved.[66] The Marines success in achieving a degree of co-ordination probably arose from a combination of two factors: their previous experience in operating in conjunction with other agencies in the past and their ability to assimilate counterinsurgency thinking of the time, particularly Robert Thompson's emphasis on unity of effort between civil and military agencies – where this did not exist, they sought to create it.

The second initiative that began in August 1965 was the establishment of the Combined Action Platoons (CAP).[67] These were small units of Marines assigned to work alongside the local militias (Regional Forces and Popular Forces, usually referred to collectively as RF/PF or Ruff-Puffs) in their own villages. The Marines lived, worked and trained alongside the RF/PF and also carried out small civil affairs projects to improve the lives of the villagers in some way. The Marines assisted the RF/PF in developing the village defences and would go on joint patrols or ambushes in the local area. If the village came under attack, the Marines fought alongside the RF/PF and also co-ordinated the supporting arms, such as air or artillery fire.

The first CAP was formally established in the Phu Bai area on 1 August 1965 as part of a plan to improve the defences of the airbase against indirect fire attacks. During the course of the summer the Commanding Officer of the 3/4 Marines at Phu Bai was advised by his civil affairs officer that the RF/PF might be able to assist in the defence of the airfield if given the right support. Lt Paul Ek, a Vietnamese-speaking officer, was sent to Phu Bai to implement a plan, put together by the CO of 3/4 Marines, the commander of the 3rd Marine Division and General Walt, which would integrate Marines into the RF/PF platoons.[68] Within two weeks of the formation of the first CAP, a total of six Popular Force platoons were placed under command of the 3/4 Marines and at the end of September 1965 the programme was publically announced, after a suitable delay to ensure the programme would not become a potentially embarrassing failure and to resolve issues around foreign military control of Vietnamese troops.[69] By the end of 1965 the CAP had

65 Richard A. Hunt, *Pacification: The American Struggle for Vietnam's Hearts and Minds* (Boulder, CO: Westview, 1995), p. 69.

66 Richard A. Hunt *Pacification*, p. 67.

67 In most of the literature the acronym CAP is used almost interchangeably for the Combined Action Platoons and the overall Combined Action Program, of which they were a part. To avoid confusion, this study will use the acronym CAP to describe the platoons and will use the term CAP Programme to describe the whole initiative.

68 Jack Shulimson and Charles Johnson, *US Marines in Vietnam: 1965*, pp. 133-135. This is perhaps the most comprehensively researched account of the formation of the first CAP, although some further details can also be found in Michael Peterson, *The Combined Action Platoons: The US Marines' Other War in Vietnam* (New York: Praeger, 1989). pp. 23-25.

69 Russell Stolfi, *US Marine Corps Civic Action Effort in Vietnam*, p. 40.

increased from one platoon to a full company, with plans for the 3rd Marine Division to 'assume control of additional PF platoons' and continue to develop the programme.[70]

The CAP programme is probably one of the most frequently examined elements of the Marines' pacification strategy and has, therefore, been attributed an exaggerated importance as the debate over the success or failure of the Marines in Vietnam has tended to become a debate over the success or failure of the CAP programme, largely fuelled by the prominence of works by former Marines such as Francis 'Bing' West (*The Village*) and William Corson (*The Betrayal*).[71] Even General Walt said that '[o]f all our innovations in Vietnam none was as successful, as lasting in effect, or as useful for the future as the Combined Action Program', even though arguably the 'innovation' that was 'most useful for the future' was in fact the Joint Co-Ordinating Council and the efforts to unite the Vietnamese, Marine and US civilian pacification programmes – presaging Civil Operations and Revolutionary Development Support (CORDS) programme, which attempted to do the same thing on a national level, by almost two years.[72] In *The Betrayal*, William Corson, a commander of the CAP programme in 1967, was harshly critical of the entire US pacification effort and his feelings about the programme in comparison to the rest of the US pacification effort are summed up in his description of the impact of a news story on the CAPs:

> Don Moser of *Life* magazine tackled the CAP story in his article 'To Keep a Village Free' (*Life*, August 25, 1967), but he was perhaps too believable because the article provoked an anti-CAP reaction in Saigon. As long as the CAPs stood quietly – and died – 'To Keep a Village Free' they were not a threat to the Westmoreland/Komer conventional wisdom; however, when Moser, without intending to, indicated *what* a CAP actually does, the contrast between it and the current Revolutionary Development fraud became too apparent for comfort. There is little doubt in the minds of those without an axe to grind as to what the CAPs have done and are capable of doing with proper support, but this potential has not been achieved.[73]

Corson's book achieved additional notoriety because he failed to clear it through proper channels – as a serving Marine the manuscript should have been vetted by the Headquarters of the US Marine Corps - and he only avoided a court martial because the Commandant of the Marine Corps wanted to avoid exacerbating the existing tensions between the Army and the Marine Corps.[74]

The momentum of attention paid to the CAP Programme that was generated by Corson's book in 1968 was given further impetus by the publication of West's *The Village*,

70 FMFPac, *Operations of the III MAF, December 1965*, p. 30.

71 Bing West, *The Village* (New York, NY: Simon & Schuster, 1972 (2003 edition)); William Corson, *The Betrayal* (New York, NY: W.W Norton & Co, 1968).

72 General Lewis Walt, *Strange War, Strange Strategy*, p. 105.

73 Corson, *The Betrayal*, pp. 195-196.

74 'The War: A Marine's Protest', *Time*, 28 July 1968.

in 1972. *The Village* was West's account of the actions of one CAP unit in Bin Nghia Village in 1966 during his time there as a junior officer. Despite being virtually ignored when it was first published the book has achieved prominence among modern counterinsurgency practitioners, having been re-published in 1985 and 2002 and has remained in print ever since. These two books, along the attention that Generals Walt and Krulak drew to the CAP Programme at the time, and later scholarly works such as Michael Peterson's *The Combined Action Platoons: The US Marines Other War in Vietnam* have narrowed the focus of analysis on the Marines' counterinsurgency strategy on to the CAPs. Even in Andrew Krepinevich's influential *The Army and Vietnam* he only examines the CAPs in any great detail when comparing the Marines' approach with that of the Army: as in most analyses of pacification in Vietnam as a whole, the focus moves straight from Saigon to the villages in ICTZ without stopping at the III MAF headquarters in Da Nang. For the Marines in 1965, however, the CAP Programme was simply one of several initiatives intended to provide defence in depth to the airfields that the Marines were defending.

The third major initiative that started in late 1965 was Operation Golden Fleece. According to General Walt, this operation started in Hoa Vang district, near Da Nang. In that district the presence of the Marines had meant that the VC could not collect the bi-annual tax they imposed on the rice harvest. Instead, they issued warnings to the local population not to harvest the rice but to let it rot in the fields, on pain of death.[75] One of the local village chiefs approached the local Marine battalion commander and explained the problem. After the initial request in early September 1965, which came in the wake of a 'search and destroy' mission in the area, the battalion commander of 1/9 Marines agreed the plan with the local village chiefs and manoeuvred his battalion to support the harvest. The rest of the 9th Marine Regiment was also ordered to support the harvest and very quickly drove away a VC Main Force unit that local villagers had reported was in the area to collect the tax. At the same time 2/3 Marines were conducting a similar operation to the north of Da Nang, also in response to a local request from the villagers in the Cu De valley. Two more operations to protect the rice harvest were carried out in October. Following the success of these operations, Walt wrote, '[i]t would have been impossible not to have expanded Golden Fleece operations. The peasants asked for it...each Marine unit at harvest time was approached ... with the same request: save our rice too'.[76] A staff study in November 1965 concluded that 'Operation Golden Fleece was an economic success and a psychological success, each being measurably important...512,400 lbs rice, threshed, was denied the VC. At the accepted rate of 1.5 lbs per person per day, this could have subsisted 1900 VC's for the six months until the next harvest'.[77] The battalion commanders who had seized upon this initiative equally understood its importance in terms of damage to the enemy and increased support from the local population. The Commanding Officer of 1/9 Marines remarked that:

75 General Lewis Walt, *Strange War, Strange Strategy*, pp. 51-52.

76 General Lewis Walt, *Strange War, Strange Strategy*, p. 53.

77 Lt Col DA Clement USMC, Staff Study to Determine Data on the USMC-Assisted Summer/Fall 1965 Rice Harvest, Enclosure 7 to III MAF *Command Chronology, Nov 1965*.

> While it is entirely probable that the VC did get away with some rice…it is believed that Golden Fleece was most effective in cutting down the volume of rice the VC was able to gain. Another great benefit/derived [sic] from Golden Fleece was in good will which it earned for Marines from the Vietnamese people of our area. Golden Fleece related our efforts in a very concrete way to aid of the Vietnamese people at a very basic level. It showed them that we were in fact here to help them…Likewise it was evident to the rice growers that all of our efforts were for them, since we did not take any of the rice for our own use – something which their culture might have expected us to do.[78]

The Commanding Officer of 1/4 Marines, who had conducted his own 'Operation Harvest Moon' in the area around Chu Lai, similarly wrote that '[l]ong lasting benefits were accrued because of the District Chief, Provincial Force, Village and Marine relationships' in addition to providing proof to the local population that the Marines were 'there to protect them against VC encroachment'.[79]

With Operation Golden Fleece the Marines once again demonstrated the extent to which the basic concepts of counterinsurgency were almost 'hardwired' into their doctrine. Not only had they recognised the situation for what it was – an opportunity to drive a wedge between the people and the insurgents while at the same time doing considerable damage to the insurgents' ability to operate – but they showed the flexibility to incorporate the protection of the rice harvest into their operational template from 1965 onwards. At the end of October 1965 General Walt promulgated Divisional Bulletin 5726 directing all Marine units to 'prepare and plan for harvest protection during periods appropriate to their locality'.[80] What is equally, or possibly even more, significant in a counterinsurgency context is how the Marines defined 'success' in Operation Golden Fleece. The first criterion was measurable – the quantity of rice that had been harvested and denied to the VC. The second was intangible and anecdotal – the gain in support from the local population and improvement in relationships between the local people, the civil authorities and the Marines. There is no mention in any of the reports on Operation Golden Fleece submitted by the battalion commanders of body counts or weapon seizures (although these are included in the usual monthly returns to headquarters). Not only had the Marines made some headway in gaining the support of the populations in the areas covered by Operation Golden Fleece but the local population had actively chosen a side – at some risk to themselves, given the threats issued by the VC prior to the harvest.

78 Statement of Commanding Officer, 1st Battalion, 9th Marines, p2. This undated document is Enclosure 1 to Lt Col DA Clement USMC, Staff Study to Determine Data on the USMC-Assisted Summer/Fall 1965 Rice Harvest.

79 Lt Col JR Fisher USMC, Operation Harvest Moon, 2nd Bn, 4th Marines, Chu Lai, p1. This undated document is Enclosure 2 to Lt Col DA Clement USMC, Staff Study to Determine Data on the USMC-Assisted Summer/Fall 1965 Rice Harvest.

80 III MAF, *Division Bulletin 5726*, 31 October 1965, p. 2.

Phase Three – The Move to Large-scale Offensive Operations

During the course of 1965, Westmoreland had been critical of the Marines' progress in their area of operations. He felt that the pacification strategy was too slow and lacked the necessary offensive spirit.[81] He also accused the Marines of 'sitting back and waiting for the enemy'.[82] Other senior army generals were even more scathing in their criticism of the Marines. General Harry Kinnard, who commanded the 1st Cavalry Division (Airmobile) in 1965 and later commanded the 1st Field Force in the area south of ICTZ, said that 'I did everything I could to drag [the Marines] out and get them to fight...They just wouldn't play...They don't know how to fight on land, particularly against guerrillas'.[83] Major General William Depuy, Chief of Staff for Operations at MACV said, 'the Marines came in and just sat down and didn't do anything. They were involved in counterinsurgency of the deliberate, mild sort'.[84] Not only does this show the depth and strength of the inter-service tensions at the time, but it also demonstrates the lack of understanding of one of the Marines' main missions throughout the war – to defend the airbases on the coast – and also ignorance of the extent to which the Marines were logistically dependent on being close to support from the sea.

General Westmoreland was concerned about the increasing number of VC and NVA units in the Central Highlands and adding to this was the problem of the Cambodian Government's acquiescence in allowing the Vietnamese to reinforce and resupply their forces along the Ho Chi Minh Trail.[85] Westmoreland believed that this was a direct threat to the area around Saigon, which could be reached from Cambodia. He believed that the North Vietnamese intended to conduct a major offensive to the north of Saigon to cut the northern provinces off from the rest of the country.[86] Although keen to move the Marines further inland, he did not want to start an 'interservice imbroglio' and therefore decided to issue a 'mission type order' to be followed up with 'orders for specific projects that as time passed would gradually get the marines out of their beachheads'[87]. Thus a new Letter of Instruction was issued on 21 November 1965 that committed Marine forces to general offensive operations throughout the I Corps area of operations. The mission paragraph stated:

> The III MAF will conduct military operations in I ARVN Corps Tactical Zone (CTZ) in support of and in coordination with CG, I ARVN Corps, and in other

81 William Westmoreland, *A Soldier Reports*, pp. 164-166.
82 William Westmoreland, *A Soldier Reports*, pp. 144-145.
83 Andrew Krepinevich, *The Army and Vietnam*, p. 175.
84 Andrew Krepinevich, *The Army and Vietnam*, p. 175.
85 General William Westmoreland, *A Soldier Reports*, p. 180.
86 General William Westmoreland, *A Soldier Reports*, p. 126.
87 General William Westmoreland, *A Soldier Reports*, p. 166.

> areas of RVN as directed by COMUSMACV, in order to assist GVN to defeat the VC and extend GVN control over all of Vietnam.[88]

The 'Execution' paragraph of the letter still placed the emphasis on operations in the coastal areas, but added a crucial element to the Marines' task in Vietnam:

> In addition, III MAF will conduct search and destroy operations against more distant VC base areas in order to destroy or drive the VC out.[89]

General Walt's response to Westmoreland was to accommodate him as far as possible, while keeping the emphasis on pacification. He did not believe the two were necessarily mutually exclusive but felt constrained by lack of intelligence. His operations officer, Colonel Edwin Simmons, commented:

> Westmoreland's view was 'Yes, we accept the Marine Corps concern about pacification, but we want you to do more'. He wanted the Marines to experiment with lighter battalions and new tactics. General Walt's position was, 'Yes, I will engage the enemy's main force units, but first I want to have good intelligence'[90].

As already pointed out, the Marines found that pacification led to an increase in the amount of information gleaned from the local population that could be processed into intelligence concerning VC unit strengths and intentions.

Acknowledging that previous estimates of time-scales for operations had been optimistic and that progress had been hampered by the increase in VC Main Force and NVA regular army units, as well as the inability of the South Vietnamese forces to follow up on gains by the Marines, Walt retained confidence in his overall strategy. He wrote that his aims for 1966 were:

1. Present secure base areas would remain essentially unchanged; i.e. that is coastal enclaves at Hue Phu Bai, Danang and Chu Lai.
2. Present TAORs would be gradually expanded; their rate of expansion governed by the ability of GVN to fill in behind.
3. Temporary bases would be established as necessary for inland operations.[91]

88 COMUSMACV, Letter of Instruction (LOI–4), 21 November 1965, enclosure 2 to III MAF, Command Chronology, November 1965, p. 2.

89 COMUSMACV, Letter of Instruction (LOI–4), 21 November 1965, enclosure 2 to III MAF, Command Chronology, November 1965, p. 2

90 Colonel Simmons comments quoted in Jack Shulimson, *US Marines in Vietnam: An Expanding War, 1966*, (Washington DC: US Marine Corps Historical Division, 1982), p. 14.

91 III MAF, *Command Chronology, February 1966*, Enclosure 18.

These aims had been first briefed to General Krulak in October 1965 and were based on the assumption that this could achieved by June 1966, if III MAF increased in strength to 18 battalions. In February 1966, III MAF had 13 battalions, but Walt assumed an increase to 21 battalions with the arrival of 1st Marine Division. The presentation also discussed how the Marines would deal with Westmoreland's orders for more inland operations but highlighted an intelligence mismatch between the MACV headquarters in Saigon and III MAF. The MACV orders to conduct operations in the inland provinces were based on a briefing given to General Westmoreland in which it was assessed that there were 22 enemy battalions operating in the Quang Tri and Thua Thien Provinces. The Marines maintained that there were only nine enemy battalions in the area.[92] This, as much as any doctrinal difference is likely to have been a major factor in the Marines' desire to keep resources in the coastal enclaves rather than chasing a relatively small VC force around the jungle highlands.

General Walt's compromise with General Westmoreland was reportedly not well received by General Krulak, who remained convinced that greater efforts should be put into pacification. In 1978 he commented that this 'balanced approach' was a compromise with Westmorland…every man we put into hunting for the NVA was wasted'. He also said that the strategy that had evolved as a result of the compromise was 'designed to pacify all shades of strategic thought; that if we persisted in such a compromise, we would bleed ourselves – and we did'.[93] Speaking in an interview in 1970, Krulak explained that he believed that the large unit operations were 'unwise and unproductive and they'd have done better to let the enemy come across the Cambodian border and extend his lines a bit and then cut him up'. [94] The compromise is, however, consistent with Walt's recognition that the war in the north and west of his area of responsibility was very different to that in the coastal enclaves. That said, Krulak was at pains to point out that despite the perception of the Marines as being tied to their enclaves, they were energetic in carrying out large unit operations. In a letter to Secretary of the Navy Paul Nitze in July 1966, Krulak responded to a criticism commented on by Nitze that the Marines were 'characterized as unaggressive [sic] and bemused by the project of passing out soap to the natives'. [95] He backed up his point with the following statistics with regard to operations in Vietnam since January 1966: the Marines contributed 28 percent of the manoeuvre battalions in Vietnam but had carried out 39% of the major operations (defined as battalion-size or larger); the Marines had carried out 35 percent of the major offensives (defined as those in which more than 125 enemy were reported killed); and they had accounted for 28 percent of the total number of casualties. He further pointed out that as four Marine battalions were not available for operations because they were dedicated

92 III MAF *Command Chronology, February 1966*, Enclosure 18.

93 General Krulak comments quoted in Jack Shulimson, *US Marines in Vietnam: An Expanding War, 1966*, p. 154.

94 Transcipt of interview with General Victor Krulak by Frank Benis, US Marine Corps Historical Division, Oral History Section, Washington DC, p. 9. Interview conducted on 22 June 1970.

95 General Victor Krulak, 'Letter to Secretary of the Navy', 17 July 1966, p. 1.

to airfield defence, 'the proportionate large unit operation effort of the Marines becomes even more impressive'.[96]

There appears to have been a 'whispering campaign' against the Marines in late 1965 and early 1966. In June 1966 the Commandant of the Marine Corps was informed that Senator Inouye of Hawaii 'had been approached by certain army officers and told that the Marine Corps was not carrying out an aggressive campaign in I Corps area'.[97] If there was a concerted campaign of disinformation about the Marines' operations, it is possible that General Westmoreland was basing his view of their strategy on a false perception; that the Marines were wholly opposed to offensive operations against large VC formations. As has been already shown Marines were committed to major operations but in the areas around the coastal plain where they felt such operations to be more useful, rather than in the highlands where these large enemy formations were largely ineffective and posed no immediate threat.

Conclusion

By the end of 1965, Marine Corps strategy had begun to evolve into a dual effort. In the area around the enclaves in the coastal plains they were carrying out a combination of pacification and 'big unit' offensives. In the central highlands, the Marines were following roughly the same path as the US Army to the south, in establishing temporary and semi-permanent fire bases from which they would operate against the VC and NVA major units. The two main tactics used were the 'sweep and block', in which the enemy were driven by mobile units onto a static blocking force, or 'find, fix and destroy', where the US forces would conduct large-scale patrols to locate an enemy force and then use air and artillery to destroy the enemy once a static engagement had been initiated.[98] This latter tactic was sometimes referred to as 'dangling the bait'.[99]

There were a number of factors that prevented this combination of strategies from achieving complete victory. First, insufficient resources were allocated to the pacification of the populated areas and therefore the Marines lacked the funds and manpower to commit to the effort. The Commandant of the Marine Corps frequently advocated an increase in the overall troop levels in Vietnam, possibly up to 1,000,000 men, an increase in the established strength of the USMC and possibly the use of reserve forces, but this was never acted upon.[100] Lack of manpower also meant that Marine units were moved

96 General Victor Krulak, 'Letter to Secretary of the Navy', 17 July 1966, p. 1..

97 General Wallace Greene, Memorandum for the Record, Developments in the Southeast Asia Situation, 24 June 1966.

98 Andrew Krepinevich, *The Army and Vietnam*, pp. 196-197.

99 Christian G. Appy, *Working-Class War: American Combat Soldiers and Vietnam* (Chapel Hill, NC: University of North Carolina Press, 1993), pp. 182-184.

100 General Wallace Greene, Record of Conference on Southeast Asia held at the White House, 221150 July 1965. Also: Conference, CMC with Vice President Humphrey, Tuesday 25 October 1966; Memorandum for the Record, I Corps Estimate (Force Requirements and Long-range

around the areas quite frequently, and therefore were unable to carry out long-term pacification operations in the more remote areas outside the enclaves. At the end of major operations, forces would be redeployed which allowed the VC to move back into the areas they had been forced out of. General Krulak, in his book *First to Fight*, summed up the situation and the mind-set of the Marines at the time:

> The Marines never gave up on their multipronged concept for victory. To the very end, and within the limits of the forces available, they strove to protect and emancipate the people. They never ceased pleading for decisive action against the North Vietnam port and logistic system. And they went into the hinterland after the large enemy units – far more than they wanted to – but in response to the strong pressures from MACV Headquarters.
>
> ...Obviously we had become involved in a self-punishing, self-defeating cycle brought on by a faulty attritional strategy. Thus, our self-declared victories in the search-and-destroy operations were not relevant to the outcome of the war.[101]

Robert Thompson said of the Marines that they 'alone made a serious attempt to achieve permanent and lasting results in their tactical area of responsibility by seeking to protect the rural population' and praised the efforts of the CAPs. He added that '[u]nfortunately the commitment of forces to this task was very limited. The selected areas were too scattered, and, in any case, the northern provinces of South Vietnam were the most vulnerable to major Vietcong and North Vietnamese unit attacks from the mountain chain'.[102]

These assessments of the Marine strategy and its effectiveness, however, ignore the primary mission allocated to their forces in Vietnam at that time. When one considers the initial primary mission allocated to the Marines, defence of the strategically-important air bases and port facilities in the I Corps area, alongside a diagrammatic representation of USMC strategy, a completely different picture emerges. Taking the enclaves as the centre of a series of concentric circles, the strategy can be determined as:

Estimates for I Corps, RVN), 7 November 1966.

101 Victor Krulak, *First to Fight*, pp. 201 – 202.

102 RobertThompson, *No Exit From Vietnam*, p. 138.

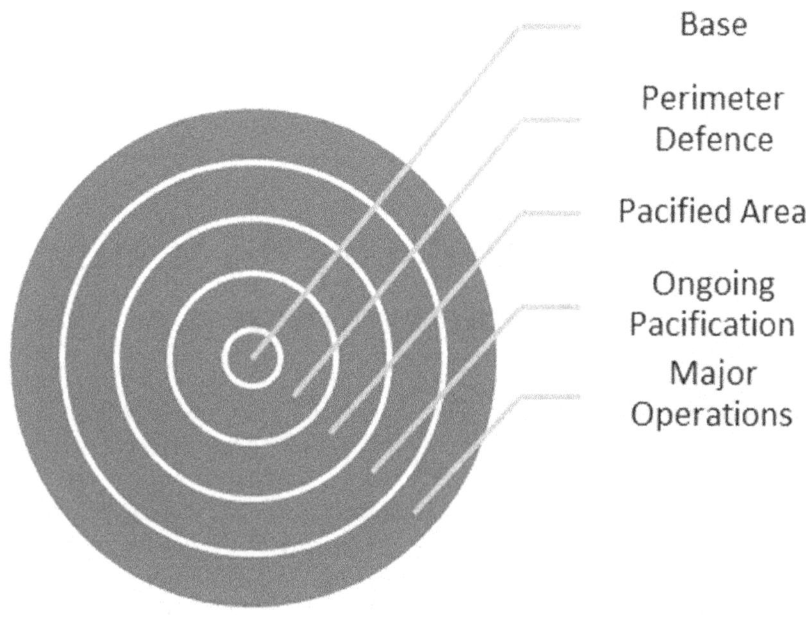

Figure 3.2: Diagram of Marine Corps Strategy.

When viewed in this way, the Marine strategy makes sense in terms of defence-in-depth of the enclaves. The criteria for success also changes from whether or not victory was achieved to whether or not the enclave areas were successfully defended against the enemy. III MAF found itself on a strategy 'fault line' that lay between senior Marine Corps officers, such as General Krulak, who felt that the emphasis in Vietnam should be on pacification and nation-building, and General Westmoreland, who felt that the main role of the US forces should be the physical destruction of the Communist forces and that pacification should be left to the Vietnamese. While trying to please both masters, III MAF also found that the enemy was fighting a campaign in which the war for the hearts and mind of the people was as important as the 'conventional' war. It also became clear that, to a large extent, the Vietnamese were unable or unwilling to carry out pacification and the Marines had to 'jump start' the process and build up the Vietnamese capacity. The 'strategy debate' that ensued between Westmoreland and the Marines was essentially a matter of deciding where to place the emphasis. Westmoreland did not believe that pacification had no place in the ground war in Vietnam, he just didn't necessarily believe that it was a matter for the US military. In fact, as this analysis will show, the situation had moved beyond the point where it was appropriate to choose between pacification and attritional manoeuvre warfare. The time had come to put equal resources into both.

4

1966 – 1967: Developing the Strategy and Measuring Progress

The period between January 1966 and December 1967 put the Marine Corps' view of the war and its counterinsurgency strategy to the test. Having been ordered to conduct full-scale offensive operations against the NVA and VC the Marines were put in the difficult position of trying to pursue both a counterinsurgency strategy in the populated coastal areas, where they were still responsible for the security of the coastal bases, and a more conventional war in the highlands and border areas. The tensions between III MAF and MACV continued because of the competing demands placed upon the Marines.

In early February 1966, President Johnson called a conference in Honolulu to reassure the South Vietnamese of continued American support, secure Vietnamese assurances of political, social and economic reform and determine a unified civil-military strategy for the war. The conference was attended by Robert McNamara, Dean Rusk, Ambassador Henry Cabot Lodge, General Wheeler, Admiral Sharp and General Westmoreland. The Vietnamese President Thieu and Prime Minister Ky also attended. The political side of the conference resulted in a number of specific agreements.

The first agreement was that the US would conduct a range of diplomatic activity that would include increased pressure on the Hanoi government to negotiate and a high level tour of Asian capitals to 'explain our position and describe the Honolulu meeting'.[1] The second agreement was that the South Vietnamese leaders would institute political reforms to include a new constitution, the immediate appointment of an advisory council 'selected from a cross-section of society and all regions of the country', the eventual democratic election of a civilian government and 'General Ky was urged to spend more time in the countryside in the role of a political leader'.[2] The final agreement was that the South Vietnamese government would make improvements in health, education and agriculture to improve the lives of the general Vietnamese population.[3]

1 Honolulu Meeting: Record of Conclusions and Decisions for Further Action (Washington, DC: State Department, 23 February, 1966) in Foreign Relations of the United States, Volume IV, Vietnam 1966, Document 83.

2 Honolulu Meeting: Record of Conclusions and Decisions for Further Action.

3 Honolulu Meeting: Record of Conclusions and Decisions for Further Action.

Although the conference was not intended to be a military conference, the senior military officers present held their own meetings in tandem with the political event, after which Westmoreland was sent a memo stating that:

> The South Vietnamese, US and third-country forces, in coordination will:
>
> 1. Defend military bases, political and population centers and food-producing areas now under government control.
> 2. Open and secure lines of communications required to support military operations and for essential support of the civilian population.
> 3. Conduct clearing and security operations to provide military security in the four selected high priority national construction areas.
> 4. Conduct intensified offensive operations against major VC/PAVN forces, bases and lines of communications--almost doubling the number of battalion-months of offensive operations from 40 to 75 a month.
> 5. Increase the level of attack on the infiltration routes through Laos and North Vietnam by more than 60 per cent--from 5,400 to 9,000 attack sorties a month.
>
> Achieve the following results in 1966:
>
> 1. Increase the population in secure areas to 60 per cent from 50 per cent.
> 2. Increase the critical roads and railroads open for use to 50 per cent from 20 per cent.
> 3. Increase the destruction of VC/PAVN base areas to 40-50 per cent from 10-20 per cent.
> 4. Ensure the defense of all military bases, political and population centers and food-producing areas now under government control.
> 5. Military security needed for pacification of the four selected high-priority areas--increasing the pacified population in those areas by 235,000.
> 6. Attrit [sic], by year's end, VC/PAVN forces at a rate at least as high as their capability to put men into the field.[4]

Westmoreland took this as an endorsement of his 'big war' attrition strategy. He later wrote:

> Nothing about these goals conflicted with the broad outline of how the war was to be fought as I had worked it out over the months of consultation with South Vietnamese officials, Admiral Sharp and the Joint Chiefs of Staff. Indeed, in setting the goals for 1966, senior civilian authorities acting for the President directed that I proceed as I had planned.[5]

4 *1966 Program to Increase The Effectiveness of Military Operations and Anticipated Results Thereof*, State Department, Washington DC, 23 February 1966. FRUS, Volume IV, Vietnam 1966, Document 70.

5 William Westmoreland, *A Soldier Reports*, pp. 160-161.

Westmoreland did understand that pacification was an essential part of the overall strategy but felt that the role of the US military forces in Vietnam was to first 'stem the tide' of insurgent infiltration and then destroy the main force NVA/VC units 'as a prelude to the progressive pacification of all of South Vietnam over the ensuing years'.[6] Westmoreland was convinced that the North Vietnamese intended to conduct a military offensive in the north and that this offensive was imminent. When asked by the President at the Honolulu conference what he thought the next move of the North Vietnamese would be, he replied 'without hesitation: capture Hue'. This belief was founded on his assessment of North Vietnamese intentions after the loss of a Special Forces camp in the A Shau valley early in 1966, together with increased intelligence reports of increased North Vietnamese infiltration across the Demilitarised Zone (DMZ). The loss of this camp left the valley, which provided access to the coast, open to the enemy and Westmoreland feared that the build-up of enemy troops was the prelude to an offensive.[7]

At least one of Westmoreland's staff officers did not believe that the goals set out in the Honolulu memo were realistic. Phillip Davidson, General Westmoreland's chief intelligence officer, criticized the goals enumerated in the Honolulu conference directive as representing 'McNamara's obsession with trying to somehow quantify the American goals in the war…These are largely meaningless numbers, a vain effort to gauge progress in a messy and unmeasurable war'.[8] Despite this, Davidson said that:

> The first objective, enemy attrition, claimed Westmoreland's immediate attention in early 1966. He was now formally charged with attriting [sic] the enemy, but not told how to do it. The answer was, of course, to focus on the enemy. Wherever he could find the enemy's Main Force units, or wherever they threatened to appear, then United States and Allied troops would go there and with superior mobility and firepower kill them. At least that was the theory. Thus, the enemy Main Force units and their intentions determined where and when Westmoreland would attempt to attrite them.[9]

Rather than simply responding or reacting to the enemy's initiatives in the border areas, where the ability to cause attrition to the enemy was largely dictated by whether or not the North Vietnamese chose to commit troops to the fight, the Marines maintained the counter-guerrilla war as their main effort. In February 1966, the Marines listed their missions as:

> Airfield Defense. Active defense of one of the most critical airfield complexes in Southeast Asia.

6 Andrew Birtle, 'PROVN, Westmoreland, and the Historians: A Reappraisal', *The Journal of Military History*, 72 (October 2008), p. 1222.
7 Westmoreland, *A Soldier Reports*, p. 167.
8 Phillip Davidson, *Vietnam at War*, p. 403.
9 Phillip Davidson, *Vietnam at War*, p. 403.

> Counterguerrilla operations. Aggressive action to comb the guerrillas out of a populous and traditionally Viet Cong infested area.
>
> Large unit actions. Attacks to destroy the Viet Cong main force units and their infrastructure.
>
> Civic action. Helping the Vietnamese, through organized compassionate effort, to achieve a higher level of health, stability and productivity.[10]

Whether by design or not, these tasks occur in the same order as the tasks given to General Westmoreland in the memo following the Honolulu conference, with the additional self-imposed task of civic action.[11]

The Marines, mindful of both the need to defend the airfields in the coastal areas and deny safe havens to the insurgents, justified their apparent lack of resolve in conducting 'big unit' operations in a May 1966 letter from General Krulak to Secretary of Defense McNamara. The letter was written in response to the implied criticism in a comment made by McNamara the previous week about the apparent lack of progress of the Marines:

> In the I Corps we have to inspire and guide the Vietnamese in the direction of stabilizing the society and developing a local militia force in those regions where we have combed the guerrillas out of the villager's hair. It has been said that this is not our job, that it is a task more properly identified with the Vietnamese themselves. As a principle this is fine. As a practical reality, it does not work. The Vietnamese are just not ready to do it all alone. They do not know how. They are learning – from us – but they do not appreciate fully the importance of ministering to the people. They do not have the resources, nor do they yet have the integrity or the compassion to administer what they resources have. As of now we have to help. If we do not, the guerrillas and political cadre will be back to re-infect the villagers and to re-establish the link with the Main Force and Hanoi.
>
> And the point of this is that the Marines are not just addressing one part of the problem, they are covering each of the four important bases. It is not a matter of their being bemused with handing out soap or bushwhacking guerrillas at the expense of attacking the main force units. To the contrary, they are treating the whole patient in the manner that the patient – the I Corps area – demands.[12]

As well as making the case for the Marines' strategy, it is also an unusually candid assessment of the shortcomings of their Vietnamese allies; most senior officers were at pains to be complimentary about the Vietnamese military in official documents, even if these were at considerable variance to their personal opinions. It is likely that this candour

10 FMFPac, *Operations of the III MAF, Vietnam, February 1966*, p. 7.

11 Although this may be an implied task resulting from the directives in the Honolulu conference memo ordering the increase of the percentage of population in pacified areas.

12 General Victor Krulak, 'Letter to Secretary of Defense Robert McNamara', dated 9 May 1966. Krulak Papers, Alfred M Gray Research Center, US Marine Corps University, Quantico, VA.

was borne out of the political unrest that was still going on in I Corps at the time the letter was written, although that situation was nearing a solution.

In October 1966, the Marines started reporting their progress in achieving the goals set at the Honolulu conference. These reports, crafted by General Krulak to emphasise the importance of counterinsurgency, were known to the US Marine Corps Historical Center staff as 'Krulak's Fables' because of their optimistic interpretation of the data.[13] The first progress report was prefaced with the following comments:

> The broad goal of the USMC in Vietnam is, in company with the RVNAF, to expel, destroy or neutralize the enemy in the I Corps Tactical Zone. Through this, it is their object to bring about a condition wherein the local government can function, farmers can harvest and market their crops, and the people can live with reasonable freedom from terrorism, extortion and oppression. A close companion to this goal is the mission of defending a number of large and valuable military installations.
>
> The key to achieving both of these goals is establishment of firm GVN/US influence throughout the coastal plain of the five northern provinces of South Vietnam.[14]

This is consistent with Marine statements regarding their strategy throughout the war; that the counterguerrilla war and pacification should be the main effort. Their reasoning, which ran contrary to Westmoreland's view, was explained in a subsequent paragraph in the October report:

> The scarcity of food in the highlands causes enemy troops there to be heavily reliant upon the guerrillas in the coastal lowlands, since the guerrilla is the vital link between the people, the food supply and the large organized units. Much of the effort of the Marines in Vietnam is directed towards breaking this link, destroying the guerrilla infrastructure, and preventing the rice, information and other essentials from reaching the main force units...To the peasant, it is the Viet Cong guerrilla who marks the difference between peace and war, and it is the guerrilla who must be eliminated in order to give permanence to programs aimed at establishing firm GVN/US control of the lowland area. Thus the coastal plain is not only a strategic terrain compartment that contains the majority of the people. It is also the essential target area for destruction of the guerrilla, and a key to the isolation of the main force units in the highlands[15].

13 The term was still in use when the author was conducting archival research for this book.
14 FMFPac, *Operations of US Marine Forces, Vietnam, October 1966*, p. 5.
15 FMFPac, *Operations of US Marine Forces, Vietnam, October 1966*, p. 7.

The protection of crops, destruction of guerrilla forces and protection of the population in the coastal plains had, by this time, become significant elements of the Marines operations in Vietnam.

Political Unrest in I Corps – March to June 1966

An outbreak of political unrest in the northern provinces of South Vietnam presented an opportunity for the North Vietnamese to attempt to bring down the South Vietnamese government. The North Vietnamese made considerable efforts to exploit the opportunity but were unable to achieve their objectives due to a combination of insufficient resources and the success of a major part of the Marine strategy; development of local security forces although pacification efforts suffered severely during the course of the crisis. As part of their overall strategy the Marines had developed effective relationships with the ARVN that prevented the South Vietnamese forces from splintering into warring factions and worsening the security situation. The Viet Cong lacked the strength in the affected areas to maximise this opportunity, even though pacification operations were affected by the crisis as Marine forces were redeployed and ARVN units ceased participation in operations due to their involvement in political events.

On his return from the Honolulu conference, Prime Minister Ky decided to remove a potential threat to his regime; General Thi, who had proved a popular leader but who appeared to dominate the northern provinces to the extent that they appeared almost autonomous. President Johnson had been impressed with the ability of the relatively young prime minister, who seemed to have a good understanding of what needed to be done in terms of political, social and economic reform but was unsure of his ability to deliver results.[16]

Prime Minister Ky had spent some months prior to the Honolulu conference trying to hold his government together in the face of various military and political factions who were competing for power. In addition to this, there was still unrest amongst the Buddhist population of the northern part of the Republic of Vietnam, who felt unfairly disenfranchised in the Catholic-dominated government. Ky felt Thi to be a particular threat, especially as he was in control of the region of the country that abutted North Vietnam, which he seemed to be ruling as a personal fiefdom; any instability there was likely to be exploited by the enemy. Ky spoke of his concerns to the US Ambassador:

> Thi was becoming more and more difficult. His judgment was poor, he had delusions of grandeur, he did none of the things that were expected of him. For example, he had done nothing about pacification/revolutionary development. He was deliberately insubordinate; he would receive orders from the government and

16 'Telephone Conversation between President Johnson and the Indian Ambassador (Nehru)', State Department, Washington DC, 10 February 1966. FRUS, Volume IV, Vietnam 1966, Document 71.

> return them, scribbling on the order 'this crazy government'. It was obvious that one fourth of the country was exempt from the control of the national government. As long as this condition obtained Viet-Nam could not really call itself a nation.[17]

General Thi had worked to establish links with civilian leaders in the provinces in his Area of Responsibility, including the Buddhists[18]. He was also accused of appointing leaders more loyal to him than the government in Saigon, including the new Mayor of Da Nang, Dr Nguyen Van Man, who had previously been suspicious of the General's motives but had come to view him as a patriot and one of the few honest leaders in the country.[19]

The Marine commanders, though, had a high opinion of General Thi. A document prepared for the Commandant of the Marine Corps outlined General Walt's opinion of Thi:

> He had considerable admiration for General Thi...They discussed all operation and no movements were undertaken until both concurred on the operation. Although they didn't always agree on the tactics, after discussion an amicable solution was always reached. General Walt described General Thi as an honest man and a patriot.[20]

Prime Minister Ky gained the support of the other generals by threatening to resign and ordered Thi removed from command on 10 March 1966. He was to be replaced by General Chuanh. Within 24 hours of this order, demonstrations organised by a new organisation called the Military Civilian Struggle Committee, which was a mainly Buddhist organisation, took place in Da Nang. In Hue, Buddhist students and teachers from the university rioted. A four-day general strike was called for 14 March. As the demonstrations progressed, they took on an anti-US tone in addition to their opposition to the Thieu/Ky regime in Saigon. General Thi addressed several rallies in an attempt to calm the situation and asked that the 'struggle' be conducted in an orderly manner. The Marines attempted to stand back from the political crisis and not get involved, although there were some incidents involving confrontations between Marines and demonstrators.[21] In the face of continuing unrest in Da Nang, Prime Minister Ky announced on 3 April that the city was in communist hands and that he intended to order South Vietnamese

17 'Telegram from the Embassy in Vietnam to the Department of State', State Department, Washington DC, 9 March 1966. FRUS, Volume IV, Vietnam 1966, Document 91.

18 Randall B Woods, *LBJ: Architect of American Ambition* (New York, NY: Free Press, 2006), pp. 722-723.

19 'Personal Evaluation of Lieutenant General Nguyen Chanh Thi by Lieutenant Lewis W. Walt, US Marine Corps', document prepared for the Commandant of the Marine Corps, HQ USMC, Washington DC, 6 April 1966, p. 2.

20 'Personal Evaluation of Lieutenant General Nguyen Chanh Thi', p. 1.

21 FMFPac, *Chronology of Political Unrest in I Corps – 9 Mar – 23 Jun 1966*, p. 11.

troops would retake the city. He also threatened to shoot the Mayor, Dr Man, despite the fact that he had offered to resign as soon as General Thi had been sacked.[22]

The Marines quite successfully prevented an armed confrontation throughout the crisis. On 5 April, General Walt persuaded the ARVN troops at the Da Nang airbase that had been sent from Saigon to remain where they were, while at the same time Marine units moved to block a convoy of troops loyal to the Struggle Movement from entering the city.[23] After a confrontation between an ARVN artillery unit and the CO of the 9th Marines on 9 April, the 'rebel' ARVN units started to move back to their original positions.[24] The new commander of I Corps, General Dinh, met with the Buddhist leaders in Hue and ordered all ARVN troops back to their original units. The barricades in Hue and Da Nang came down and the situation appeared calm.[25] On 14 April, the Saigon government announced a series of political reforms aimed towards a general election later in the year and granted amnesties to all involved in the recent unrest.[26]

The situation did not remain calm for long. General Thi continued to call for the removal of the government in Saigon, supported by former Mayor Man and the Buddhist leadership in Hue. The demonstrations flared up again, some of which were extremely violent and resulted in a number of deaths, but there was no further action by ARVN troops to support opposition to the central government. According to the Marine chronology of the period there was some concern at the extent to which Buddhist chaplains within the ARVN were exerting their influence over the troops including the establishment of a 'shadow' Buddhist command structure.[27] On 7 May, Ky appeared to renege on some of the promises made by his government on 14 April and announced that the constitutional assembly, which was to have formed the basis of a new democratic government, would be dissolved and elections would not be held until 1967. More violent demonstrations broke out almost immediately in Da Nang and Hue.[28] On 15 May, ARVN units arrived in Da Nang from the south and took control of various strategic facilities. General Walt, with full support of General Westmoreland, moved to prevent fighting between ARVN units, especially those with US advisors attached, even to the extent of threatening to shoot down Vietnamese Air Force jets that were attacking columns of dissident troops from I Corps. In one confrontation between the factions on 18 May, General Walt placed himself on a bridge separating loyal and dissident troops, which had been rigged with explosives, to prevent its destruction. The order to detonate the bridge was given, but due to the unseen intervention of a US Army engineer who cut the wires under the bridge,

22 FMFPac, *Chronology of Political Unrest in I Corps – 9 Mar – 23 Jun 1966*, p. 15.

23 General Lewis Walt, *Strange War, Strange Strategy*, p. 118.

24 FMFPac, *Chronology of Political Unrest in I Corps – 9 Mar – 23 Jun 1966*, p. 21.

25 FMFPac, *Chronology of Political Unrest in I Corps – 9 Mar – 23 Jun 1966*, p. 23.

26 FMFPac, *Chronology of Political Unrest in I Corps – 9 Mar – 23 Jun 1966*, pp. 26-27.

27 FMFPac, *Chronology of Political Unrest in I Corps – 9 Mar – 23 Jun 1966*, pp. 41-43.

28 FMFPac, *Chronology of Political Unrest in I Corps – 9 Mar – 23 Jun 1966*, p. 41.

the explosives failed to function. Both factions were then persuaded to stand down in the ensuing negotiations.[29]

Buddhist demonstrations continued in Hue, critical of American support for the Saigon government. These demonstrations forced an evacuation of the Consulate in Hue, which together with a wave of self-immolations by Buddhists, persuaded the government to grant concessions.[30] Although they continued to press for the removal of President Thieu and Prime Minister Ky, this was enough to satisfy the Buddhist leaders and they agreed to stop the demonstrations on 2 June.[31] By 18 June the situation had almost returned to normal and all the key Struggle Movement leaders in the military had been arrested, although most members were granted an amnesty as part of the government concessions.[32]

The unrest had several major effects on Marine Corps operations. The most immediate effect was its negative impact on ongoing operations against the Viet Cong. In April 1966 the Marines reported that 'the unfavourable effect on logistic operations was considerable, and the adverse impact on pacification and Popular Force development was serious and is still visible'. [33] Port operations and construction work were affected by the unrest in Da Nang. The number of Popular Force units raised was 'practically halted during the month by the civil unrest'.[34] Civic action was almost brought to a halt as most of the American NGOs ceased operations for the first three weeks of April due to the evacuation of American personnel from Hue and Da Nang.[35] The 9th Marines were forced to halt offensive operations in April and assume a defensive posture when local ARVN units abandoned their posts, allowing the Viet Cong to seize considerable quantities of ammunition and explosives.[36] Similar effects were reported in May 1966, with logistics and civil affairs being the most affected areas of operation, although it was remarked that the population in the more rural areas seemed determined to continue with projects despite the lack of support from the government; the Marines reported increases in the number of villages that had completed their census, increases in the number of villages working on defence plans and increases in the number of villages with public information programmes.[37]

Between March and May 1966, despite the unrest, the number of large operations (multi-battalion operations) dropped only slightly (see Table 4.1 below). The only major change in trend throughout the period is a drop in the number of confirmed enemy KIA,

29 General Walt, *Strange War, Strange Strategy*, pp. 125-132.
30 FMFPac, *Chronology of Political Unrest in I Corps – 9 Mar – 23 Jun 1966*, pp85-8 and Stanley Karnow, *Vietnam: A History*, p. 464.
31 FMFPac, *Chronology of Political Unrest in I Corps – 9 Mar – 23 Jun 1966*, p. 102.
32 FMFPac, *Chronology of Political Unrest in I Corps – 9 Mar – 23 Jun 1966*, p. 125.
33 FMFPac, *Operations of US Marine Forces Vietnam, April 1966*, p. 3.
34 FMFPac, *Operations of US Marine Forces Vietnam, April 1966*, p. 3.
35 III MAF, *Command Chronology, April 1966*, p. 16.
36 Jack Shulimson, *The US Marines in Vietnam: An Expanding War 1966* (Washington, DC: History and Museums Division, HQ United States Marine Corps, 1982). p. 80.
37 FMFPac, *Operations of US Marine Forces Vietnam, April 1966*, p. 4.

which dropped by around 50% for April and May. What is of significance is that there is no real increase in the estimated enemy strength within 25 miles of the Marine enclaves, which would be expected if the VC were planning a major operation to maximise their opportunities during the instability in the region. The number of incidents initiated by the VC did not increase significantly until June, when most of the trouble was over.

Table 4.1: Marine and NVA/VC Activity During 1966 Political Unrest[38]

	Enemy Initiated Incidents	Enemy KIA (Confirmed)	USMC Large Unit Operations	USMC Company Size Operations	Estimated Enemy Strength (Within 25 miles of major airbase)
March	1045	1382	15	96	15649
April	1000	593	14	202	14640
May	1064	658	12	127	16740
June	1217	1021	11	227	13940

In his memoirs, General Walt summed up the political unrest in the spring of 1966 as representing a failed opportunity for the Viet Cong:

> This much is plain: the fledgling government of Vietnam showed remarkable resilience under extreme pressure. Whoever it was that wanted it toppled was disappointed. And the Viet Cong had shown how weak and ineffective they were. All of I Corps – and the nation itself – had solidified again. What opportunity existed for the Viet Cong during those three long months, when we felt we were making no more headway but reeling from crisis to crisis, had been beyond their reach and now had disappeared. They had failed to capture the Struggle Movement, the Buddhist revolt, the Army, or the people.[39]

Although Walt might have been over-optimistic about the resilience of the Saigon government, in that it was propped up by the United States and opposition had largely crumbled when faced with that reality, his comment about the North Vietnamese inability to exploit the situation bears further analysis. In May, the III MAF intelligence section reported an increase in the number of VC political cadres sent into the major cities to

38 Figures derived from III MAF Command Chronologies for March, April, May and June 1966.
39 General Lewis Walt, *Strange War, Strange Strategy*, p. 134.

exploit the ongoing unrest.[40] In June, III MAF reported that the VC, 'appear to have been slow in taking the initiative to exploit the recent political unrest, however, they gained some momentum during the month of June'.[41] The report goes on to list some of the VC activities; persuading troops to desert, subverting local politicians, spreading dissension amongst the religious and political groups, and spreading anti-US propaganda. In July, it was reported that VC propaganda, although more sophisticated in terms of dissemination (with regular indoctrination classes being held) and production quality, had reverted to a mainly anti-US message. Reports also indicated that the VC had made influencing and disrupting the planned elections in September 1966 its main effort, indicating that they had abandoned attempts to exploit the political turmoil that existed in the northern provinces.

The VC had failed to mount an effective campaign during the political unrest despite signs that they had tried to make the most of it. There are a number of possible reasons for this. First, although there were suspicions that the Buddhist monks were naively heeding communist-inspired advice, the fact that the Saigon government was able to provide sufficient concessions to ensure the rapid collapse of the Struggle Movement show that this was in fact an internal struggle more concerned with the lack of democracy.[42] This inability to exploit the political situation is made more pointed by the fact that President Johnson was actively preparing a US withdrawal from Vietnam if Ky's government should fall. State department documents from the time show clear evidence that Johnson was considering the collapse of the government as a pretext for withdrawal with honour, or at least using the threat of withdrawal as a spur for Ky's government to carry out the reforms.[43] Second, the increased presence of US and GVN military forces in the northern provinces and the pacification effort in the rural areas around Da Nang and Hue was likely making the environment too hostile for the VC forces to operate with any degree of effectiveness.

There are two schools of thought regarding the political unrest in early 1966. Some in the US and Vietnamese governments believed it was wholly inspired by the Communists. Others believed that the Communists seized the opportunity to renew their efforts to undermine and weaken the GVN. In either case, the attempt failed. Arguably, when measuring success in counterinsurgency one useful indicator is how effective the insurgents are at achieving their aims. In this case they failed due to a combination of: political reforms instituted just in time by the central government; the Marine Corps' efforts to prevent fighting between the elements of the ARVN; counterguerrilla operations disrupting the movement of NVA/VC units in the contested areas; and major operations in the hinterland preventing an offensive by the NVA.

40 III MAF, *Command Chronology, May 1966*, p. 10.

41 III MAF, *Command Chronology, June 1966*, p. 12.

42 'Telegram from the Embassy in Vietnam to the Department of State, State Department', Washington DC, 23 March 1966. FRUS, Volume IV, Vietnam 1966, Document 100.

43 FRUS, Volume IV, Vietnam 1966, Documents 109, 111 and 114.

Dual Strategy

Although the Honolulu conference memo was an attempt to produce a unified strategy for the ground war in Vietnam, in fact commanders chose to emphasise different elements. General Westmoreland fixed upon the goals related to destruction of enemy forces while the Marines, by pointing out that the factors affecting the enemy's ability to deploy troops were outside their control, minimised the importance of this goal. The Marines' campaign plan was outlined in *Operations of III MAF, Vietnam, February 1966*.[44] Then, the four elements of the plan were airfield security, counter-guerrilla action, large unit operations and civic action. After the Honolulu conference the Marines began to align the reporting of the success of its operations in Vietnam with the goals stated in the Honolulu memo, but their strategy remained essentially the same. In *Operations of the III MAF July 1966* the Marines produced a more comprehensive document showing the three main elements of the strategy they intended to follow. Airfield defence was dropped from the list, probably because this was part of the mission rather than a strategy in itself. The campaign plan consisted of three main functional areas, each with a number of programmes and subprogrammes. The first of these functional areas was 'Counterguerrilla Operations', which had the aim of destroying VC forces. Its supporting programmes were the destruction of VC forces and infrastructure and the development of local security forces. The second functional area was 'Large Unit Operations', which had the aim of destroying VC and NVA main forces. Its supporting programmes were divided into two categories; 'Watch' (the use of reconnaissance forces to locate enemy units) and 'Strike' (conducting major search and destroy operations). The third, and the most complex functional area, was 'Pacification', which had the aim of nation-building, a term that did not gain wide usage until the 21st century. The supporting programmes for this functional area were the establishment of village security, establishment of village government, improving the local economy, improving public health and improving public education.[45] The table is reproduced below, without the statistical information on progress since February 1966, which was included in the original.

44 FMFPac, *Operations of the III MAF, February 1966*, p. 7.
45 FMFPac, *Operations of US Marine Forces Vietnam, July 1966*, p. 6.

Table 4.2: III MAF Campaign Plan

MAJOR FUNCTIONAL AREAS	SUPPORTING PROGRAMS	SUBPROGRAMS
Counterguerrilla: Aim – Destroy Guerrilla Forces	1. Kill VC Guerrillas And 2. Destroy VC Infrastructure	Ambush
		Snipe
		Patrol
		Search and Destroy
		Collect Intell (sic) from Civilians
		Conduct County Fairs
	Phase-in VN Local Security Forces	Demonstrate Proper Security
		Train Local Security Forces
Large Unit Operations: Aim – Destroy VC and NVA Main Forces	Watch	Man Deep Recon Posts
		Reconnoitre By Air
		Execute Stay Behind Recon
	Strike	Conduct Large Unit Search and Destroy Operations
Pacification: Aim – Assist in Nation Building	Establish Village Security	Train Village Local Defense Forces
		Complete Village Defense Plans
		Establish Village Intel Networks
		Establish Village Psy-War Public Information Programs
	Establish Village Governments	Encourage Village Census
		Assist in Installing Government Officials
		Restore Security for Village Officials
		Maintain Close Contact with Village Officials
	Improve Local Economy	Assist in Establishing Local Markets
		Protect Rice Harvest
		Improve Communications
		Assist in Local Construction Projects
	Improve Public Health	Give Medical Treatment
		Evacuate Critically Ill
		Give Medical Training
		Feed Hungry Vietnamese
	Improve Public Education	Support Students
		Teach English Language
		Help Build Schools
		Give Vocational Training

Implementation of the campaign plan required a complex balancing act involving three factors. The first was the Marines' emphasis on the counterinsurgency war amongst the people in the coastal area. The second was the drive from General Westmoreland to conduct large-scale offensive operations, which became even more pronounced when the NVA started to cross the DMZ and the Laotian border in ever-increasing numbers since 1965. The third factor was the lack of manpower available to the Marines. Even with the deployment of the 1st Marine Division in 1966 and the enhancements provided by the US Army and the Republic of Korea Marines, the Marines did not have the manpower to satisfy effectively the requirements of all the elements of its strategy. The situation was further complicated by the decision to construct a barrier along the DMZ to prevent incursions by the NVA.

Paradoxically, the more successful a counterinsurgency campaign is the more resources it requires. The Marines decided to increase the number of CAP platoons and maintain the efforts in support of pacification, including operations such as Golden Fleece and County Fair (an initiative to assess individual villages while ridding them of VC guerrillas in a combined Marine and ARVN operation).[46] At the same time, the increasing incursions by the NVA required more effort in the border areas. The Marines took this as a sign of success of their counterinsurgency campaign as Generals Krulak and Walt believed the NVA was trying to draw units away from the coastal areas and tie them up near the border so that the insurgency, which was the real main effort could continue and flourish.[47]

Counterinsurgency Operations

The management of the counterinsurgency elements of the Marine's campaign remained the same during 1966 and 1967 as it had been in 1965. The Joint Co-Ordinating Council (JCC) continued to meet approximately every week, even during the political unrest in early 1966.[48] The JCC committees concentrated on public health, distribution of aid, the port at Da Nang and education.[49] The membership of the JCC continued to reflect the importance placed upon co-ordination of the civil affairs effort. The meetings were usually chaired by the deputy commander of III MAF and the Chief of Staff of the ARVN I Corps was also in attendance.

In May 1967 a new American organisation was formed to co-ordinate civil affairs, or 'Revolutionary Development' at the national level. Under Robert Komer, appointed as an Ambassador, Civil Operations and Revolutionary Development Support (CORDS) took control over the entire American military and civilian pacification effort. Komer's position in the American hierarchy was that of deputy to General Westmoreland.[50] The creation of

46 FMFPac, *Operations of the III MAF, Vietnam, February 1966*, p. 37.
47 General Lewis Walt, *Marine Corps Bulletin 5700* dated 31 March 1969.
48 III MAF, *Command Chronology, May 1966*, p22.
49 III MAF, *Command Chronologies, January 1966 – December 1967*, passim.
50 Richard A. Hunt, *Pacification: The American Struggle for Vietnam's Hearts and Minds* (Boulder:

CORDS had little more than a cosmetic effect on the JCC, which continued to operate as the interface between the Marines, the Vietnamese and American civil efforts. The membership of the JCC remained the same but the job titles of some of the members changed and they attended their first meetings as representatives of CORDS in July 1967.[51] But apart from the JCC meetings, co-operation between CORDS and III MAF was almost non-existent. From the point of view of the III MAF civil affairs staff, this was because the CORDS representatives tended to work directly to their headquarters in Saigon and did not pass information back to III MAF.[52] It is characteristic of the American effort in Vietnam that even when two co-ordinating agencies were located in the same building, they reported to different chains of command and did not share information.

This state of affairs did not bode well for the war in Vietnam as a whole but the Marines of III MAF had little or no control over matters at a national level. Their pacification effort, therefore, should be assessed in light of what the Marines could actually control and what was possible. In reality, III MAF was only responsible for relatively small areas around the bases at Phu Bai, Da Nang and Chu Lai even though their subordinate units operated further afield when taking action against NVA/VC main force units. These latter operations, however, only involved the temporary deployments of the units conducting them. Thus, the only permanent presence during the war was the Marine units protecting the air bases, which included the CAPs. The population of these areas was relatively small, consisting of the villagers who were mainly involved in agriculture. The Marines did not operate in the main towns or provincial capitals – Hue, Da Nang, Quang Tri and Quang Ngai.

Thus, the 'ink blot' strategy was as much about defence in depth as it was an attempt to follow the strategies propounded by such experts as David Galula and Sir Robert Thompson. The problem of the Rocket Belt around Da Nang, puts this into particular perspective. The Rocket Belt was the effective range from which the deadliest of the rockets in the NVA/VC arsenal, the 122 mm rocket, could be launched against Da Nang airbase. Despite these efforts the NVA/VC were still able to carry out large scale rocket attacks against the base in July 1967, when 50 rockets were fired destroying '10 aircraft, 13 barracks and a bomb dump'.[53] Further attacks occurred against all of the airbases during August 1967 as part of the NVA/VC effort to disrupt the elections and gain a propaganda victory by demonstrating the vulnerability of the bases.[54] During the course of the rest of 1967, the Marines fought off numerous efforts by the 2nd NVA Division to infiltrate the area.[55] By the end of 1967 it was reported that:

Westview, 1995). pp. 87-88.

51 Annex D to III MAF, *Command Chronology, July 1967.*

52 Major G. Telfer, Lt. Col. Lane Rogers and V. Fleming, *US Marines in Vietnam: Fighting the North Vietnamese: 1967* (Washington, DC: History and Museums Division, HQ USMC, 1984). pp. 184-185.

53 Major G. Telfer, Lt. Col. Lane Rogers and V. Fleming, *The US Marines in Vietnam: 1967*, p. 109.

54 FMFPac, *Operations of the III MAF, Vietnam, August 1967*, p. 35.

55 Major G. Telfer, Lt. Col. Lane Rogers and V. Fleming, *The US Marines in Vietnam*: 1967, pp.

> Although III MAF's extensive program of counter-measures has diminished the enemy's chances for successful attacks against the ICTZ bases, he still possesses the capability of launching mortar and rocket attacks against these installations. Further, as his chances for success in both large unit and guerrilla operations continue to diminish, he may elect to increase his attempts of indirect fire attacks on the bases.[56]

Counterinsurgency was an important part of the defence of the coastal airbases because popular support was recognised as an important force multiplier. The pacified areas had already germinated around the airbases and the Marines were still tied to the coast to a large extent due to their reliance on seaborne assets such as logistics (approximately 80% of their supplies still came by sea during 1966 and 1967) and the Special Landing Force, which was an important strategic reserve that was used to support operations against the NVA/VC and preserve the Marines' amphibious ethos.[57]

The aim of the Counterguerrilla Operations functional area in the Marine strategy was to destroy guerrilla forces, as opposed to the Main Force VC or NVA units. This was broken down into three supporting programmes, but effectively split into two main efforts. The first two programmes, which involved direct action against the guerrilla forces were intended to buy the space and time needed to allow the third, which was to create a long-term solution to the security situation, to proceed. As well as providing long-term security, it also provided a significant indicator of progress in the counterinsurgency campaign; increased participation by the in local population in security forces shows that they have made their choice and intends to defend itself against the insurgents.

The first two counterguerrilla programmes included ambushes, sniping operations, patrols, company size search and destroy operations, collection of intelligence from civilians and conducting County Fair operations. Most of these were fairly standard small-unit operations and often form part of conventional warfare when destruction of the enemy and seizing ground are the main aims. County Fair, however, was a step beyond that, since one of its aims was also to address the long-term welfare of the local population, a key factor in increasing support for local and national government, which in turn was intended to reduce support for the insurgency. County Fair was designed to destroy the VC infrastructure in a village or hamlet and, at the same time, start to re-establish local government. The first operations were carried out in August 1965, but it was not until February 1966 that the programme was refined sufficiently to be of general use. In April 1966, the progress of these operations was reported on for the first time. County Fair operations were conducted in three phases. First, a cordon of Marines would

111-124.

56 FMFPac, *Operations of the III MAF, Vietnam, November 1967*, p. 34.

57 For more precise figures see Major G. Telfer, Lt. Col. Lane Rogers and V. Fleming, *The US Marines in Vietnam: 1967*, p. 226. The figures for quantities of supplies in November 1967 can be found at *Operations of US Marine Forces Vietnam, November 1967*, p. 61. This source also shows the reliance on sea supply routes to move materiel between the Marines' bases.

be established in the early hours of the morning to prevent any VC escaping. The second and third phases ran concurrently. ARVN and GVN officials would conduct a census of the population, issue identity and ration cards, enquire about absent family members and segregate any VC suspects for questioning. Marine Corps teams would provide medical and dental treatment, while other teams would entertain the villagers with films, concerts and plays, often with psychological operations (psyops) messages to persuade the villagers to stop supporting the insurgents and support the government instead. ARVN troops would carry out the third phase, which was a systematic search of the village for arms caches, hiding places and tunnels. The first operations were considered a success in terms of the number of VC killed or captured and the number of weapons seized (61 killed, 35 captured and 25 weapons seized in April 1965). [58] One operation captured an entire village VC cadre (command element).[59] By the end of the first year of the program (and the end of the Marines' second year in Vietnam) 107 County Fair operations had been conducted. The number of operations varied widely each month, depending on the weather, number of troops available and, during the Tet celebrations in 1967, the desire not to cause any ill feeling.[60] The Marines appear to have stopped recording the number of these operations in July 1967. After this time there is mention of individual County Fair operations if they were particularly successful, but there is no running total reported as in previous months. By this time, though, only a few County Fair operations were being conducted per month. While they achieved some short term success, the operations were criticised for the fact that the forces left at the end of the operation with no plan for long-term security, leaving a vacuum that was often soon filled by the VC.[61] Without a permanent security presence, the local population was fearful of reprisals by insurgents if they were seen to be collaborating with government security forces by receiving aid or providing information. The population also the insurgents as the more permanent presence, offering greater long-term stability, and therefore such operations are of limited success unless there is some kind of follow-up. Greater success might have been achieved if a CAP platoon had been established in the villages after a County Fair operation, but there is no evidence that the two programs were ever linked in this way.

In addition to more traditional methods of destroying enemy guerrilla forces, such as ambushes, patrols and sniping operations, the Marines also sought to persuade guerrillas to surrender. The *Chieu Hoi* or 'Open Arms' programme had been started under the Diem regime in 1963 but had been neglected for a number of years following the coup in that year. It was originally planned as part of a wider initiative to resettle surrendered guerrillas, who would be housed in Strategic Hamlets and allowed to farm.[62] The programme was resurrected by the Marines, who used the 'ralliers' (i.e. those who had

58 FMFPac, *Operations of US Marine Forces Vietnam, April 1965*, p. 7.

59 FMFPac, *Operations of US Marine Forces Vietnam.*

60 FMFPac, *Operations of US Marine Forces Vietnam, February 1967*, pp. 53-54.

61 Major G. Telfer, Lt. Col. Lane Rogers and V. Fleming, *The US Marines in Vietnam: 1967*, p. 186.

62 Captain Russell Stolfi, *US Marine Corps Civic Action Effort in Vietnam March 1965-March 1966*, p. 65.

'rallied' to support the government) or '*Hoi Chanhs*' as they were called, in psychological operations persuading other guerrillas to surrender or giving lectures to villagers during County Fair operations on VC methods and intentions. The Marines found that villagers had little or no faith in the South Vietnamese government and would not believe that former VC would really be welcomed with open arms. The presence of ralliers who could tell their own stories of disillusionment with the VC and good treatment by the government would help persuade others who were considering surrendering.[63] The South Vietnamese set up *Chieu Hoi* centres to resettle the ralliers, but the Marines found other employment for some of them. The *Hoi Chanhs* who had participated in County Fair operations had proved useful in identifying VC members in their home villages. In 1966, 1,653 *Hoi Chanhs* rallied and in 1967 the figure increased to 2,989. It is worth noting that in December 1967, the month immediately preceding the Tet Offensive, there were 375 ralliers, the highest total ever recorded.[64] *Operations of US Marine Forces Vietnam, November 1967* stated 'Every indication points to a continuing upward trend in enemy defections in ICTZ, as the potential rallier, similar to the refugee, becomes progressively wearier of VC oppression'.[65] Psychological operations personnel assigned to the *Chieu Hoi* programme found that 'fear of air strikes and lack of food, clothing and medicine continue to be the primary vulnerabilities', although leaflets containing letters from other ralliers were also an influence on their decision, while the Safe Conduct Pass (a document guaranteeing safe conduct signed by a government official) was a prized possession amongst VC members.[66]

In October 1966, six *Hoi Chanhs* were selected to work alongside Marine patrols, using their local knowledge and experience with the VC to assist them in locating guerrilla units. They were known as 'Kit Carson Scouts', after the famous frontier guide and Indian fighter of the 19th Century. In addition to their military duties they also explained the benefits of the *Chieu Hoi* program to the families of VC members.[67] In February 1967 the programme was formally extended throughout III MAF. By the end of 1967 there were 132 Kit Carson Scouts serving with Marine units. Between them, they were held to be responsible for 58 VC dead, 37 captured, and 82 weapons seized.[68] While these figures are not large by any means, a more meaningful assessment of the usefulness of the Kit Carson Scouts can perhaps be derived from the number of patrols they accompanied and the classes they

63 'Returnee Exploitation; The Kit Carson Scout Development Program, Annex to III MAF', *Command Chronology, February 1967*, p. 2.

64 Figures combined from *Operations of US Marine Forces Vietnam, November 1967* and *III MAF Command Chronology December 1967*.

65 FMFPac, *Operations of US Marine Forces Vietnam, November 1967*, p. 33.

66 III MAF, *Command Chronology, September 1967*, p. 34.

67 III MAF, *Command Chronology, October 1966*, p. 27.

68 Major G. Telfer, Lt. Col. Lane Rogers and V. Fleming, *The US Marines in Vietnam: 1967*, p. 192. There is no reference to how these figures were arrived at. The III MAF Command Chronologies only recorded these figures for Nov 1966 – Jun 1967, then Nov and Dec 1967. There is no reason given in the narrative for the gap, but the figures in the Command Chronologies for KIA, detainees and weapons for those months are 43, 120 and 14 respectively.

gave on VC tactics. Between November 1966 and December 1967, Kit Carson Scouts accompanied over 3,000 patrols and gave more than 78 classes.[69] Thus many thousand Marines would have had some exposure to VC tactics and had the chance to interact personally with a former member of the VC, thus gaining greater understanding of their enemy. More importantly, however, this program was a clear demonstration that changing sides from the insurgency to support for the government, or at least ceasing the struggle against it, was a viable option. It was also an option that did not necessarily incur any penalty; *Hoi Chanhs* were integrated back into the community or employed by the security forces rather than being tried for crimes against the state or incarcerated.

The third program in the Counterguerrilla functional area of the campaign plan was to phase-in Vietnamese local forces, which were a militia style force intended for local defence. There were two branches of local forces, Regional Forces and Popular Forces, commonly grouped together under the acronym RF/PF. The difference between the two was that the RF companies were under the command of the Province Chief, while the PF units (usually platoon level) were under the command of the District Chief and tended to remain in their own villages or hamlets, almost as an armed 'neighbourhood watch'. During 1966 and 1967, one model for developing the Popular Force units was the CAP programme. The other model was to assist the RF/PF with training and provide 'mentoring' by partnering RF/PF units with Marines units on operations on a temporary basis. The Marines decided to use PF units to provide security in 'pacified' areas in order that they could release units for offensive action against the VC and NVA. In *The Combined Action Platoons: The US Marines' Other War in Vietnam*, Michael Peterson described this policy as a 'filler tactic to enhance base defence'.[70]

The RF/PFs suffered from a number of severe problems that hindered their performance: they were not allowed to recruit males aged between 20 and 35 since that age group was reserved for regular military service; they were considered low status and therefore got little support from the regular forces; lack of support, training and equipment meant they were generally ineffective against the NVA/VC; and the lack of support for widows, orphans and injured veterans was also a bar to recruitment and motivation. The Marines implemented a wide range of reforms to improve the effectiveness and quality of life of the RF/PFs, as well as other units that lay outside the regular ARVN structure. They asked for improvements to pay, conditions of service, training and equipment in order to improve the recruitment, retention, status, morale and effectiveness of these units. The Marines argued that the RF/PF took greater losses than the ARVN, but their pay and conditions were considerably lower, so men often deserted from the RF/PF to join the ARVN for more money, prestige and slightly less risk. While many of the measures were outside the control of the Marines, since they required that MACV ask the General Staff of the RVNAF to take action, there were things the Marines could do to improve

69 Figures derived from III MAF Command Chronologies Nov 1966 to December 1967. For an unknown reason, figures for Kit Carson Scout activities were not recorded between July and October 1967 inclusive.

70 Michael Peterson, *The Combined Action Platoons*, p. 32.

the lot of the RF/PF. These problems and the recommendations of the III MAF G3 (Operations Branch) to solve them were contained in a loose minute attached to the III MAF Command Chronology. The main recommendations were:

1. Standardize, throughout each enclave, operational cooperation presently being instituted in Quang Nam Special Sector with RF/PF.
2. Continue to focus attention at all levels on the importance of Popular Forces and the necessity of expanding the recruiting program.
3. Insure [sic] that advisory personnel are thoroughly familiar with the aims of the program and thus advising their counterparts.
4. Improve prestige and security of PF units whenever possible by making available supporting fires, reserve forces and helicopter resupply.[71]

The first point was a reference to operations being conducted in Quang Nam Province, where a sector consisting of five villages had been designated for special attention by the government. Although some limited success was achieved, the project was hampered by a lack of security. Although perimeter security was provided by 3/9 Marines, the VC concentrated their efforts on the RF/PF within the hamlets themselves and their attacks eventually forced the reconstruction effort to stop. Recognising the need for greater integration and co-operation between the Marines and RF/PF, III MAF managed to institute more formalised training in the Da Nang area by attaching units of the RF/PF to Marine units. Popular Force Platoons were attached to companies of the 1/3 Marines for training in marksmanship and patrolling, while a Regional Force platoon was put through a two week basic training course by the 1/3 Marines at battalion level.[72] This training became more formalised in 1966, with the creation of training centres in each of the provinces in the ICTZ, staffed by a mixture of US Army, Australian Army and Marine Corps personnel. There were five training centres with a maximum capacity of 2100 recruits at any one time. In order to maintain close links with the training schools, the Marines assigned a further Senior NCO to each school.[73] By the end of the first year of operation, in March 1967, 521 PF platoons had been trained, with a total of 19,978 personnel.[74] The following month, the Vietnamese Joint General Staff authorised a further 15 new Regional Force companies and 41 new Popular Force platoons in the ICTZ.

During 1966 and 1967, the Marines continued in their attempts to improve conditions of service for the RF/PF troops. Alongside the lifting of recruitment restrictions by the

71 III MAF, G3 Section, *Agenda Subject: RF/PF Status and Improvement*, 5 Jan 1966, pp. 4-5, Enclosure to III MAF *Command Chronology Jan 1966*.

72 Russell Stolfi, *US Marine Corps Civic Action Effort in Vietnam, March 1965 to March 1966*, pp. 45-48.

73 III MAF G3 Section, 'Popular Force Training Center', enclosure 12 to III MAF *Command Chronology, February 1966*, p. 3.

74 III MAF, *Command Chronology, March 1967*, p. 54.

Vietnamese General Staff, improved supplies and increased direct support to RF/PF operations the Marines also allocated resources to widows and RF/PF veterans. This was in the form of food aid, medical supplies and provision of materials to start small businesses.[75] The RF/PF forces were not entirely successful and, on their own, often lacked the capability to stand up to the NVA/VC. In October 1966, for example, it was recorded that they lost almost twice as many weapons as they captured.[76] Figures for April to December 1966 show that approximately 25% of the total strength of the PF deserted and that the kill ratio for PF units operating on their own was 3:1 (three VC for each PF soldier killed), whereas PF units operating alongside Marine units the ratio was 14:1.[77]

The Combined Action Platoons could be counted as a part of the phasing in of local security forces, even though they also fall within the establishment of village security in the 'Pacification' functional area. From January 1966 the Marines continued to develop the programme but as a result of these manpower shortages there were only 80 CAPs in place by the end of 1967 instead of the 114 that were planned.[78] There were three CAP Groups, headquartered in Phu Bai, Da Nang and Chu Lai although 50% of the platoons were in the area around Da Nang.[79] Table 4.3, below, shows the level of CAP activity during 1966 and 1967, with steady increases in the number of patrols and enemy killed (although there was an unaccounted-for drop in the number of enemy captured). These demonstrated the military benefits of the CAPs, which were in line with the Marines' preference for effective small unit activity. In addition to these measurable activities, the Marines believed that CAPs delivered more intangible benefits. The FMFPac monthly report for November 1967 stated that 'the platoons provide openings through which GVN and US sources initiate programs to strengthen GVN's position among the people; they also encourage people to provide information about the enemy, his activities and his intentions. In addition, the combined PF/Marine platoon serves as a constant reminder to the enemy of his inability to assert a strong influence within the CAP's area of influence'.[80]

75 Details reported each month in III MAF Command Chronologies from March 1966 to July 1967. These activities were not reported on much after that period, probably due to the change of command at II I MAF. Reporting formats changed slightly and almost certainly reflected the priorities of the new Commanding General. It is likely, however, that the activities continued but were not included in the statistics.

76 III MAF *Command Chronology, October 1966*, p. 29.

77 FMFPac, *The Marine Combined Action Program, Aug 1965 – Jan 1967*, summarised in Jack Shulimson, *The US Marines in Vietnam: 1966*, p. 240.

78 FMFPac, *Operations of US Marine Forces, Vietnam November 1967*, p. 29.

79 FMFPac, *Operations of US Marine Forces, Vietnam November 1967*, p. 29.

80 FMFPac, *Operations of US Marine Forces, Vietnam November 1967*, p. 28.

Table 4.3: Combined Action Platoon Activity Nov 1965 – Nov 1966. (US Marine Corps: FMFPac)

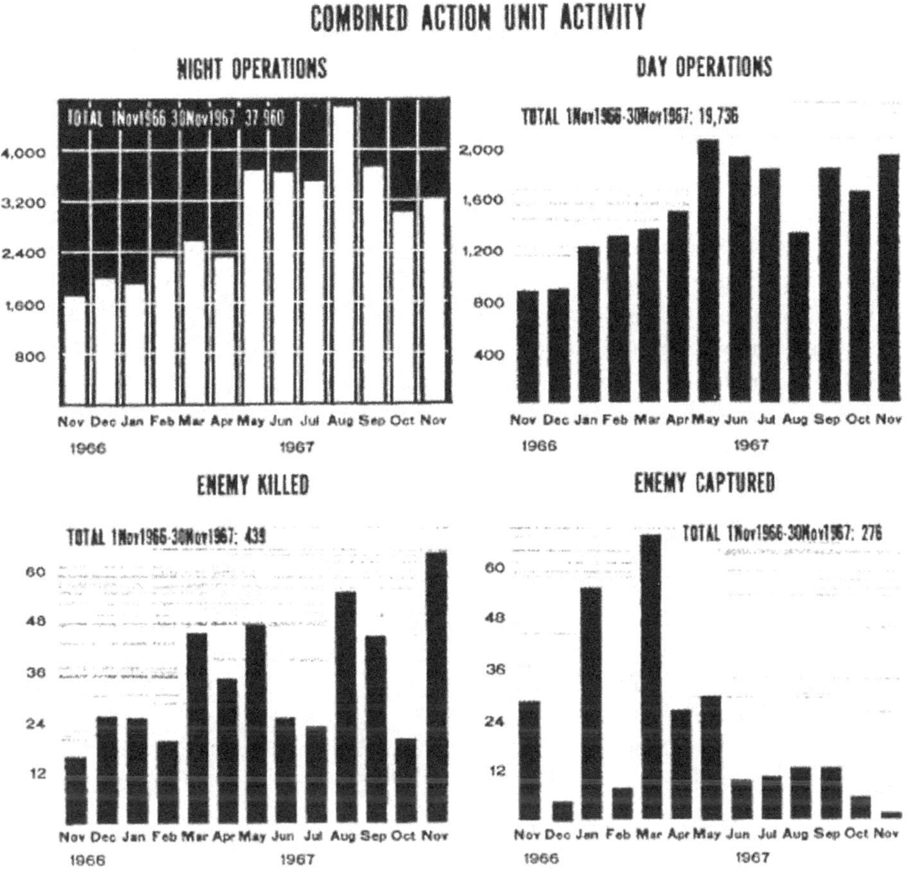

The CAP Programme became more formalised in mid-1967 under the command of its first Director, Lieutenant Colonel William Corson. On 17 July 1967 the programme was formally established by the promulgation of *III MAF Force Order 3121.4A*. The burden of logistics and command and control was removed from the respective parent Marine battalions of each team. As a result the teams became better equipped and co-ordination was significantly improved.[81] Despite these improvements and the importance of the programme to the Marines, there are some significant criticisms of the CAPs that Michael Peterson lists in his study of the programme: poor training; racism; lack of effectiveness in

81 Michael Peterson, *The Combined Action Platoons*, pp. 35-36.

dealing with VC personnel present in their villages; and that ultimately, the Marines opted for a more conventional approach to the war in general and failed to devote sufficient resources to the CAP.[82] As a former CAP Marine, Peterson's study contains useful insights and is based upon a wealth of first-hand accounts and primary sources. The CAP Marines certainly did not receive a great deal of training – only two weeks, with little or no language instruction – and there was a certain amount of racism among Marines serving in Vietnam, as the III MAF 'Personal Response' study in 1967 showed.[83] But his charge that the Marines opted not to put resources into the CAPs ignores the fact that this was forced upon them by the requirement to increase the number and scale of operations in the inland border areas. In fact senior Marine officers continued to press to be allowed to devote more resources to pacification generally, but to no avail.

Unfortunately, one possible measure of success in the counterinsurgency campaign relating to improvement in local security forces was not recorded in the III MAF monthly reports. There appear to be no records of recruitment or retention figures for the Popular Forces. This is another example where the Marines measured the effort that was being put in to a programme, in that the numbers of units put through re-training programs is recorded, as is the level of support given to PF units in terms of food and supplies, but there is no indication of the effect this had on recruitment and retention. This would have been an important indicator of the level of support for security forces and the extent to which the local population had chosen to defend themselves against the insurgents.

The Marines considered small-unit counterguerrilla operations to be the most important element of their offensive operations against the VC guerrillas. Certainly between January and June 1966, small-unit counterguerrilla operations had been at least as successful as major operations. Of the 4,672 VC killed in that period, 2,428 had been killed in small-unit operations. After June, however, the ratio began to change with an increasing number of VC killed in major operations as these became more frequent. The move of Marine units northward in the late summer and early autumn of 1966 also had a detrimental effect on small unit counterguerrilla operations, since fewer units were available.[84] A chart produced by CG FMFPac showed that the number of attacks initiated by the NVA/VC during 1966 of company size or smaller increased during the year and, in fact, made up the vast bulk of all attacks. Documents captured during the year and summarised in FMFPac *Operations of US Marine Forces Vietnam, January 1967* also show that guerrilla action and revolutionary warfare was still the main effort at that time.[85] In light of the apparent successes of small unit operations and the continued efforts of the VC to conduct revolutionary guerrilla warfare, it made sense to

82 Michael Peterson, *The Combined Action Platoons*, pp. 37-51 and pp. 124-125.

83 Michael Peterson, *The Combined Action Platoons*, p. 48 and Major G. Telfer, Lt. Col. Lane Rogers and V. Fleming, *The US Marines in Vietnam: 1967*, pp. 191-192.

84 FMFPac, *Operations of US Marine Forces Vietnam, September 1966*, p. 3.

85 FMFPac, *Operations of US Marine Forces Vietnam, January 1967*, p. 16.

the Marines that they should continue to place an emphasis on their pacification and counterinsurgency efforts.[86]

During 1967, small-unit counterguerrilla operations remained a mainstay of III MAF operations in Vietnam. In January 1967 there were 20,927 small-unit operations (ambushes, patrols and sniper missions), the highest number of such operations in a single month since the arrival of the Marines in March 1965, but was an increase of over 7,000 on the average number of small unit operations per month for the last three months.[87] Between January 1967 and the end of January 1968 small unit operations accounted for 8,519 confirmed VC or NVA killed.[88] Total VC and NVA killed for the same period was 29,126. VC and NVA killed in small unit operations therefore accounted for around 30 percent of all enemy fatalities inflicted by the Marines in the I Corps Tactical Zone. During the first half of 1967, the number of small-unit operations continued to increase monthly, reaching a peak of 40,846 in July 1967. There were also more major operations that month than any previous month, with eighteen named operations either started, ongoing or terminated.[89] After that, the number of operations declined to just above 20,000 in December 1967. During August and October this was due to allocation of units to duties connected with the South Vietnamese national and congressional elections, which were held in September and October respectively. After that time, the reduction in NVA/VC activity, largely due to interdiction of supplies by operations around the DMZ and bad weather, led to a reduced number of small unit operations.[90] It is also likely that guerrilla forces had expended a considerable portion of locally-available resources during the campaign to disrupt the elections and interdiction of supplies considerably reduced their ability to operate.

Unfortunately for the Marines, their progress was not only measured in terms of enemy killed or captured. Their level of activity was also recorded as' large unit operations' and 'battalion days of operations'. Large unit operations were defined as battalion size (or larger) operations or operations involving three or more company size units of any type under control of the reporting unit. These operations were named operations, such as Operation Hastings or Operation Prairie. Battalion days of operations were the number of days a battalion was involved in operations or a figure obtained by adding up the number of company size units involved in an operation, dividing by three and multiplying by the number of days an operation lasted. The Marines were reporting fewer battalion days in the field than the US Army but were reporting more 'small unit' operations. As well as appearing to be less active than the US Army, the Marines were

86 FMFPac, *Operations of US Marine Forces Vietnam, January 1967*, p. 17.

87 III MAF *Command Chronology, January 1967*, p. 6.

88 FMFPac, *Operations of US Marine Forces Vietnam, January 1968*, p. 28. Since the December 1967 report did not contain operational details, figures for 1967 were produced as part of the report for January 1968 and included figures for that month.

89 III MAF *Command Chronology, July 1966*, p. 9.

90 According to *Operations of US Marine Forces Vietnam, September 1967*, p. 4. The monsoon season commenced early in 1967 and seriously hampered operations.

concerned that these figures could have an effect on appropriations and force levels. The difference in figures was partly a result of the Marines' emphasis on small unit operations, but also resulted in different reporting criteria. The Marines were only reporting infantry battalions actively engaged on search and destroy operations, whereas the US Army also counted route clearance, route security, rice harvest security, border surveillance and some reconnaissance operations for the purposes of battalion days of operations. In order to redress the balance the Marines considered a number of options such as: including battalions other than infantry battalions in their reports; increasing the number of named operations; or 'whether it would be wise or proper to increase battalion days [of] operation by combining actions presently reported as small unit actions and reporting them as battalion size operations'.[91] From August 1966, the number of battalion days in the field reported by Marine units increased from 177 in August to 306 in October of the same year.[92] It is likely that one (or more) of these solutions was employed although the available material does not indicate which. Counterguerrilla actions of the type listed in the sub-programs of the overall strategy document, most of which were conducted at the small unit level, were most likely underreported for the rest of the war and therefore it is almost impossible to accurately quantify the effectiveness of counterguerrilla operations in destroying or defeating the VC.

All of the actions taken by the Marines as part of their counterguerrilla line of operations are entirely consistent with their existing doctrine and with the conventional wisdom on counterinsurgency promulgated by experts at the time. The use of small units to locate and destroy insurgent forces was well entrenched in Marine doctrine and experience. They attributed much of their success in the Banana Wars of the early 20th Century to the use of small units patrolling deep into the guerrillas' territory. General Walt particularly favoured the use of small patrols to locate enemy forces, upon which artillery and air power could be brought to bear. These were known as Stingray patrols. He wrote that '[t]he particular advantage of Stingray was its severe toll on the enemy with no significant loss of our own men. The Marines of the reconnaissance units came to know the hills and valleys of their areas as well as the Viet Cong themselves, and the weapons they used struck with stunning suddenness. The size of the opposing forces meant nothing: a Stingray patrol could take on a thousand men as long as their own location remained a secret'.[93] The use of patrols in this way, ensuring that firepower was used in a controlled and focussed manner rather than indiscriminate carpet bombing, was also consistent with lessons learned from the British Army experience in Malaya where it was concluded that 'given accurate information as to a target there would be merit in

91 Signal from Lt. Gen. Krulak to Major General Fields, 270822Z Aug 66. III MAF Incoming Message File August 1966. Held at US Marine Corps Historical Center, Washington DC at time of writing. Major General Fields was in temporary command of III MAF at the time during General Walt's absence.

92 III MAF *Command Chronology, October 1966*, p. 4.

93 Lewis Walt, *Strange War, Strange Strategy*, p. 49.

considering bombing as a means for attacking it. But to use bombing on a random basis would really be far too costly. And could well perhaps do more harm than good'.[94]

There was, therefore, nothing really new or innovative about the Marines approach to counter-guerrilla warfare. Their actions during 1966 and 1967 were those of an organisation that had assimilated its own historic experience for use by a generation that had never previously conducted such a campaign before and that had absorbed the lessons from more recent campaigns in Malaya and Algeria.

Large Unit Operations

During 1966 the requirement to conduct more large-scale operations began to absorb more of the Marines' resources. While Westmoreland saw operations of this nature as the mainstay of his campaign plan, to the Marines they were simply a means to allow the other elements of their campaign plan to succeed. This was certainly reflected in the way in which they used large scale operations to engage enemy forces in the coastal areas and then slowly move further afield once the immediate vicinity of the major bases had been cleared of Main Force VC or NVA units. For the first half of 1966, the Marines large-scale operations were conducted close to their coastal enclaves. In January 1966 the Marines conducted two large scale units within their existing TAORs around the coastal bases and two outside their TAORs (with a third ongoing at the time of the report).[95] By May 1966 the number of large operations outside the Marine TAORs had increased to ten, with two conducted inside TAORs.[96] The Marines' operations were also conducted increasingly further inland. All five operations in January were conducted near the coast, with only Operation Mallard being conducted at any great distance from the Marine TAORs.[97] In May, only four of the large unit operations were conducted on the coast but most of the remainder were within 20 km of the coast.[98] Only one operation was conducted in the border highlands: Operation Virginia, which was a battalion operation in the Khe Sanh area.[99] Despite General Westmoreland's insistence that there was a large NVA/VC presence in that area, the Marines reported that Operation Virginia was the 'most frustrating' operation that month because 'two weeks of aggressive effort in an area where large VC units had been reported resulted in only minor contact'.[100] The commander of the operation, Lt Col Bell, did acknowledge the fact that among other factors the enemy could have refrained from attacking his force in order to 'inspire overconfidence in the area later'.[101]

94 Lt. Colonel Ian Hywel-Jones, quoted in John Nagl, *Learning to Eat Soup with a Knife*, p. 105.
95 III MAF, *Command Chronology, January 1966*, Part 2, p. 1.
96 III MAF, *Command Chronology, May 1966*, Part 2, p. 1.
97 FMFPac, *Operations of the III MAF, Vietnam, January 1966*, pp. 9-10.
98 FMFPac, *Operations of the III MAF, Vietnam, May 1966*, p. 13.
99 FMFPac, *Operations of the III MAF, Vietnam, May 1966*. p. 13.
100 FMFPac, *Operations of the III MAF, Vietnam, May 1966*. p. 14.
101 1/1 Marines 'After Action Report Operation Virginia', quoted in Jack Shulimson, *US Marines in*

Operation Hastings, launched in July 1966 was the largest operation conducted by the Marines in the war to date.[102] It was also the first major operation to be conducted in the Vietnamese hinterland, near the border with Laos where it abuts the DMZ. The operation began as a reconnaissance operation but rapidly expanded to seven Marine battalions and five ARVN battalions when reconnaissance units reported contact with large formations of NVA, later assessed to be the 324B Division of the NVA. When the operation finished, the Marines claimed 783 confirmed NVA killed in action and another 909 unconfirmed killed.[103] This may not seem a large number when compared to the estimated strength of the division, which was 5,000 regular troops, and in the context of a war of attrition this would hardly be considered a success. In counterinsurgency terms, however, the effect of Operation Hastings was considerable. First of all, the operation was intelligence-led; although Westmoreland later said that the Marines had 'rudely bumped into North Vietnamese troops only seven miles from Dong Ha'.[104] In fact, the operation was based on an interrogation report that led to a reconnaissance operation that in turn led to the capture of documents and further interrogations that confirmed the presence of the NVA division.[105] The plan of the 324B Division was assessed to be the establishment of logistic bases from which attacks could be launched against targets in the northernmost province of South Vietnam.[106] The Marine operation succeeded in driving the division back across the DMZ, severely disrupting the planned operations in the coastal region to the north of Hue city. Even Westmoreland credited it as being a 'highly successful spoiling attack'.[107]

At a meeting between Westmoreland, CINPAC, and other senior commanders, including General Krulak in August 1966, Westmoreland laid out his strategy. Westmoreland told the meeting that he was working on a National Campaign Plan, in which US forces would conduct most of the offensive operations while the ARVN concentrated on civil affairs and reconstruction. Krulak pointed out that this was at odds with Robert McNamara's view that 'we must not end up in a position where we expend most of the blood in carrying the major offensive burden, while the ARVN contents itself with less costly activities'. Westmoreland's reply is not recorded, but Krulak commented that he felt that Westmoreland was 'a little out of focus with high command'. Westmoreland told the meeting that he had been working on a force structure plan to fight an indefinite war of attrition 'with a minimum effect on the economy, avoiding mobilisation and avoiding movement of forces from Europe' and that he was willing

Vietnam: An Expanding War 1966, p. 143.

102 FMFPac, *Operations of US Marine Forces Vietnam, July 1966*, p. 8.

103 III MAF *Command Chronology, July 1966*, p. 6.

104 General William Westmoreland, *A Soldier Reports*, p. 197.

105 FMFPac, *Operations of US Marine Forces, Vietnam, July 1966*, p9 and III MAF *Command Chronology, July 1966*, p. 6.

106 III MAF *Command Chronology, July 1966*, p. 10.

107 Message from CG FMFPAC to Commandant of the Marine Corps, DTG 130222Z Aug 66, III MAF Incoming Message file, August 1966, p. 2.

to accept a protracted war rather than rely on more troops. At the close of the meeting Krulak was left with the impression that Westmoreland did not 'have a plan of campaign on paper or in his mind yet' but that he was 'moving slowly towards acceptance of our approach to the war'.[108] Nonetheless, the Marines were ordered to move a division north to deal with the threat of North Vietnamese infiltration and the construction began of a barrier along the DMZ to enhance border security.[109]

Secretary of Defense Robert McNamara had already ordered a barrier to be built along the DMZ, following a study in August 1966 by the Institute for Defense Analyses, known as the 'JASON Summer Study'. The study recommended the construction of a foot and vehicle barrier consisting of minefields and acoustic sensors, supported by monitoring aircraft that could call in airstrikes when an incursion was detected. Although General Westmoreland was receptive to the idea, he felt the barrier concept envisioned by McNamara and his scientists would require the use of 'a battalion every mile or so in conventional defense'.[110] He persuaded McNamara to modify his plan from a linear barrier, to a series of strongpoints with minefields and wire to 'canalize' the enemy into areas where they could be engaged with airstrikes, artillery and mobile defense units. Although Westmoreland claimed in *A Soldier Reports* that he and General Walt were in agreement, in fact Walt was opposed to the plan because of the drain on his resources.[111] General Walt stated that if he had the forces that the planners said he would have during its construction 'a far better job of effectively sealing the DMZ could be accomplished without the barrier itself'.[112] Walt's position was that the Marines were already doing an effective job of preventing infiltration of NVA and VC Main Force units across the border, since the Marines 'beat these units handily each time we encounter[ed] them'.[113] Throughout 1967 the project, named Operation Dye Marker in June 1967, remained a bone of contention between III MAF and MACV. III MAF continued with the construction, but too slowly as far as Westmoreland was concerned, although Lt Gen Cushman (who replaced Lt Gen Walt as commander of III MAF in April 1967) was of the opinion that the faster the strong points were built and the project completed the better, as this would then release troops for other, more useful operations.[114]

The Marines had considerable success with their major operations during 1967 in that they managed to prevent the NVA from linking up with the civilian population in the coastal plains. In April and May a battalion of Marines at Khe Sanh, which had

108 Message from CG FMFPAC to Commandant of the Marine Corps, DTG 130222Z Aug 66, III MAF Incoming Message file, August 1966..

109 General William Westmoreland, *A Soldier Reports*, p. 199.

110 General William Westmoreland, *A Soldier Reports*, p. 200.

111 General William Westmoreland, *A Soldier Reports*, p. 200.

112 General Lewis Walt, 'CG III MAF Letter to LtGen Buse', dated 29 Dec 1966, quoted in Jack Shulimson, *US Marines in Vietnam; 1966*, p. 318.

113 General Lewis Walt, 'CG III MAF Letter to LtGen Buse' dated 29 Dec 1966, quoted in Jack Shulimson, *US Marines in Vietnam; 1966*, p. 319.

114 Major G. Telfer, Lt. Col. Lane Rogers and V. Fleming, *The US Marines in Vietnam: 1967*, p. 91.

been developed as a combat base on Westmoreland's orders, managed to destroy the better part of an attacking force consisting of two NVA Regiments.[115] This was followed up with a successful defence of other base camps along the DMZ in the second week of May.[116] A series of offensive operations against the remaining NVA/VC forces in the area immediately south of the DMZ prevented 'a major enemy effort to move south into Quang Tri Province'.[117] The 'Prairie' series of operations, which ran from August 1966 to April 1967, repulsed a series of invasion attempts across the DMZ by two NVA divisions.[118] They followed on from Operation Hastings, which had turned back the 324B NVA Division in July 1966. Operations Union I, Union II and Operation Swift, in the Spring and Autumn respectively, were conducted to deny the NVA and VC access to the rice growing areas in the area south of Da Nang. In addition to its success in denying important food supplies, Operation Union I had a considerable psychological impact on the NVA/VC due to loss of prestige.[119] Operation Swift managed to prevent the NVA/VC from disrupting both the rice harvest and the national elections in the Que Son district.[120]

By the end of 1967, the Marines concluded, the NVA/VC could no longer rely on the local population for logistic support and were forced to transport their own food 'over long supply lines from both Cambodia and North Vietnam'.[121] The Marines also conceded that the barrier had caused the NVA/VC to use routes further west adding to the 'logistic and time-space problems confronting the infiltration effort'.[122] That said, senior Marine officers were still concerned that the physical barrier relied too heavily on the presence of troops in static locations. General Krulak argued with Westmoreland about the need for combat bases such as Khe Sanh because he believed that they would have little or no effect on the NVA/VC who had already demonstrated the ability to move without using major highways and could easily enter South Vietnam at almost any point further south along the border. He also debated the point about monitoring enemy activity since there were 'US Army Special Forces, with several hundred irregular scouts, doing a competent job in the area'. Krulak finished by pointing out that 'every Marine tied to the Khe Sanh area would be one less involved in pacification of the critical coastal area'.[123] Sir Robert Thompson made the point that these static defences 'did [the North Vietnamese] more good than harm' because while forces were tied down manning and defending them, they could not manoeuvre to block infiltration routes further south.[124] In the end, Krulak and Thompson were vindicated: after the siege of Khe Sanh in 1968

115 Phillip Davidson, *Vietnam at War*, p. 429. Marine estimates of casualties were 807 confirmed killed and 611 probably killed. III MAF, *Command Chronology, May 1967*, p. 14.
116 III MAF, *Command Chronology, May 1967*, p. 14.
117 III MAF, *Command Chronology, May 1967*, p. 14.
118 Major G. Telfer, Lt. Col. Lane Rogers and V. Fleming, *The US Marines in Vietnam: 1967*, p. 3.
119 Major G. Telfer, Lt. Col. Lane Rogers and V. Fleming, *The US Marines in Vietnam: 1967*,, p. 68.
120 III MAF, *Command Chronology, September 1967*, pp. 17-18.
121 FMFPac, *Operations of US Marine Forces, Vietnam, October 1967*, p. 6.
122 FMFPac, *Operations of US Marine Forces, Vietnam, November 1967*, p. 17.
123 Victor Krulak, *First to Fight*, p. 208.
124 Sir Robert Thompson, *No Exit From Vietnam*, p. 69.

the base was destroyed and the strategy changed to one of reliance on mobility to detect and prevent infiltration.[125]

Conclusion

The Marines transitioned from a largely defensive posture to an offensive one during 1966 and 1967. This transition demonstrated the real limitations upon counterinsurgency; it is time consuming and resource intensive. Thus, it is not an approach that could have been used to defeat both the NVA and the VC in the northern provinces. That required more conventional means, but even then the senior commanders were unable to agree on how best to achieve this. Clearly the Marines felt the pressures imposed on them by their force structure and their reliance on the sea for logistic support. Large scale operations not only detracted from what was still the main mission of defending the coastal bases but were far more difficult for the Marines than they would have been for the US Army, with its larger logistical support infrastructure and airmobile capabilities. The Marines still maintained that counterinsurgency was the best means of providing defence in depth for the coastal bases but, apart from large calibre rocket attacks, this had not yet been tested to any great extent. That test was to come, in 1968 during the Tet Offensive.

125 Lt Gen Robert Cushman, 'Foreword' in Captain Moyers Shore, *The Battle for Khe Sanh*, (Washington DC: Historical Branch, G-3 Division, HQ USMC, 1969), pp. ix-x.

5

1968: The Start of the General Offensive – General Uprising

At the beginning of 1968, the Marines had two divisions in country, the 1st and 3rd Marine Divisions, consisting of 18 infantry battalions with supporting arms; a total of around 76,000 men.[1] Senior Marine Corps officers felt that this was not enough to support the two very different missions that III MAF had been assigned; the 'big unit' war in the north and defence of the coastal enclaves. General Greene's estimate in early 1965 that it would take two divisions to clear the coastal strip appeared to be optimistic in 1968; even with the addition of a US Army division to the south of Da Nang, the Marines were still unable to achieve all they wanted.[2] Westmoreland's requests for more troops were cut almost in half and in 1967 he had only received 46,000 of the 80,000 that was the minimum he had asked for.[3] Although reluctant to use reservists, because they were not a sustainable force but could only be used once for a limited duration, the Marines drew up plans to mobilise an entire Marine Expeditionary Force before the Tet Offensive. Afterwards, under instructions from the Secretary of Defence, there were plans to send a reduced force of 18,000 Marines. In the end, however, when President Johnson finally announced the call up of reservists in March 1968 he did not include any Marines.[4] The Marines, therefore, found themselves unable to rely upon MACV for any more troops and could not draw upon their own resources in the United States.

As a result of these manpower shortages the cornerstone of the pacification program, the Combined Action Platoons, had not expanded as expected during 1967. The plan was to have 114 CAPs in place by the beginning of 1968 but by November 1967 there were only 80.[5] Reinforcements consisting of elements of three US Army divisions were

1 III MAF, *Command Chronology January 1968*, pp. 2, 7.

2 General Wallace Greene, Memorandum for the Record, 28 April 1965.

3 Jack Shulimson, Lt. Col. Leonard Blaison, Charles Smith and Captain David Dawson, *US Marines in Vietnam: The Defining Year: 1968*, History and Museums Division, HQ USMC, Washington, DC, pp. 11-12.

4 Jack Shulimson, Lt. Col. Leonard Blaison, Charles Smith and Captain David Dawson, *US Marines in Vietnam: The Defining Year: 1968*, pp. 574-575.

5 FMFPac, *Operations of US Marine Forces Vietnam, January 1967*, p. 6 and FMFPac *Operations of*

sent to III MAF, but the bulk of these went to the north and west to fight the 'big unit war', rather than the coastal areas. The 23rd Infantry Division (Americal), previously designated Task Force Oregon, was assigned to the south of Da Nang in September 1967. The remaining two US Army formations were in the process of moving north to assist the 3rd Marine Division along the DMZ at the start of 1968. Two brigades of the 1st Cavalry Division (Airmobile) arrived towards the end of January 1968 and a brigade of the 101st Airborne Division arrived at the end of February 1968. The 1st Cavalry Division (Airmobile), the 101st Airborne Division and the 3rd Marine Division were designated the Provisional Corps, Vietnam on 10 March 1968, subordinate to III MAF but under command of a US Army officer. In July 1968 the Provisional Corps was re-designated XXIV Corps when it became a permanent formation.[6] General Cushman, the III MAF commander, summarised the situation in his end of year report for General Westmoreland in January 1968:

> Generally, en[emy] hoped his 1967 campaigns would gain significant tactical victories with minimum losses, while imposing heavy losses on ARVN and Allied forces. Intention was to utilize victories as psychological tool in undermining morale and prestige of friendly forces. Attendant long-range political aim was to create polit[ical] situation in US paralleled to that in France in 1953, thus influencing world public opinion and confronting public with endless war of attrition…Dichotomy which exists is evidence by conventional type war in North and counter-insurgency struggle in remainder of ICTZ.[7]

The flaws in fighting on two under-resourced fronts were exposed in the onslaught that occurred in early 1968 when the North Vietnamese decided that the time had come to begin the third phase of their war to re-unite Vietnam; the General Offensive – General Uprising. The start of the General Offensive – General Uprising, more commonly known as the Tet Offensive, was signalled by a wave of attacks throughout South Vietnam during the Tet holiday that celebrated the Vietnamese New Year at the end of January 1968. This offensive was followed by two smaller offensives during the course of 1968 that were intended to continue the process of the transition from guerrilla warfare to the general offensive – general uprising phase.

Relations between the Marines and General Westmoreland at this time were possibly at their lowest ebb than any other time during the war. General Westmoreland considered the forthcoming battle for the Northern provinces to be so crucial that he ordered a new headquarters be established at or near Phu Bai in late January 1968 so he could monitor

US Marine Forces Vietnam, November 1967, p. 29.

6 III MAF, *Command Chronology, September 1967*, p2; III MAF, *Command Chronology January 1968*, p. 2; III MAF, *Command Chronology February 1968*, p. 2; III MAF, *Command Chronology March 1968*, p. 2 and III MAF, *Command Chronology August 19 68*, p. 2.

7 General Robert Cushman, message to General Westmoreland, *CY67 Assessment*, pp. 2-3, III MAF Outgoing Message File, Jan 1968.

the situation more closely. The new headquarters, designated MACV Forward, was to be under the command of his deputy, General Creighton Abrams. Unfortunately this became the cause of yet another rift between Westmoreland and the Marines because, although General Cushman understood that a commander would want to be able to monitor a key battle more closely, he was concerned that the establishment of MACV Forward was a demonstration of lack of confidence in his ability and that MACV Forward would eventually take control of all the US Army assets in ICTZ.[8] General Abrams managed to placate Cushman somewhat by informing him that the new HQ would only be in existence for 60 to 90 days, after which it could be downgraded to a corps headquarters for the units in the DMZ area.[9] US Army criticism of the Marines' performance in the DMZ area in the latter part of 1967 had already created an atmosphere in which any action by Westmoreland was likely to be seen in a negative light. General Westmoreland reassured General Krulak that he had 'absolute confidence in [Cushman's] professional judgement and leadership'.[10] General Krulak, ever suspicious of Westmoreland's motivations, told Cushman that he was of the opinion that the decision to establish MACV Forward was because Westmoreland did not think that III MAF could handle the extra responsibility for the additional US Army divisions and that he 'probably cannot endure the thought of a Marine commanding so many soldiers'.[11] Perhaps the most telling indicator of just how bad relations between the US Army and the Marines had become was Krulak's final thought on why Westmoreland had decided to establish MACV Forward. He told Cushman that there might be the possibility that Westmoreland 'doesn't want the Marines to end up with all the bouquets when the victory materializes'.[12] This was typical of Krulak and reflected his concern that Westmoreland and the Army would do all they could to minimise the Marines' achievements in Vietnam.

The issue of the establishment of MACV Forward came at an unfortunate time in relations between Westmoreland and the Marines as it also occurred in the middle of an inter-service row concerning management of tactical air assets. By mid-January 1968 Westmoreland already had some concerns about the performance of III MAF and the apparent inability of the Marines to integrate with the other services. During a meeting

8 General Robert Cushman, MACV Forward, Top Secret SPECAT Exclusive message for General Chapman and General Krulak, dated 27 Jan 1968, FMFPAc SPECAT Exclusive Message File Dec 1967-20 Feb 1968, p. 157.

9 General Robert Cushman, 'Gen Abrams' Visit to Discuss MACV Forward', Top Secret SPECAT Exclusive message for General Chapman and General Krulak, dated 27 Jan 1968, FMFPAc SPECAT Exclusive Message File Dec 1967-20 Feb 1968, p. 160.

10 General Victor Krulak, 'Last Night's Discussion with Westy re Organizational Changes in ICTZ',Top Secret SPECAT Exclusive message for General Cushman, dated 27 Jan 1968, FMFPAc SPECAT Exclusive Message File Dec 1967 – 20 Feb 1968, p. 164.

11 General Victor Krulak, Top Secret SPECAT Exclusive message for General Cushman, dated 27 Jan 1968, FMFPAc SPECAT Exclusive Message File Dec 1967-20 Feb 1968, p. 163.

12 General Victor Krulak,Top Secret SPECAT Exclusive message for General Cushman, dated 27 Jan 1968, FMFPAc SPECAT Exclusive Message File Dec 1967-20 Feb 1968, p. 163.

with III MAF at Da Nang Westmoreland wrote that Cushman appeared reluctant to use the US Army units put at his disposal. In frustration, Westmoreland felt he had to act:

> For almost two hours, I listened to reports of the various commanders, becoming more and more shocked at things that virtually begged to be done yet remained undone. Local decisions were urgently needed. I ended up giving direct orders myself to General Cushman's subordinate forces, an unusual and normally undesirable procedure.[13]

Of particular concern to Westmoreland was the lack of co-ordination between the Marines' organic air assets and other services. The US Army units assigned to ICTZ were still relying on the US Air Force for support rather than the Marine Air Wing under command of III MAF. General Westmoreland ordered his Deputy Commander for Air, General Momyer, to establish a system under which all tactical air assets (apart from helicopters) would come under a single manager. He thought that III MAF would understand the need for it and comply but, due to the 'close supervision that Marine Corps headquarters exercised over anything involving the III Marine Amphibious Force', they did not. On being informed of the decision, Krulak immediately ordered Cushman to stand firm and refuse to allow III MAF's air assets to come under command of MACV's single manager system.[14] His suggestions to Cushman regarding how to proceed were followed almost to the letter, an indication that Westmoreland was right to be concerned about the level of informal influence exerted upon III MAF by the Marines' own chain of command rather than the formal one through MACV.[15] This highly complex issue eventually took another two years to resolve (to the pre-1968 arrangement of Marine control of their own assets under nominal control of the US Air Force) but it highlights the fact that command relationships had not changed since the arrival of the Marines in Vietnam in 1965.[16] There was constant pressure upon III MAF to satisfy the requirements of its in-country commander at MACV and the Marine Corps chain of command that detracted from the ability to comply with one of the basic principles of counterinsurgency war – unity of command.

13 General William Westmoreland,, *A Soldier Reports*, p. 342

14 General Victor Krulak, Secret SPECAT Exclusive Marine Corps Eyes Only message to General Cushman, dated 17 Jan 68, FMFPac SPECAT Exclusive Message File Dec 1967-20 Feb 1968, pp. 68-74.

15 General Robert Cushman, 'Discussion of General Cushman and General Momyer as directed by MACV 171206Z Jan 68', Secret SPECAT Exclusive Message for General Westmoreland, dated 18 Jan 1968, III MAF Outgoing Message file, pp. 36-38.

16 The issue is referred to in order to show the dysfunctional nature of the command arrangements. The III MAF message files contain three volumes of messages on the subject spanning the period Dec 67 to Jan 69. For a summary of the single manager issue see General William Westmoreland, *A Soldier Reports*, pp. 343-345; Alan Millett, *Semper Fidelis*, pp586-588.

Aims of the Tet Offensive

All levels of command within the US forces in Vietnam were expecting a major attack in early 1968, even if it was not clear that it would be a nationwide effort. General Phillip Davidson, the chief of intelligence at MACV in January 1968 summed up the general feeling in his account of the offensive:

> First, the major element of tactical surprise was not the timing of the assault, but the fact that the enemy attacked so many cities and did so simultaneously. General Westmoreland and I confidently expected the enemy offensive to be launched either just before or just after Tet. The fact that the enemy attacked *during* Tet was therefore only a mild surprise. Much more unexpected were the assaults on the many cities and towns. Although United States intelligence had dredged up several reports dealing in exhortative terms with the 'Great Uprising', no responsible American or South Vietnamese official believed that the enemy would throw himself at the heart of Allied strength – the cities ... Giap's coordination of the simultaneous attacks against almost forty towns and cities was also unexpected. The Allies believed that the Communists lacked the staff expertise and signal communications necessary to coordinate so many far flung attacks. Actually, the Allies were right. The premature attack in mid-South Vietnam (a breakdown of coordination) provided the key tip-off to the waiting Allies.[17]

The premature attack referred to by Davidson was the result of poor communication amongst the Communist forces and lack of uniformity throughout Vietnam on when the Tet holiday actually began. Although Giap intended the offensive to begin on the night of 30/31 January, some units in central South Vietnam commenced their attacks in the early hours of the morning of 30 January.[18]

III MAF expected that the forthcoming offensive would be another attempt at severing the Northern provinces from the rest of South Vietnam, with the main effort being directed against the city of Hue. A III MAF periodic intelligence report (PERINTREP) dated 14 January 1968 made the following assessment:

> Throughout the ICTZ, a strong effort to interdict main routes of friendly movement is anticipated, particularly in the TRI THIEN Region, as the enemy continues in his attempt to sever the ICTZ from SVN. The enemy is expected to continue limited attacks against CAP units and friendly installations in the PHU LOC area, while preparing for a major offensive against the HUE – PHU BAI complex...Provincial jails, CAP units and District HQ's, such as DAI LOC, TAM

17 Phillip Davidson, *Vietnam at War*, p. 479.

18 James Willbanks, *The Tet Offensive: A Concise History*, (New York, NY: Columbia University Press, 2007), pp. 26-30.

> KY and QUANG NGAI city, remain the most probable targets in central and southern I Corps.[19]

According to Ang Cheng Guan, in *Decision Making Leading to the Tet Offensive – The Communist Perspective,* the decision to launch the Tet Offensive, or the 'General Offensive – General Uprising' as the North Vietnamese called it, was taken during a series of meetings in 1967 after General Nguyen Chi Tranh (Commander in Chief of the Communist forces in South Vietnam) presented a proposal to the Political Bureau and Military Central Commission in Hanoi in July of that year.[20] Although planning began almost immediately, the date was not settled until October 1967 and final confirmation of the order to attack was not given until January 1968, a mere two weeks before the offensive was due to start. The decision makers in Hanoi were torn between concerns that the US build-up of forces in the South would soon make a general offensive impossible and the need to get the timing right. It is important to note that the offensive was not intended to be a single knock-out blow, but the start of the last phase of the Communist revolutionary war strategy – the General Counteroffensive.[21] Le Duan, First Secretary of the Vietnamese Communist Party (and *de facto* deputy to Ho Chi Minh) wrote in a letter, in January 1968, that the specific aims of the Tet Offensive were 'to deal [the enemy] thundering blows so as to change the face of the war, further shake the aggressive will of US imperialism, compel it to change its strategy and de-escalate the war'.[22] Le Duan foresaw a number of outcomes for the Tet Offensive, ranging from total victory in the Saigon area to limited success, the worst of which would only cause the Communists to revert to a protracted war.[23] The point is that military failure of the offensive would not necessarily translate into a strategic political or diplomatic failure for the Communists.

The Tet Offensive was clearly about more than simply gaining military advantage. The intention was to begin the process of the general offensive-general uprising and a large part of that was undermining the credibility of the Allied forces while also intimidating the South Vietnamese people through a show of strength. The Tet Offensive was entirely in keeping with the principles of Communist revolutionary warfare and exposed the critical weakness caused by the failure to devote equal attention and resources to the conventional war in the northern part of ICTZ and the pacification program in the populated coastal areas.

The communist objectives for the Tet Offensive can also be inferred from analysis of a training document produced by COSVN in March 1968. The document lists the

19 III MAF *Periodic Intelligence Report 2-68,* dated 14 January 1968, pp. 2-3. III MAF Periodic Intelligence File 1 Jan – 25 Feb 1967.

20 Ang Cheng Guan, 'Decision-Making Leading to the Tet Offensive – The Communist Perspective', *Journal of Contemporary History,* Vol. 33, No. 3 (Jul 1998), p. 346.

21 Ang Cheng Guan, *Decision-Making Leading to the Tet Offensive,* pp. 341-353.

22 Le Duan, *Hanoi: Letters to the South* (1986), pp 93-100, quoted in Ang Cheng *Decision-Making Leading to the Tet Offensive,* p. 351.

23 Ang Cheng Guan, *Decision-Making Leading to the Tet Offensive,* p. 351.

successes and the failures of the Tet Offensive, from which an assessment of the objectives can be made. These were as follows:

> *Destruction of US and South Vietnamese military forces and administrative infrastructure.* The document claims that 30% of the ARVN and 20% of the US military force was destroyed and that they have been forced into a defensive posture but that overall the Communist forces 'have not fulfilled their role as a 'lever' and have not created favourable conditions for motivating the masses to arise in towns and cities'.[24]
>
> *'Liberate' the population and persuade the people to join in an uprising against the South Vietnamese government.* Although the document claims that 1.5 million people were liberated, it points out that the 'organized popular forces were not broad and strong enough' and that 'we have not had specific plans for motivating the masses to the extent that they would indulge in violent armed uprisings'. A minimum objective is also revealed as the document states that in liberating the 1.5 million people, the Communists also managed to 'consolidate and widened... rear areas' and moved considerable resources into front line areas.[25]
>
> *Undermine the capability of the South Vietnamese armed forces by creating a 'military revolt movement in which the troops would arise and return to the people's side'.* The document states that 'inadequate attention' had been paid to this task and therefore they failed to achieve this objective.[26]
>
> *Quantitative and qualitative improvement of the Communist armed forces.* In a clear indication that for the Communists the Tet Offensive was the start of a process rather than a single event, the authors of the document claim that their armed and political forces 'have become outstandingly mature during the struggle in the past months. Our armed forces have progressed in many respects, political organizations are being consolidated and have stepped forward; much progress has been realized in leadership activities and methods and we have gained richer experiences'.[27]

Two elements of Communist thinking can be seen in the training document. First, it conforms to the principles of Communist revolutionary warfare in that as well as addressing the armed *dau tranh* it also discusses all three elements of the political *dau tranh*; the action among the population controlled by the enemy (the efforts to persuade them to take part in an uprising), action among the people (consolidation of the 'rear areas') and the non-military action among the enemy troops (the efforts to persuade the

24 'Lao Dong Party Training Document on COSVN Resolution No 6, March 1968' extracted from Gareth Porter, *Vietnam: A History in Documents* (New York, NY: New American Library, 1981), p. 364.

25 *Lao Dong Party Training Document on COSVN Resolution No 6, March 1968*, p. 364.

26 *Lao Dong Party Training Document on COSVN Resolution No 6, March 1968*, pp. 364-365.

27 *Lao Dong Party Training Document on COSVN Resolution No 6, March 1968*, p. 364.

troops to 'return to the side of the people'). The document is also a classic piece of 'self-criticism', an important element of Maoist and Vietnamese communist practice.

The Tet Offensive in the III MAF Area of Operations

The General Offensive – General Uprising in the III MAF area of operations had five distinct phases during 1968. These are described in detail below, but in short they consisted of operations around Da Nang in early January 1968, a siege of the combat base at Khe Sanh that started in the middle of January and then three waves of offensives during the course of the rest of the year.

NVA/VC Precursor Operations Around Da Nang

In ICTZ the expected Winter/Spring offensive began in early January with a series of attacks in the Da Nang area. A US Army brigade in the Que Son Valley, southwest of Da Nang, was attacked by a sizeable force on 3 January. The NVA unit responsible was intent on destroying the brigade even though its plans had been compromised by capture a month previously.[28] At the same time there were attacks against district headquarters, CAP locations and various outposts followed by a rocket attack against the Da Nang airbase. Further attacks took place to the north of Da Nang on the night of 7 January. Some of these attacks were successful, with CAP units suffering particularly high casualty rates. One CAP unit to the south of Da Nang was completely overrun and all 14 Marines in the platoon were either killed or wounded in an attack on 3 January and 13 Marines were killed and 25 wounded in attacks against three CAP units on 7 January.[29]

Although no assessment of the reason for these attacks is given in the command chronologies or the intelligence reports, it is highly likely that these were intended as a precursor to the attack against Da Nang city on 31 January. At the time of the Tet Offensive the Da Nang area contained the biggest proportion of the civilian population of any of the areas under direct III MAF control, with over 800,000 people living within 50km of the airbase, and had 40 CAP units providing defence in depth, which was around 50% of the total number of CAPs.[30] It is not surprising therefore that the NVA/VC felt the need to conduct preliminary operations in the area. The fact that the commander of the 2nd NVA Division was ordered to conduct his attack against the brigade in the Que Son valley despite his plan being compromised seems to indicate that these attacks were either intended to soften up the heavy defences around Da Nang or to establish the likely

28 III MAF, *Command Chronology, January 1968*, p. 23.

29 Jack Shulimson, Lt. Col. Leonard Blaison, Charles Smith and Captain David Dawson, *US Marines in Vietnam: 1968*, p98 and pp. 102-105.

30 CAP unit data from FMFPac, *Operations of US Marine Forces Vietnam, November 1967*, p. 29. Population data from FMFPac, *Operations of US Marine Forces Vietnam*, Jan 1968, pp. 41-45.

response to attacks in the area.[31] III MAF also assessed the attacks as being part of the continuing effort to close Route 1 between Da Nang and Hue.[32] Since Da Nang was the closest base with sufficient forces to support Marine and ARVN operations in Hue during the Tet Offensive this road would later become a vital part of the battle for Hue.

Battle For Khe Sanh and its Significance

No treatment of the Marine Corps in Vietnam during the Tet Offensive is complete without a discussion of the siege of Khe Sanh Combat Base. For nearly three months 20,000 NVA/VC besieged the 6,000 defenders of the base but their reasons for doing so have long been debated by military historians. The two prevailing opinions are that the NVA/VC either intended to overrun the base and force a humiliating defeat upon the Americans in a repeat of the battle for Dien Bien Phu or that the siege was an attempt to divert attention and resources away from the Tet Offensive. Both of these opinions, however, assume that the siege at Khe Sanh had the same importance for the NVA/VC that it did for the Americans, for whom it became essential that the base be defended at all costs. It became a matter of national pride with President Johnson following the battle closely, having extracted promises from the Joint Chiefs of Staff that the base would not fall.[33] Each of these aims is consistent with the idea of maximum and minimum aims for the Tet Offensive and each one is consistent with the principles of Communist revolutionary warfare. That is, the NVA/VC may have wanted to overrun the base if at all possible, but if this was not possible then they at least wanted to ensure that the battle was a drain on resources by maintaining the siege for as long as possible. The political aims could easily run in parallel with the military aims; mounting such an attack and maintaining the siege would demonstrate that the NVA/VC remained a potent force despite the best efforts of the American forces. Actually managing to overrun the base would be a significant propaganda coup.

There is a possible third explanation for the siege of the base, which is that the siege of Khe Sanh was necessary to suppress operations in that area in order to support the main effort in Hue. This explanation is based upon research into North Vietnamese sources by Ang Cheng Guan, for his article *Khe Sanh from the Perspective of the North Vietnamese*, and analysis of the overall NVA/VC activity during Tet to establish whether it supports the hypothesis.[34] The fact that the Americans became fixated upon the base to the extent

31 Reference to 2nd NVA Division Commander's orders from McGarrigle, 'The 2nd North Vietnamese Division', Working Papers Americal Division, manuscript, p. 43 and quoted in Jack Shulimson, Lt. Col. Leonard Blaison, Charles Smith and Captain David Dawson, *US Marines in Vietnam: 1968*, p. 99.

32 III MAF *Periodic Intelligence Report 2-68*, dated 14 January 1968, p. 1.

33 Randall B. Woods, *LBJ: Architect of American Ambition* (New York: Free Press, 2006), p. 823; General William Westmoreland, *A Soldier Reports*, pp. 316-317.

34 Ang Cheng Guan, 'Khe Sanh from the Perspective of the North Vietnamese', article in *War in History*, Vol. 8, Number 1, (2001), pp. 87-98.

that they did was an unexpected propaganda bonus for the North Vietnamese. Before exploring these ideas, though, it is worth examining the reasons for establishing the base in the first place because it provides a good example of the strategic differences between Westmoreland and the senior Marine Corps officers in Vietnam.

Khe Sanh combat base was established in the northwest corner of South Vietnam, near the main highway from Laos to the coast. The base was first established in September 1966, at General Westmoreland's insistence and despite the objections of senior Marine officers. General Westmoreland and his intelligence staff at MACV believed that there was a sizeable NVA/VC presence in the area around Khe Sanh as early as April 1966 and that therefore a military presence was required to monitor enemy activity, prevent infiltration and anchor the western end of the DMZ defence system that had been established during 1967. Westmoreland also believed that the base at Khe Sanh would provide an opportunity to bring the NVA/VC into a large scale battle in an area where the Americans could use artillery and air power without their use 'being complicated by the proximity of civilian population'.[35]

General Krulak disagreed with the importance of establishing a base at Khe Sanh and thought that the opportunity to fight a major pitched battle was more important to Westmoreland than any other reason because it 'represented his own conception of how to defeat the large North Vietnamese forces' and, as far as Krulak was concerned, Westmoreland believed that 'firepower was the classic answer – locate the enemy formations, fix them, then back off and beat them to death with air and artillery'.[36] Here Krulak also seems at odds with his fellow Marine Generals; both Walt and Cushman were happier with this approach than trying to conduct large scale operations. At a meeting with Westmoreland at the Chu Lai airbase Krulak argued that holding Khe Sanh would have little or no effect on NVA/VC infiltration because they had already demonstrated the ability to move without using major highways and could easily enter South Vietnam at almost any point further south along the border. He also debated the point about monitoring enemy activity since there were 'US Army Special Forces, with several hundred irregular scouts, doing a competent job in the area'. Krulak finished by pointing out that 'every Marine tied to the Khe Sanh area would be one less involved in pacification of the critical coastal area'.[37]

During 1967 the Marines and the NVA/VC built up their forces in the Khe Sanh area, which led to heavy fighting both sides fought for the hills surrounding Khe Sanh.[38]

35 General William Westmoreland comments on draft manuscript dated 27 May 1978 quoted in Jack Shulimson, *The US Marines in Vietnam: 1966*, p. 196.

36 Victor Krulak, *First to Fight*, p. 208.

37 General Victor Krulak, *First to Fight*, p. 208. Krulak covers the meeting in his book but no official record can be found. The passage implies that the meeting occurred at Chu Lai in the autumn of 1966, prior to the establishment of the base on 29 Sep. The III MAF Command Chronology shows that the only time both General Krulak and General Westmoreland visited at the same time during that period was 6 Sep so this is the most likely date for the meeting.

38 III MAF *Command Chronology, April 1967*, pp. 16-18a; May 1967, pp. 13-14, June 1967, p. 13;

A III MAF intelligence report in May 1967 assessed that the attacks against Khe Sanh were an attempt to gain a morale-boosting victory that would also have a significant impact upon the South Vietnamese and American people. The report noted that NVA/VC 'capacity to initiate such major action undoubtably [sic] stems from being able to fight from a relatively safe base with his supply and support immediately behind him and never far away'.[39]

By the time of the Tet Offensive, III MAF was committed to defending the base at Khe Sanh regardless of any misgivings about whether the base should have been established in the first place. A week before the assault on Khe Sanh General Krulak made his feelings clear in a message to the Commandant of the Marine Corps. Krulak had been directed to respond to a message from the Chairman of the Joint Chiefs of Staff, General Wheeler, to General Westmoreland. In his message Wheeler had expressed concern that two opposing but somewhat simplistic views on Khe Sanh were 'being given prominent attention' in 'high non-military quarters' in Washington. The first view was that the base should be defended and used as a springboard for attacks against the enemy's rear areas in Laos. The second was that the Marines were likely to suffer a defeat at Khe Sanh and that, therefore, a withdrawal was the best course of action, partly because it could be achieved 'without much public notice'. The message had been passed to Krulak, as the senior Marine Corps officer in the Pacific theatre, to formulate a response. Krulak dismissed the idea of operations in Laos because there were no clear targets for a large scale offensive, since the NVA/VC were widely dispersed with no easily identifiable centres of mass, and because 'the impact upon other productive COMUSMACV programs resulting from a diversion of forces of the magnitude required, could be unfavourable'.[40] This was consistent with the Marines' line that pacification was more worthwhile than the constant drain on resources resulting from operations in the border areas. The last thing Krulak or the III MAF commander would have wanted was additional large scale operations even further inland.

Regarding the idea of withdrawing from Khe Sanh, Krulak said, 'I come out with the obvious conclusion that to withdraw would save lives that would otherwise be lost in a battle for Khe Sanh, but that no-one ever won anything by backing away'. He disputed that a withdrawal could be carried out unnoticed because 'there are newsmen at Khe Sanh every day...In nothing flat a withdrawal from Khe Sanh would be ballooned all over the world. While it is dangerous to try and think like an Asian, I believe the [North Vietnamese] would have to characterize such an act as an exhibition of weakness on our part'. Although he believed any assault would occur 'shortly after Tet' he asserted his support for COMUSMACV's decision to keep the Marines at the base.[41]

July 1967, p. 13.

39 III MAF, 'Periodic Intelligence Report 20-67', dated 21 May 1967, pp. 4, 13-14. III MAF Periodic Intelligence Report File No. 17.

40 General Victor Krulak, Top Secret exclusive SPECAT message for General Chapman, dated 13 Jan 1968. III MAF Incoming Message file, Jan 1968, pp. 32-37

41 General Victor Krulak, Top Secret exclusive SPECAT message for General Chapman, dated 13

General Cushman, writing after the battle for Khe Sanh, stated that he also agreed with the decision to defend Khe Sanh because it was an effective block to any full scale invasion of the south, it dominated the main route from the Laotian border to the coast and it was a vital part of the defensive screen along the DMZ that provided cover for the pacification efforts in the coastal region. Cushman added, however, that Khe Sanh became redundant once more troops and helicopters became available later in 1968 allowing III MAF to conduct mobile operations rather than relying on fixed defensive positions.[42] Mobile operations were more in keeping with the Marines' strategy in Vietnam, which emphasised detecting and preventing infiltration rather than pitched battles to destroy enemy forces.

The battle for Khe Sanh lasted from 20 January (the date of the first large scale attacks against the base) until 15 April, when Operation Pegasus (the operation to relieve the base) officially ended.[43] During that time the North Vietnamese committed two of its regular army divisions to the fight and lost between 3,000 and 10,000 personnel killed, many of them as a result of the 110,022 tons of bombs and 142,081 artillery rounds the Americans had used in defence of the base.[44] Allied losses amounted to around 330 killed and 2,200 wounded.[45]

Although the Johnson administration feared another Dien Bien Phu, the American military leaders in Vietnam were confident that the base could be held.[46] Generals Westmoreland and Krulak agreed on this point. The Marines held all the high ground around the base, the road (when open) was of good quality, massive air power was available and the base could be well supplied by air when the road was closed; this included the delivery of forty-three tons of mail during February, the worst month of the

Jan 1968, III MAF Incoming Message file, Jan 1968, pp. 32-37.

42 Lt General Robert Cushman, 'Foreword' in Captain Moyers Shore, *The Battle for Khe Sanh*, pp. ix-x.

43 FMFPac *Operations of US Marine Forces Vietnam, January 1968*, p. 11, and III MAF *Command Chronology, January 1968*, p. 13, both date the start of the battle as 20 January when the first major attacks began. III MAF *Command Chronology, April 1968*, p. 12, gives 15 April as the date the base was secured and the main route opened. Most histories give a figure of 77 days for the battle but this would put the end date as 4 or 5 April (for example see General Victor Krulak, *First to Fight*, p213, and Captain Moyers Shore, *The Battle for Khe Sanh*, p144).

44 FMFPac, *Operations of US Marine Forces Vietnam, April 1968*, p. 12. The lower limit of 3,000 reflects the actual confirmed 'body count'. The upper limit of 10,000 is an extrapolation based on the number of casualties caused by the airstrikes in areas where they could not actually be counted or whose bodies were literally disintegrated in the attacks.

45 Compiled from Captain Moyers Shore, *The Battle for Khe Sanh*, p. 130 and 143; III MAF *Command Chronology, March 1968*, p 13; III MAF *Command Chronology, April 1968*, p. 12. A note in Shulimson, Blaisol, Smith and Dawson, *The US Marines in Vietnam 1968*, p. 283, points out that official casualty figures were on the low side because they did not include personnel not actually engaged in Operation Scotland (the defence of Khe Sanh) or Operation Pegasus (the relief of Khe Sanh). This would have included air crew and personnel killed in aircraft approaching the base who had been assigned there but had not actually reported in.

46 Randall B Woods, *LBJ: Architect of American Ambition* (New York: Free Press, 2006). p. 823.

battle.[47] Westmoreland even considered a possibility that was definitely not available to the French; the use, or threat, of tactical nuclear weapons in the northern part of ICTZ.[48] The units in the base also never considered themselves truly besieged because they were not restricted to the perimeter of the base and were able to patrol out to a distance of 500 metres or more.[49] In one ten day period in February, for example, the defenders were able to conduct forty patrols outside the perimeter, including one ARVN patrol that resulted in the capture of a recoilless rifle.[50] A telling point though, regarding NVA/VC intentions is that they never attempted to cut off the water supply to the base. Khe Sanh's water supply came from a river approximately 1km to the east of the combat base and the pipeline from this to a water point 150 metres outside the base was crucial to the ability of the troops to remain because water was the one thing that could not be transported in sufficient quantity to sustain them. Colonel Knight, the 3rd Marine Division's intelligence officer called this 'the most puzzling aspect of the siege' and General Krulak took it as an indication that the NVA/VC had no intention of overrunning the base.[51] It is also worth noting that III MAF identified another two divisions in the ICTZ at the time of Khe Sanh, but it appears that neither of these was used to reinforce the attacks against the base, which would have been expected if the NVA/VC really intended to press home their attack.[52] In fact one of these divisions was sent to Hue to reinforce the effort there.[53]

If it is unlikely that Khe Sanh would have been another Dien Bien Phu, the possibility that it was a diversion must be considered. Certainly the timing would seem to support the idea that it was a diversionary attack because it occurred ten days before the main offensive itself. General Westmoreland's attention was certainly concentrated on the ICTZ, and Khe Sanh in particular, because he was convinced that the NVA/VC plan was to seize the two northernmost provinces.[54] Westmoreland wrote later that '[m]uch of the attention of the press, my own command, and Washington officials understandably focused on Khe Sanh. It was an obvious objective, essential to the enemy if he were to get

47 General William Westmoreland, *A Soldier Reports*, p. 337; General Victor Krulak, *First to Fight*, p. 216.

48 General William Westmoreland, *A Soldier Reports*, p. 338.

49 General Victor Krulak, *First to Fight*, p216; Captain Moyers Shore, *The Battle for Khe Sanh*, p. 63 and p. 140; Shulimson, Blaison Smith and Dawson, *US Marines in Vietnam, 1968*, pp. 480-485. The commanding general of 3rd Marine Division visited the base on an almost daily basis during the battle and General Krulak visited during February and March.

50 General Creighton Abrams, Message for General Cushman, dated 17 Feb 1968, III MAF Incoming Message file, Feb 1968, p. 154.

51 Colonel Frederic Knight, comments on manuscript, Shulimson, Blaison, Smith and Dawson, *US Marines in Vietnam: 1968*, p289; Krulak, *First to Fight*, pp. 218-219. Peter Brush, a Khe Sanh veteran and writer on Vietnam is, however, convinced that in fact the NVA/VC were unaware of this vulnerability. Peter Brush, "Perspectives -- Khe Sanh Could Have Been Another Dien Bien Phu if the NVA Had Cut Off the Marines' Water Supply" in *Vietnam*, August 1997, pp. 58-60.

52 III MAF *Command Chronology, January 1968*, p. 23.

53 FMFPac, *Operations of US Marine Forces, Vietnam, February 1968*, p. 8; III MAF *Command Chronology, February 1968*, p. 11.

54 Westmoreland, General William, *A Solder Reports*, p. 313-316 and 337.

behind the defensive posts facing the DMZ and move deep into Quang Tri province'.[55] It was only on 10 January, when General Fred Weyand (commander of II Corps) and General Davidson drew Westmoreland's attention to activity further south, that he began to prepare for a more widespread offensive by the NVA/VC.[56]

The siege of Khe Sanh was also a drain on resources at a time of impending national crisis. The defence of Khe Sanh required considerable resources; in addition to the four infantry battalions there was an artillery battalion, two 'provisional' artillery batteries, seven Marine helicopter squadrons, ten US Air Force transport squadrons and forty-two supporting units of company size or smaller. There was also a fifth infantry battalion comprised of around 300 ARVN troops.[57] At the end of the siege there was also a relief force of approximately 30,000 men from the 1st Cavalry Division 12 miles east of Khe Sanh at Ca Lu. The NVA/VC employed two divisions against the base, with another two in the area.[58] Arguing against the idea that Khe Sanh was intended to tie down large numbers of American troops, General Westmoreland pointed out that there were two NVA/VC divisions of between 15,000 and 20,000 soldiers 'tying down' a force of approximately 6,000 American and South Vietnamese troops, which represented 'sixtieth of the 299 US and Allied combat battalions operating in South Vietnam'. Based upon that he questioned, 'who was tying down whom?'[59] Even taken as a proportion of III MAF (at that time consisting of five divisions plus a Korean Marine Brigade) it is a little under 5 percent, although the Marines had long argued that these troops would be better employed in mobile operations or pacification than defending a single position.[60] As for detracting from the pacification effort, the damage was already done; the requirement to move troops to the DMZ had deprived the Marines of much of their available manpower. Of the extra three Army divisions sent to ICTZ in late 1967 and 1968 only one had gone to the coastal area while the other two had gone north with the 3rd Marine Division. The units involved in the fight for Khe Sanh were all from the 3rd Marine Division and the units used in the relief of the base in April were from the 1st Cavalry Division, both of which were already assigned to the DMZ area.[61] Therefore the defence of Khe Sanh had little extra impact on the pacification effort on top of that already suffered as a result of the Tet Offensive. The presence of the forces at Khe Sanh was more the result of Westmoreland's insistence upon establishing the base than anything else. As General Krulak later pointed out that once more helicopters became available for mobile operations

55 Westmoreland, General William, *A Solder Reports* p. 316.

56 Westmoreland, General William, *A Solder Reports*, p. 318.

57 Captain Moyers Shore, *The Battle for Khe Sanh*, p. 192.

58 Phillip Davidson, *Vietnam at War*, p. 552, III MAF, *Command Chronology, March 1968*, p20 lists two divisions in the area around Khe Sanh. These are the 325 and 304 NVA divisions.

59 General William Westmoreland, *A Soldier Reports*, p. 339.

60 III MAF, *Command Chronology, January 1968*, p. 7. Adding the total strength gives a figure of just over 117,000 USMC, US Army, US Navy and US Air Force personnel under command of III MAF.

61 III MAF, *Command Chronology, January 1968*, pp. 8-9.

the base was abandoned 'in a reversal that deserves Olympic honors for inconsistency... the piece of ground that had been characterized a few months previously as terrain of the utmost importance was abandoned as having no great tactical significance'.[62] If the siege of Khe Sanh was intended as a diversion, it is one that the Americans had imposed upon themselves.

Neither of these two reasons is entirely satisfactory for explaining the siege of Khe Sanh. The NVA/VC put considerable effort into the battle, but not enough to overrun the base in the face of the overwhelming air power that the American forces could bring to bear. The attack also failed to a large extent as a diversion. Even though Westmoreland's attention was focused on the north he realised enough of the big picture in time to begin preparing for a countrywide offensive ten days before the attack on Khe Sanh.

Ang Cheng Guan makes the argument that Khe Sanh was no more or less important than any other installation at the time of the Tet Offensive; in fact it was of secondary importance.[63] Based upon North Vietnamese sources contemporaneous with the battle he explains that the area around Khe Sanh was a key part of the plan for the Tet Offensive because of its position on the western end of the main route to the coast but, according to an account by the NVA Chief of Staff, it was just 'one of the many fronts of the general offensive-general uprising with the objective of either destroying or surrounding part of the US forces. The most important targets were Saigon, Hue and Danang'.[64] Guan's examination of the North Vietnamese documents appears to show that the attack on Khe Sanh was planned to take place at the same time as the main Tet Offensive.[65] There then appears to have been a rush to start the attack on Khe Sanh before the Tet Offensive. The North Vietnamese had become aware that American strength in the area around Khe Sanh was increasing in line with their own and became concerned that this might disrupt one of the main lines of communication between the Laotian border and the coast.[66] Guan argues that there was 'the possibility – although this is nowhere explicitly stated in the official history – that the Khe Sanh siege, which eventually took place 10 days ahead of the Tet Offensive (31 January 1968), *might* have been inadvertently forced upon the North Vietnamese by Westmoreland's counter-actions'.[67] His argument continues that the idea of another Dien Bien Phu was entirely a construct of the American political establishment, military command and media, which the North Vietnamese played on for propaganda purposes.[68] This argument has a great deal of merit. Although the NVA/

62 General Victor Krulak, *First to Fight*, p. 221.

63 Ang Cheng Guan, *Khe Sanh from the Perspective of the North Vietnamese*, pp. 87-98. .

64 Ang Cheng Guan, *Khe Sanh from the Perspective of the North Vietnamese*, p. 95.

65 Ang Cheng Guan, *Khe Sanh from the Perspective of the North Vietnamese*, p. 95. See also Ang Cheng Guan, *Decision-Making Leading to the Tet Offensive – The Communist Perspective*, pp. 341-353

66 Ang Cheng Guan, *Khe Sanh from the Perspective of the North Vietnamese*, pp. 93-94.

67 Ang Cheng Guan, *Khe Sanh from the Perspective of the North Vietnamese*, p. 93. The italics are present in the original article.

68 Ang Cheng Guan, *Khe Sanh from the Perspective of the North Vietnamese*, pp. 96-97.

VC attacked almost every military installation in the country, as well as a large number of minor ones, the main effort during the Tet Offensive was the attempt to gain control of major towns and cities and generate a popular uprising. The attacks against the military installations all appear to have been supporting actions, with the intention of suppressing the ability to react to the offensive. Evidence of the importance of the effort in the cities over that against the military can be seen in the relative value applied to the fight in Hue compared to Khe Sanh, which are close enough geographically for NVA/VC resources to be diverted from one to the other. When the NVA/VC forces in Hue started to lose the battle it appears that Giap diverted resources from around Khe Sanh to assist them. Had Khe Sanh have been the more important of the two it is unlikely he would have done this. The following chronology, which shows activity at Khe Sanh, Da Nang and Hue, it is clear that that Hue was the main effort and attacks against the other bases were intended to cover movement of NVA/VC forces or prevent III MAF from reinforcing its units in Hue:

20 January 1968 – NVA/VC forces began the large scale attack on combat base at Khe Sanh using two regular NVA divisions.
31 January 1968 – Tet Offensive began with attacks against Hue and Da Nang as well as other major population centres. The NVA/VC attacked in Hue with eight battalions (equal to almost one division) under regular NVA command. The NVA/VC succeeded in gaining control of almost the entire city, but the ARVN and Marine counterattack began immediately, despite severely underestimating the size of the NVA/VC force. The extent to which Hue had been infiltrated only became apparent once the battle commenced and units from III MAF and the ARVN found themselves fighting well equipped and well trained troops in greater numbers than the three battalions initially assessed to be present in the city.[69] At the same time significant fighting lasted around Da Nang until 9th February.[70]
6 February – NVA/VC launched a division-size attack against Da Nang. The attack was beaten back, and the NVA/VC withdrew to nearby base areas.[71] This attack occurred the day before a similar attack at Khe Sanh and during the time when NVA/VC were reinforcing Hue. It is therefore likely that this attack was intended to prevent any disruption to the movement of the reinforcements.
7 February – NVA/VC attacked and overran the Special Forces camp at Lang Vei, five and a half miles from Khe Sanh, using tanks. The following day NVA/VC made one attack against Khe Sanh but it was beaten back. The tanks were not used, but this may have been because there was no covered avenue of approach for them. Although the NVA/VC prepared for a second wave to attack it did not take place.[72] This was the last major attack made against the base until the end of

69 FMFPac, *Operations of US Marine Forces, Vietnam*, February 1968, p. 8.
70 FMFPac, *Operations of US Marine Forces, Vietnam*, February 1968 pp. 22-23.
71 III MAF, *Command Chronology, February 1968*, p. 19.
72 III MAF *Command Chronology*, *February 1968*, p. 11.

February.[73] This attack, like the one against Da Nang on the previous day, may well have been intended to screen the arrival of reinforcements in Hue (see below).
9-12 February – NVA/VC units in were Hue reinforced by elements amounting to another division of troops. By this time the Marines were in control of most of the south of the city and the ARVN had forced the NVA/VC into a corner of the old Citadel.[74] The NVA units reinforcing Hue were identified as elements of the 324B NVA Division and the 5th NVA Regiment, both of which had been in the Quang Tri province, where Khe Sanh is located.[75] This is an indication that the North Vietnamese had chosen to reinforce Hue at the expense of the effort around Khe Sanh.
22-25 February – Final battle for Hue. The final assault on NVA/VC positions in the Citadel began on 22 February. The city was declared secure and handed back to South Vietnamese civil government control on 25 Feb.[76]
23 February – Khe Sanh was subjected to heaviest bombardment of the battle so far.[77] This bombardment coincided with the final assault by Marine and ARVN troops against the NVA/VC in Hue. Since there were no signs that this was the precursor to an attack the reasons behind it can only be guessed at, but the timing indicates that it may have been co-ordinated with the attack against Da Nang to maintain pressure during the final battle for Hue and allow the last remaining units to escape the vicinity of the city.
24-25 February – NVA/VC attacked Da Nang for the third and last time during the Tet Offensive. The III MAF Command Chronology described this attack as 'an attempt to maintain the façade of an offensive'.[78] This attack may well have been a last attempt to relieve the pressure on NVA/VC units in Hue.
29 February-1 March – The last major attack against Khe Sanh combat base. III MAF estimated at least one NVA regiment participated and was destroyed in the attack.[79] The Tet Offensive had clearly run its course by this time and this attack may have been intended to prevent units in Khe Sanh from moving against NVA/VC formations withdrawing into base areas in ICTZ or across the DMZ.
10-15 March – 26th Marine Regiment intelligence section noted start of an exodus of NVA/VC from Khe Sanh area. One of the NVA divisions surrounding Khe Sanh moved across border to Laos while the other moved southwest but

73 Captain Moyers Shore, *The Battle for Khe Sanh*, p. 71.
74 FMFPac, *Operations of US Marine Forces, Vietnam, February 1968*, p. 8.
75 FMFPac, *Operations of US Marine Forces, Vietnam, February*, p. 8; III MAF *Command Chronology, February 1968*, p. 11.
76 FMFPac, *Operations of US Marine Forces, Vietnam, February 1968*, p. 18.
77 III MAF *Command Chronology, February 1968*, p. 11; Shore, Captain Moyers, *The Battle for Khe Sanh*, p. 122.
78 III MAF *Command Chronology, February 1968*, pp. 19-20.
79 Captain Moyers Shore, *The Battle for Khe Sanh*, pp. 124-125.

remained within Vietnam. Electronic sensors also detected significant movement of NVA/VC forces away from Khe Sanh.[80]
31 March – Siege of Khe Sanh effectively over as Marine and ARVN operations around the base cleared the last remaining NVA/VC units from the area.[81]

The timing of the attacks against Khe Sanh and Da Nang would seem to indicate that they were being used as cover or a diversion for movements in or out of Hue and not as attempts to overrun the bases themselves. The fact that troops in Quang Tri province were moved to Hue rather than being used as reinforcements for Khe Sanh would also indicate that Hue was the main effort and that Khe Sanh was not an objective to be overrun.

Tet Offensive

On 31 January the Tet Offensive began with attacks against Hue, Da Nang and two provincial capitals (Quang Tri City and Quang Ngai City), in addition to several smaller towns. Hue and Da Nang will be dealt with in due course, but first it is worth exploring events in the other four cities, where the ARVN was responsible for security. The Marines noted that the ARVN units 'returned to duty and, by and large, fought as well disciplined units – a factor which the enemy undoubtedly thought inconceivable'.[82] In Quang Tri particularly, the ARVN division acquitted itself well and repulsed the NVA/VC attack quickly and, according to a message from General Abrams (Westmoreland's Deputy), the population of the town held a victory parade in which the ARVN and local forces marched through the town.[83] There was a similar story in Quang Ngai City, where another ARVN division stood its ground and the NVA/VC attack was over by the end of the day, having begun at 0400.[84] These two examples belie the common belief that the ARVN could not, or would not, stand and fight.[85] In fact, the resilience of the ARVN even came as a surprise to the North Vietnamese, who admitted to themselves that the propaganda effort among the ARVN ranks had proved insufficient.[86]

Nowhere was this resilience more apparent than in Hue City. The city was virtually undefended, with only one company of regular ARVN troops present ('Black Panther Company'). The remainder had been placed outside the city, some five miles to the northwest. The ARVN attempted to re-take the city themselves, but quickly found that

80 Captain Moyers Shore, *The Battle for Khe Sanh*, p126; III MAF *Command Chronology, February 1968*, p. 19.
81 FMFPac, *Operations of US Marine Forces, Vietnam, February 1968*, p. 8.
82 FMFPac, *Operations of US Marine Forces, Vietnam, January 1968*, p. 26.
83 FMFPac, *Operations of US Marine Forces, Vietnam, January 1968*, p. 26; General Creighton Abrams, 'Civilian Situation in Quang Tri City', Message for General Westmoreland, dated 22 Feb 1968, III MAF Outgoing Message File, Feb 1968, p. 185.
84 Shulimson, Blasiol, Smith and Dawson, *US Marines in Vietnam: 1968*, p. 155.
85 Gabriel Kolko, *Anatomy of a War*, p. 310.
86 Phillip Davidson, *Vietnam at War*, p. 475.

the NVA/VC force was much larger than expected and had adopted a strong defensive posture. The ARVN commander asked for assistance from the Marines.[87] For the rest of the month the ARVN and Marines fought side-by-side to retake the city, the Marines operating mainly south of the river while the ARVN operated in the old part of the city to the north. The battle raged until 24 February, when the flag of the Republic of Vietnam was raised over the Citadel, the ancient capital of Vietnam, after the final assault by the Black Panther Company.[88] That the ARVN had fought hard alongside the Marines was indicated in the relative casualty figures. The ARVN suffered 384 killed and 1,800 wounded compared with the Marines' 142 killed and 857 wounded.[89] 169 of the ARVN casualties were caused in the first eleven days of the battle, before the Marines deployed forces north of the river to provide assistance.[90] While it is certainly true that the Marines were instrumental in the re-capture of Hue City, the performance of the ARVN deserves recognition during the Tet Offensive and the relative capabilities need to be put into perspective.

The real test of the Marine pacification programme during the Tet Offensive came in the enclaves around the air bases at Phu Bai, Da Nang and Chu Lai. While there were indirect fire attacks against all of the bases, using rockets and mortars, it was only the area around Da Nang that was subjected to a significant ground assault. The attack against Da Nang started with a rocket attack against the air base on the night of 30 January. This was followed by a co-ordinated attack by NVA forces consisting of the 31st NVA Regiment, a VC local force battalion, a rocket regiment and elements of the 2nd NVA Division that were moving to the south of Da Nang.[91] The assault against the city of Da Nang was held off by ARVN forces and a CAP. Subsequent operations by the ARVN and Marines located the rest of the attacking force, which was broken up by artillery and air strikes.[92] During the battle for Da Nang, which lasted in the main until 9 February, the CAPs made a significant contribution to the defence of the city as they remained in place and provided early warning of NVA/VC movements.[93] There were repeated attacks in the Da Nang area during February but at no time was there a danger of the NVA/VC overrunning the city or the air base and it is more likely that these attacks were intended to prevent Marine and ARVN forces from Da Nang reinforcing Hue City.

The strength of the Marine pacification and counterinsurgency effort lay not so much in the effect it had on the Tet Offensive, but in the capability that it provided in the recovery and reconstruction effort afterwards. The population of the South did not rise up and take part in the General Offensive – General Uprising and even the North Vietnamese accept that they did not have the level of support among the population

87 FMFPac, *Operations of US Marine Forces, February 1968*, pp. 9-10.
88 FMFPac, *Operations of US Marine Forces, February 1968*, p. 18.
89 FMFPac, *Operations of US Marine Forces, February 1968*, p. 19.
90 FMFPac, *Operations of US Marine Forces, February 1968*, p. 15.
91 FMFPac, *Operations of US Marine Forces, January 1968*, pp. 21-22.
92 FMFPac, *Operations of US Marine Forces, January 1968*, p. 22.
93 FMFPac, *Operations of US Marine Forces, January 1968*, p. 22.

that they had expected.[94] But it is difficult to quantify the extent to which the Marines' pacification efforts contributed to this – after all, they were only operating in relatively small areas and had no programmes operating in the major cities themselves, which were the target of the Tet Offensive. The FMFPac monthly report for February 1968 noted the level of support the population showed for their 'duly-elected government' but did not claim the credit for this success.[95] The infrastructure put in place for pacification did, however, play an invaluable role in 'Project Recovery', the South Vietnamese government plan for reconstruction of the damage caused by the Tet Offensive. The Joint Co-ordinating Council became the basis for the committees and sub-committees involved in Project Recovery, under the chairmanship of the Commanding General of I Corps.[96] By April, the civil affairs branch of III MAF headquarters reported that pacification programmes had recovered to almost the pre-Tet levels and that the local population seemed more supportive of pacification efforts. In several villages, they were even spontaneously providing twenty-four hour protection for US Navy reconstruction teams.[97] This trend continued and in May, the civil affairs branch reported an increase in the weapons found and turned in by villagers, while in Quang Tri province (immediately south of the DMZ) 'several separate battalions…have reported an increased interest in implementing civic action projects and it is anticipated that the pacification status of the area immediately around the base will measurably improve in the near future'.[98] The FMFPac monthly reports showed considerable improvement in the pacification status in Quang Tri province by November 1968. In May 1968, for the whole of the Marines' area of operations approximately 24,000 people lived in areas where pacification was rated at less than 20% - a significant increase on the 2,000 prior to the Tet Offensive – while the percentage of the population living in areas between 40% and 80% decreased.[99] By November 1968, the percentage of the population living in areas that were rated at less than 20% pacified had gone back down to around 2,600 and the percentage of population living in areas that were between 40 and 80 percent pacified had increased; the Marines were regaining the ground lost during the Tet Offensive.[100]

Conclusion

The Marines judged their performance in 1968 to have been a success. The FMFPac monthly report for December 1968 said that the NVA/VC's 'exaggerated claims of an

94 'Lao Dong Party Training Document on COSVN Resolution No 6, March 1968', extract in Gareth Porter, *Vietnam: A History in Documents*, (New York, NY: New American Library, 1981), p. 364.
95 FMFPac, *Operations of US Marine Forces, February 1968*, pp. 9-10.
96 III MAF, *Command Chronology, March 1968*, p. 31.
97 III MAF, *Command Chronology, April 1968*, p. 30.
98 III MAF, *Command Chronology, May 1968*, p. 35.
99 FMFPac, *Operations of US Marine Forces, May 1968*, p. 45.
100 FMFPac, *Operations of US Marine Forces, November 1968*, p. 36.

overall substantial victory during the 1968 Tet Offensive notwithstanding, the enemy sustained a costly – and serious – defeat…However…he had gained no victories, occupied no new terrain, nor strengthened appreciably his standing with the local populace, and had wasted the equivalent of three divisions in the process'.[101] To support this assertion, the Marines presented the following evidence: there 100,000 NVA/VC casualties in the ICTZ area during 1968 (a total of the number killed, captured or defected); after an initial shock, the ARVN had responded 'with an assertive performance'; and that the South Vietnamese government had solidified its position with the people by responding to the Tet Offensive 'with timely energy to restore order, repair enemy-caused damage, and renew the advance of pacification and revolutionary development'.[102]

There is little doubt that the Tet Offensive was a military defeat for the North Vietnamese in conventional terms. The NVA/VC had failed to achieve their main objective in ICTZ; they did not gain control of Hue City or any other urban area. The Viet Cong, which had been extensively used in the urban battles, was crippled after 1968 and resulted in the greater use of regular North Vietnamese Army troops in subsequent operations. At the end of the year the Marines reported that although local forces 'continued to maintain a limited degree of pressure' in ICTZ, 'most major enemy tactical units remained withdrawn and out of contact'.[103] An expected Winter/Spring offensive failed to materialise and the Marine analysts assessed that this was either due to 'the enemy's desires exceeding his capabilities' or the effectiveness of the operations conducted by the Marines and allied forces in ICTZ.[104] Having accepted for themselves that the Tet Offensive was a failure, a strong faction in the North Vietnamese government argued for a reduction in military effort in the South and that their forces should revert to guerrilla warfare, making greater efforts in political action.[105]

Marine pacification efforts and their large-scale operations against the NVA/VC main force units had undoubtedly played a key role in preventing the Tet Offensive from being more successful than it was. The pacification measures to provide defence in depth in the coastal enclaves had helped prevent the air bases, in particular the airfield at Da Nang, from being overrun. The large unit operations in the border areas and south of the DMZ had inflicted heavy casualties on the NVA/VC units as they tried to infiltrate south.

The assessment in the FMFPac monthly report for October 1967, that time was the most important thing that the North Vietnamese could gain was remarkably prescient. The North Vietnamese did indeed view their opponents, the Americans in particular, as an 'irresolute adversary' as the process to withdraw from Vietnam had already begun.[106] Richard Nixon won the 1968 presidential election with a supposed secret plan to end the

101 FMFPac, *Operations of US Marine Forces, Vietnam, December 1968*, p. 25.

102 FMFPac, *Operations of US Marine Forces, Vietnam, December 1968*, p. 3.

103 III MAF, *Command Chronology, December 1968*, p. 18.

104 III MAF, Command Chronology, December 1968, p. 18.

105 Phillip Davidson, *Vietnam at War*, pp542-544.

106 FMFPac, *Operations of Marine Forces Vietnam, October 1967*, p. 10.

war, which included the withdrawal of American troops.[107] In 1969 the Marines increased their pacification efforts, increasing the number of CAPs and conducting ambitious mobile offensive operations of the type they had always advocated in the highlands, such as Operation Dewey Canyon.[108] But, for them, the war was ending and in mid-1969 the first Marine units withdrew from Vietnam.[109]

107 Phillip Davidson, *Vietnam at War*, p. 587. In fact the reference to the 'secret plan' was an insertion into Nixon's comments by an over-zealous reporter; Stanley Karnow, *Vietnam: a History*. (London: Pimlico, 1994), p. 597.

108 FMFPac, *Operations of US Marine Forces, Vietnam, December 1969*, pp15-17 and 32.

109 FMFPac, *Operations of US Marine Forces, Vietnam, July 1969*, p1.

Conclusion

The United States Marine Corps counterinsurgency strategy in Vietnam provides a number of lessons for counterinsurgency generally. It demonstrates the importance of quickly assimilating lessons from the past and applying appropriate ones to the situation at hand. It also shows the limitations of counterinsurgency and supports the arguments in the literature on more recent wars that the claims made for it have overreached themselves; counterinsurgency is not nation-building nor is it a war winning tool in its own right.

Intellectual Antecedents of Marine Counterinsurgency

There were two main strands within the antecedents of the Marines' strategy in Vietnam. The first was their own experience in the small wars era of the 1920s and 1930s. The lessons learned were captured, retained and disseminated to such an extent that the institutional knowledge was still present among the generation of officers who were senior commanders in Vietnam. During the 1930s in particular the lessons learned in Haiti and the Dominican Republic were widely disseminated through the *Marine Corps Gazette* and *Naval Institute Proceedings* so even those officers who did not participate in the wars could assimilate the knowledge gained. [1] Small wars doctrine was also increasingly taught at company and field level schools in the late 1930s, often by the 'larger than life' characters who had fought in the wars.[2] In fact, officers such as 'Chesty' Puller and 'Red Mike' Edson had a profound effect within a relatively small Marine Corps and were able to ensure that their ideas received a 'disproportionate' level of attention.[3] Later Marine commanders, such as General Walt, who vividly remembered the lessons they had been taught during training in the late 1930s.[4] Finally, there was the *Small Wars Manual* produced in 1940 which distilled all of the lessons from the 1920s and 1930s and provided the foundation for much of the Marine Corps' approach in Vietnam. Although there is some debate over whether or not many Marines were actually aware of the *Manual* in the years immediately preceding their involvement in Vietnam, it is certainly clear that the doctrine contained within it was employed in Vietnam.[5] The Marines' experience

1 Keith Bickel, *Mars Learning*, pp. 179, 184, Table 5.2.
2 Keith Bickel, *Mars Learning*, p. 1846.1.
3 Ben Connable, *Culture Warriors*, p. 3.
4 Lewis Walt, *Strange War, Strange Strategy*, p. 29.
5 Ronald Schaffer, *The Small Wars Manual*, p. xii.

in creating and development of *Gendarmeries* in Latin America and the Caribbean are reflected in Vietnam. The creation of the Combined Action Platoons and the extent of the Marines' involvement in training and developing the Regional Forces/Popular Forces show a direct linkage with the past. These were all solid, operational level lessons that stood the Marines in good stead in Vietnam.

The second strand within the antecedents of the Marines' strategy consists of the contemporary thinking on counterinsurgency in the early 1960s. General Krulak paid particular attention to the ideas of Sir Robert Thompson, and Thompsons 'Principles of Counterinsurgency' can be seen in the Marines' management and planning of their pacification campaign.[6] The Joint Co-ordinating Council, established in the early stages of the Marines' deployment, is certainly the type of organization that Thompson had in mind in *Defeating Communist Insurgency* and that another British expert, Frank Kitson, advised in his first principle of counterinsurgency – 'good coordinating machinery'.[7] The plan that the Marines developed in early 1966, which drew together all of the elements of their campaign – pacification and destruction of enemy forces – also conformed to Thompson's third principle of counterinsurgency; that 'the government must have an overall plan'.[8] There are also signs of the French influence in some of the methods used by the Marines. This second strand, however, was the more dangerous one because this is where the overstated claims for the effectiveness of counterinsurgency lay. The key figures based their theories on sound experience, but once these theories moved beyond the operational realm they lacked solid foundations. In becoming so dogmatic about counterinsurgency General Krulak was an outlier within the Marine Corps and his zealotry undermined the sound arguments that Generals Walt and Cushman made for their approach on the ground.

These antecedents were in place because the Marine Corps was a 'learning organisation'. In *Learning to Eat Soup with a Knife* John Nagl established five criteria to determine whether the British Army in Malaya and the US Army in Vietnam were 'learning organizations'.[9] Nagl used Richard Downie's definition of a learning organization as one that 'uses new knowledge or understanding gained from experience or study to adjust institutional norms, doctrine and procedures in ways designed to minimize previous gaps in performance and maximize future success'.[10] Nagl's five criteria are as follows: Does the organization promote suggestions from the field?; Are subordinates encouraged to question superiors and policies?; Does the organization regularly question its basic assumptions?; Are high-ranking officers routinely in close contact with those on the ground and open

6 Victor Krulak, *First to Fight*, p. 180.

7 Frank Kitson, *Bunch of Five*, (London, UK: Faber and Faber, 1977), p. 284. See also Robert Thompson, *Defeating Communist Insurgency*, pp. 70-72, 81-83.

8 Robert Thompson, *Defeating Communist Insurgency*, p. 55.

9 John Nagl, *Learning to Eat Soup with a Knife*, p. 5.

10 Richard Downie, *Learning from Conflict: The US Military in Vietnam, El Salvador and the Drug War* (Westport, CT:Praeger, 1998), quoted in Nagl, *Learning to Eat Soup with a Knife*, p. 5.

to their suggestions?; Are Standard Operating Procedures (SOPs) generated locally and informally or imposed from the centre?[11]

The Marine Corps continued to develop as a learning organization during the Vietnam War, with a clear evolution of counterinsurgency doctrine driven by lessons and initiatives from the field – one of the more well-known being the Combined Action Platoons but an equally good example is Operation Golden Fleece, which was a suggestion from the local population. Senior officers were in close contact with personnel on the ground. General Walt made a habit of visiting units and villages frequently and General Krulak was a regular visitor to Vietnam and visited Khe Sanh several times during the battle in February 1968.[12] The *Marine Corps Gazette* also provided a means by which officers could make suggestions and give constructive criticism of Marine strategy.

Choice of Strategy

The decision of the senior Marine commanders to adopt a pacification strategy along the lines of the 'ink blot' approach promulgated by French and British counterinsurgency experts was the result of the reality they faced on the ground. General Walt realised that the security of the bases he was assigned to protect could be greatly improved if the population supported the Marines (and, by extension the South Vietnamese government) rather than the VC.[13] Within a few months of the Marines' arrival, officers at battalion level realised that pacification of the population was an important element in the defence of the bases and civic actions programmes began to proliferate throughout the Marines' areas of operations.[14] The 'spreading ink blot' was a product of the need to improve security, particularly around Da Nang which was subjected to bombardment by rockets with increasingly longer range.[15] As the war progressed and the Marines were ordered to conduct offensive operations against the NVA/VC, they continued to argue that the emphasis should remain on pacification of the populated areas. General Westmoreland attempted to alleviate the tensions caused by the difference in approaches by issuing a 'mission type order' to be followed up with 'orders for specific projects that as time passed would gradually get the marines out of their beachheads'[16]. These 'specific projects' included the establishment of fixed 'strong points' south of the DMZ and along the Laotian border, including the Khe Sanh combat base. The issue of Khe Sanh in particular re-ignited the tensions between Westmoreland and the Marines, who believed that using small patrols and other means to detect enemy formations, which could then be destroyed

11 John Nagl, *Learning to Eat Soup with a Knife*, p. 10.

12 General Lewis Walt, *Strange War, Strange Strategy*, passim; III MAF, *Command Chronology*, passim.

13 Life Magazine, *General Lewis Walt on Vietnam's Hottest Spot*, 26 May 1967.

14 Russell Stolfi, *US Marine Corps Civic Action Effort in Vietnam*, p. 34.

15 Major G. Telfer, Lt. Col. Lane Rogers and V. Fleming, *The US Marines in Vietnam: 1967*, p. 109.

16 General William Westmoreland, *A Soldier Reports*, p. 166.

by mobile operations or superior firepower, was preferable to tying up resources defending fixed locations.[17] By the time of the battle for Khe Sanh, however, the point had become moot and even Krulak admitted that withdrawal would be worse than standing and fighting at the base.[18] The Marines view was, however, vindicated after the battle when the combat base was demolished and a strategy of mobile operations was adopted.[19] But the Marines never forgot the need to secure the areas around the air bases on the coast and the work they put in to pacifying the surrounding areas certainly appeared justified during the Tet Offensive.

The final reason for the Marines' preference for concentrating their efforts in the coastal areas was entirely practical. They are, after all, a seaborne expeditionary force and the 'Force in Readiness' concept that resulted from the Hogaboom Board left them without the ability to fight inland for long periods of time.[20] The deployment to Vietnam placed a severe strain on the Marines' logistic capability.[21] Even in late 1967, the Marines were still reliant on seaborne logistics for up to 80 percent of their supplies.[22] As a light infantry force, therefore, the Marines would have been unable to sustain large scale operations deep inland until the arrival of the US Army units in 1967 and 1968, with the logistic support they brought with them. In the early part of the Marines' involvement in the Vietnam War, therefore, it was almost pre-determined that they would engage in a 'coastal enclave' strategy as their approach would have been a function of their mission (to protect the bases) and their capabilities (a light seaborne expeditionary force).

Effectiveness of Counterinsurgency

One of the most difficult aspects of counterinsurgency is measuring progress. The world's leading experts in the early 1960s found this difficult to agree on, because there were so many variables.[23] The Marines developed a set of indicators to measure progress that were tied to their plan, which in itself was something of an innovation at the time.[24] Unfortunately, these indicators tended to measure the effort that was being put into the campaign (the creation of village defence plans, establishment of information programmes, creation of education facilities and establishment of markets) but did not

17 General Victor Krulak, *First to Fight*, p. 208.

18 General Victor Krulak, Top Secret exclusive SPECAT message for General Chapman, dated 13 Jan 1968. III MAF Incoming Message file, Jan 1968, pp. 32-37.

19 Lt General Robert Cushman, 'Foreword' in Captain Moyers Shore, *The Battle for Khe Sanh* (Washington, DC: Historical Branch, G-3 Division, HQ USMC, May 1969), pp. ix-x.

20 United States Marine Corps, 'FMF Organization and Composition Report: Service Elements', reproduced in the *Marine Corps Gazette*, April 1957, p. 22.

21 Jack Shulimson and Major Charles Johnson, *The US Marines in Vietnam: 1965*, pp. 181-182.

22 Major G. Telfer, Lt. Col. Lane Rogers and V. Fleming, *The US Marines in Vietnam: 1967*, p. 226; FMFPac *Operations of US Marine Forces Vietnam, November 1967*, p. 61.

23 RAND Corporation, *Counterinsurgency: A Symposium, April 16-20, 1962*, pp. 141-142.

24 FMFPac, *Operations of US Marine Forces Vietnam, February 1966*.

really measure how effective these efforts were. 'Krulak's Fables' were in fact indicating that the Marines were performing as their commanders intended and, therefore, were giving a 'false positive' in terms of progress towards actual pacification.

The Marine Corps, however, only had a limited control over the war. The geopolitics of the Vietnam War were beyond even the influence of the Corps and, due to the inter-service rivalries and the nature of the command structure, they were unable even to influence much of the ground strategy in Vietnam. It is probably fair to say that no matter how effective the Marines' strategy was, it was unlikely to affect the eventual outcome of the war; had the Commandant's advice to either fully commit to a war in the north and Laos or to not get involved at all been heeded, then history may well have played out very differently. But it is well beyond the scope of this work to speculate what that outcome might have been. Any assessment of Marine Corps' performance, therefore, has to be judged against the objectives they were given and the areas in which they did have control. For the Marines, as foreign force involved in counterinsurgency, counterinsurgency becomes the 'art of the possible'. The Marines' main tasks in Vietnam were; to secure and defend the bases at Phu Bai, Danang, Chu Lai and 'others that may be established'; conduct search and destroy operations against VC forces and bases that pose an immediate threat to those bases; conduct clearing operations in areas contiguous to those bases; and to conduct other operations 'as directed by CMUSMACV'.[25] The resources available were sufficient to achieve the first three elements of the mission and the Marines were largely successful in achieving them through the use of counterinsurgency techniques.

The experience of the US Marine Corps in Vietnam clearly demonstrates that counterinsurgency is an effective tool at an operational or tactical level, when the intent is to achieve a specific objective, within a specific area, and (ideally) for a specific period of time. If any of those parameters is absent or counterinsurgency is expected to operate beyond them, it becomes ineffective. It is possible to create the 'ink blots' and even spread them but counterinsurgency overreaches itself when it claims to be able to join them all up.

25 COMUSMACV, 'Letter of Instruction (LOI – 4)', 21 November 1965, enclosure 2 to III MAF, Command Chronology, November 1965.

Bibliography

Primary Sources

United States Marine Corps Documents

Regular Reports

These reports formed the basis for most of the original research for this study. The Fleet Marine Force Pacific (FMFPac) monthly reports were prepared by HQ FMFPac in Honolulu, Hawaii. These tended to be more narrative in nature and contained most of the statistics on pacification. The III Marine Amphibious Force (III MAF) reports were prepared by HQ III MAF in Da Nang and tended to contain more narrative detail regarding pacification and had numerous reports and studies as enclosures. The 3rd Marine Division Command Chronologies (3d MARDIV) were also prepared in Da Nang. Until Feb 1966, this was the only major unit of the Marines in country.

FMFPac CDR's Combat Readiness Report FY 1965

FMFPac CDR's Combat Readiness Report FY 1966

FMFPac CDR's Combat Readiness Report FY 1967

FMFPac CDR's Combat Readiness Report FY 1968

FMFPac Operations of the III MAF, Vietnam Mar-Sep 1965 (One single report covered all seven months).

FMFPac Operations of the III MAF, Vietnam Oct 65 to Feb 66

FMFPac Operations of US Marine Forces, Vietnam Mar 66 – Dec 68

III MAF Command Chronology May 65 – Dec 68

3D MARDIV Command Chronology Apr 65 – Feb 66

Message Files

These are original messages sent between senior Marine Corps officers. These messages often contained sentiments that were not recorded in official reports. SPECAT messages are Special Category messages, which are personal messages between senior officers, also referred to informally as 'back channel' messages. These provided a means by which senior officers could debate issues freely. The Air Control messages specifically related to the issue of control over US Marine Corps air assets in Vietnam, which was a particularly thorny issue. Unless otherwise specified all signals and messages referred to in this work have come from these files.

Commanding General's Personnel/Exclusive – Incoming 5 Sep 1965 - 7 Aug 1966
Commanding General's Personnel/Exclusive – Incoming 10 Feb - 8 Mar 1966
Commanding General's Personnel/Exclusive – Incoming 9 Mar - 19 Apr 1966
Commanding General's Personnel/Exclusive – Incoming 20 Apr - 26 Jun 1966
Commanding General's Personnel/Exclusive – Outgoing 26 Aug 1965 - 8 May 1967
Commanding General's Personnel/Exclusive – Outgoing 9 Mar - 22 Apr 1966
Commanding General's Personnel/Exclusive – Outgoing 22 Apr - 3 Jun 1966
FMFPac Messages Nov - Dec 67 11/1/1967
FMFPac SPECAT Exclusive – In and Out [Apr 1965] Jan - Aug 1965
FMFPac SPECAT Exclusive – In and Out Sep - Nov 1967
FMFPac SPECAT Exclusive – In and Out Dec 1967 - 20 Feb 1968
FMFPac SPECAT Exclusive – In and Out 21 Feb - Apr 1968 2/21/1968
FMFPac SPECAT Exclusive – In and Out May - Jun 1968 5/1/1968
FMFPac SPECAT Exclusive – In and Out Jul - Sep 1968 7/1/1968
FMFPac SPECAT Exclusive – In and Out Oct 1968 - Jan 1969 10/1/1968
III MAF Incoming Messages Sep 1965 - Dec 1968
III MAF Outgoing Messages Sep 1965 – Dec 1968
III MAF Air Control SPECAT Messages Volumes 1-3

General Wallace Greene Papers – Commandant of the Marine Corps

These papers were made available to the author at the US Marine Corps Historical Center, Washington DC. General Greene was not supposed to have kept notes on the meetings of the Joint Chiefs of Staff because the convention of 'collective responsibility' applied. After the Cuban Missile Crisis in 1961, however, the Chiefs of Staff did begin to keep their own notes in order to avoid the situation whereby they were accused of taking certain positions and could not provide any evidence to the contrary.

Notes from Joint Chiefs conference with the President, dated 4 March 1964.
Memorandum for the Record: Conference with the President 081530 – 1740April65.
Memorandum for the Record, 28 April 1965.
Memorandum for the Record, HQ USMC, Washington DC, 28 Jun 1965.
Memorandum for the Record written on 10 July 1965.
Record of Conference on Southeast Asia held at the White House, 221150 July 1965.
Memorandum for the Record, Developments in the Southeast Asia Situation, 24 Jun 1966.
Conference, CMC with Vice President Humphrey, Tuesday 25 October 1966.
Memorandum for the Record, I Corps Estimate (Force Requirements and Long Range Estimates for I Corps, RVN), 7 November 1966.

Signals and Messages

Abrams, General Creighton, *Civilian Situation in Quang Tri City,* Message for General Westmoreland, dated 22 Feb 1968, III MAF Outgoing Message File, Feb 1968, p185.

Cushman, General Robert, message to General Westmoreland, *CY67 Assessment*, pp2-3, III MAF Outgoing Message File, Jan 1968.

Cushman, General Robert, *Discussion of General Cushman and General Momyer as directed by MACV 171206Z Jan 68*, Secret SPECAT Exclusive Message for General Westmoreland , dated 18 Jan 1968, III MAF Outgoing Message file.

Cushman, General Robert, *MACV Forward*, Top Secret SPECAT Exclusive message for General Chapman and General Krulak, dated 27 Jan 1968, FMFPac SPECAT Exclusive Message File Dec 1967 – 20 Feb 1968, p157.

Cushman, General Robert, Gen *Abrams' Visit to Discuss MACV Forward*, Top Secret SPECAT Exclusive message for General Chapman and General Krulak, dated 27 Jan 1968, FMFPac SPECAT Exclusive Message File Dec 1967 – 20 Feb 1968.

Krulak, General Victor, Message from CGFMFPac to CG III MAF dated 23 2215Z Mar 66. Commanding General's Personnel/Exclusive Incoming Message File – 9 Mar – 19 Apr 1966. Held at US Marine Corps Historical Division at time of writing.

Krulak, General Victor, Message from CG FMFPAC to Commandant of the Marine Corps, DTG 130222Z Aug 66, III MAF Incoming Message file, August 1966.

Krulak, General Victor, Signal to Major General Fields, 270822Z Aug 66. III MAF Incoming Message File August 1966.

Krulak, General Victor, *Planned Operations – Substance of III MAF's Campaign Plan for 4th Quarter, CY 67*, SPECAT Exclusive Marine Corps Eyes Only Message to General Greene, 19 Sep 1967, FMFPac SPECAT Exclusive message file Sep – Nov 1967.

Krulak, General Victor, Top Secret exclusive SPECAT message for General Chapman, dated 13 Jan 1968. III MAF Incoming Message file, Jan 1968.

Krulak, General Victor, Secret SPECAT Exclusive Marine Corps Eyes Only message to General Cushman, dated 17 Jan 68, FMFPac SPECAT Exclusive Message File Dec 1967 – 20 Feb 1968.

Krulak, General Victor, 'Last Night's Discussion with Westy re Organizational Changes in ICTZ', Top Secret SPECAT Exclusive message for General Cushman, dated 27 Jan 1968, FMFPac SPECAT Exclusive Message File Dec 1967 – 20 Feb 1968.

Krulak, General Victor, Top Secret SPECAT Exclusive message for General Cushman, dated 27 Jan 1968, FMFPac SPECAT Exclusive Message File Dec 1967 – 20 Feb 1968.

Krulak, General Victor, CG FMFPac message to CG III MAF (General Chapman) dated 27 Feb 1968, contained in FMFPAC SPECAT Exclusive Message file 21 Feb to Apr 1968.

Sharp, Admiral U.S.G. , message to Commander Amphibious Forces Pacific (COMPHIBPAC), dated 14 October 1967. FMFPac SPECAT Exclusive Message File, Sep – Nov 1967.

Miscellaneous Documents

3rd Marine Division, OPPLAN 37-64 for RLT CO, dated 18 Aug 1964. Obtained from US Marine Corps Historical Center, Washington DC.

3rd Marine Division (Forward), *G-3 Journal, May 1965*. Obtained from US Marine Corps Historical Center, Washington DC.

3rd Marine Division, *Lessons Learned* (Da Nang, Vietnam: May 1965, 3rd Marine Division Lessons Learned File 1965. Obtained from US Marine Corps Historical Center, Washington DC.

III MAF Force Order 5401.1 dated 5 Sep 1966, *Establishment of the Psychological Operations Section*, attached to Annex E, Part II, Section IX, III MAF *Command Chronology, Feb 1967*. Obtained from US Marine Corps Historical Center, Washington DC.

III MAF, *Division Bulletin 5726*, 31 Oct 1965. Obtained from US Marine Corps Historical Center, Washington DC.

III MAF *Periodic Intelligence Report 20-67* dated 21 May 1967, pp4 and 13-14. III MAF Periodic Intelligence Report File No 17. Obtained from US Marine Corps Historical Center, Washington DC.

III MAF, *Periodic Intelligence Report 2-68*, dated 14 January 1968. III MAF Periodic Intelligence File 1 Jan – 25 Feb 1967. Obtained from US Marine Corps Historical Center, Washington DC.

III MAF, G3 Section, *Agenda Subject: RF/PF Status and Improvement*, 5 Jan 1966, pp 4-5, Enclosure to III MAF *Command Chronology Jan 1966*. Obtained from US Marine Corps Historical Center, Washington DC.

Clement, Lt. Col. D. A. *Staff Study to Determine Data on the USMC-Assisted Summer/Fall 1965 Rice Harvest*. Da Nang, Vietnam: HQ III MAF, 26 Nov 1965. Enclosure 7 to III MAF *Command Chronology, Nov 1965*. Obtained from US Marine Corps Historical Center, Washington DC.

FMFPac, *Chronology of Political Unrest in I Corps – 9 Mar – 23 Jun 1966*. Obtained from US Marine Corps Historical Center, Washington DC.

Walt, General Lewis B., *Marine Corps Bulletin 5700: The Nature of the War in Vietnam*, HQ US Marine Corps, Washington, DC, March 1969. Obtained from US Marine Corps Historical Center, Washington DC.

United States Marine Corps, "FMF Organization and Composition Report: The Division", *Marine Corps Gazette*, April 1957

United States Marine Corps, "FMF Organization and Composition Report: Fire Support", *Marine Corps Gazette*, June 1957

United States Marine Corps, "FMF Organization and Composition Report: Service Elements", *Marine Corps Gazette*, July 1957

United States Marine Corps Field Manuals

Department of Defense. *Counterinsurgency Field Manual*. Chicago, IL: University of Chicago Press, 2007.

United States Marine Corps. *Operations Against Guerrilla Forces, FMFM 21.* Washington, DC: HQ USMC, 1962.

United States Marine Corps. *Operations against Guerrilla Forces, FMFM 8-2.* Washington, DC: HQ USMC, 1964.

United States Marine Corps, *Operations against Guerrilla Forces, FMFM 8-2.* Washington, DC: HQ USMC, 1967.

United States Army Manuals

Department of the Army. *Field Service Regulations–Operations, Field Manual 100-5.* Washington, DC: Department of the Army, 1954.

United States Army. *Operations against Irregular Forces, FM 31-15.* Washington, DC: Department of the Army, 1961.

United States Army, *Guerrilla Warfare and Special Forces Operations, FM 31-21.* Washington, DC: Department of the Army, 1961.

HQ Department of the Army, *Field Manual 3-24: Counterinsurgency* (Washington DC: HQ Department of the Army, 2006). Simultaneously published by the US Marine Corps as *Marine Corps Warfighting Publication 3-33.5: Counterinsurgency.*

Correspondence

Krulak, General Victor, Letter to Secretary of Defense Robert McNamara, 9 May 1966. Krulak Papers, Alfred M Gray Research Center, US Marine Corps University, Quantico, VA

Krulak, General Victor, Letter to Secretary of the Navy, 17 July 1966. Krulak Papers, Alfred M Gray Research Center, US Marine Corps University, Quantico, VA

Interviews

General Victor Krulak, US Marine Corps Historical Division, Oral History Section. Interview conducted by Frank Benis on 23 June 1970. Transcript at US Marine Corps Historical Center, Washington DC.

General Victor Krulak. US Marine Corps Historical Division, Oral History Section. Interview conducted by Frank Benis on 22 June 1970. Transcript at US Marine Corps Historical Center, Washington DC.

Papers and Articles

RAND Corporation. *Counterinsurgency: A Symposium, April 16-20, 1962.* Santa Monica, CA: Rand Corporation, 1963.

Krulak, General Victor. *A Strategic Concept for the Republic of Vietnam.* Strategic Paper. June 1965. Held at US Marine Corps University Archives, Quantico, Virginia.

Miscellaneous Documents

Military

COMUSMACV, "Letter of Instruction Governing Operations of the III Marine Expeditionary Force in the Republic of Vietnam" dated 5 May 1965 held as Enclosure 1 to III MAF *Command Chronology, July 1965*. Obtained from US Marine Corps Historical Center, Washington DC.

COMUSMACV, *Letter of Instruction (LOI – 4)*, 21 November 1965, enclosure 2 to III MAF, *Command Chronology, November 1965*. Obtained from US Marine Corps Historical Center, Washington DC.

Lemnitzer, General Lyman. *Counterinsurgency Operations in South Vietnam*, Memorandum for General Taylor, 18 October 1961 <http://www.mtholyoke.edu/acad/intrel/pentagon2/doc102.htm>

Thi, Brigadier General Nguyen Chanh, Letter to CG III MAF authorizing expansion of Da Nang TAOR, 20 July 1965. Enclosure 4 to III MAF *Command Chronology, July 1965*. Obtained from US Marine Corps Historical Center, Washington DC.

Walt, General Lewis, *Personal Evaluation of Lieutenant General Nguyen Chanh Thi by Lieutenant Lewis W. Walt, US Marine Corps*, document prepared for the Commandant of the Marine Corps, HQ USMC, Washington DC, 6 April 1966. Obtained from US Marine Corps Historical Center, Washington DC.

Foreign Relations of the United States Series (FRUS)

Notes of Meeting attended by President Johnson, Dean Rusk, Robert McNamara, Jack Valenti and Bill Moyers, Document 109, FRUS, Volume IV, Vietnam 1966,

General William Westmoreland, Telegram to the Joint Chiefs of Staff, Saigon, Vietnam, 6 Mar 1965. FRUS, Volume II, Vietnam. Available at

Ambassador Maxwell Taylor, *Telegram From the Embassy in Vietnam to the State Department*, Saigon, Vietnam, 7 Mar 1965, FRUS, Volume II, Vietnam.

Honolulu Meeting: Record of Conclusions and Decisions for Further Action, FRUS Volume IV, Vietnam 1966, Document 83

Notes of Meeting, White House, 2 April 1966. FRUS, Volume IV, Vietnam 1966, Document 109.

1966 Program to Increase The Effectiveness of Military Operations and Anticipated Results Thereof, State Department, Washington DC, 23 February 1966, FRUS Volume IV, Vietnam 1966, Document 70.

Telephone Conversation between President Johnson and the Indian Ambassador (Nehru), , State Department, Washington DC, 10 February 1966, FRUS, Volume IV, Vietnam 1966, Document 71.

Telegram from the Embassy in Vietnam to the Department of State, State Department, Washington DC, 9 March 1966, FRUS, Volume IV, Vietnam 1966, Document 91.

Telegram from the Embassy in Vietnam to the Department of State, State Department, Washington DC, 23 March 1966, FRUS, Volume IV, Vietnam 1966, Document 100.

Mount Holyoke College Online Vietnam Archive

Pentagon Papers, Gravel Edition, Volume Two, Chapter Two <http://www.mtholyoke.edu/acad/intrel/pentagon2/pent4.htm>

General Lyman Lemnitzer, *Counterinsurgency Operations in South Vietnam,* Memorandum for General Taylor, 18 October 1961. The Pentagon Papers, Gravel edition, Volume Two <http://www.mtholyoke.edu/acad/intrel/pentagon2/doc102.htm>

Political

US Congress, House, *Joint Resolution to Promote the Maintenance of International Peace and Security in Southeast Asia,* HR 1145, 88th Congress, 2nd Session, introduced in House August 10, 1964.

General David Petraeus, 'Report to the US House of Representatives on the Situation in Iraq', *Testimony to the US House of Representatives Committee on Foreign Affairs and Armed Services Committee,* 10 September 2007 <https://20012009.state.gov/p/nea/rls/rm/2007/91966.htm>

Books

Adams, Sam, *War of Numbers* (Hanover, NH: Steerforth, 1998).

Allison, William. *The Tet Offensive.* (New York, NY: Mayflower Books, 2008).

Appy, Christian G, *Working-Class War: American Combat Soldiers and Vietnam* (Chapel Hill: University of North Carolina Press, 1993).

Bickel, Keith, *Mars Learning: The Marine Corps Development of Small Wars Doctrine 1915-1940* (Boulder: Westview Press, 2001).

Buzzanco, Robert, *Masters of War* (Cambridge: Cambridge University Press, 1997).

Cable, Larry, *Unholy Grail* (New York, NY: Routledge, 1991).

Callwell, Colonel C. E., *Small Wars: Their Principle and Practice* (London: HMSO, 1906).

Chang, Jung and Jon Halliday, *Mao: The Unknown Story* (London: Vintage, 2006).

Corson, Colonel William, *The Betrayal* (New York, NY: W.W Norton & Co, 1968).

Daddis, Gregory A., *Westmoreland's War: Reassessing American Strategy in Vietnam* (Oxford: Oxford University Press, 2014)

Davidson, Phillip, *Vietnam at War* (Oxford: Oxford University Press, 1991).

Fall, Bernard, *Street Without Joy* (Mechanicsburg: Stackpole Books, 1994).

Fawcett, Bill, *Hunters and Shooters* (New York, NY: W. Morrow and Co, 1995).

Finch, Michael P.M., *A Progressive Occupation? The Gallieni – Lyautey Method and Colonial Pacification in Tonkin and Madagascar, 1885-1900* (Oxford: Oxford University Press, 2013)

Freedman, Lawrence, *Kennedy's Wars* (Oxford: Oxford University Press, 2000).

Galula, David, *Counterinsurgency Warfare* (Westport: Praeger Security International, 2006 reprint of 1964 edition).

Galula, David, *Pacification in Algeria, 1956-1958* (Santa Monica: RAND Corporation, 2006 reprint of 1963 edition).

Gentile, Gian, *Wrong Turn: America's Deadly Embrace of Counterinsurgency* (New York: The New Press, 2013).

Gettleman, Marvin, *Vietnam and America* (New York, NY: Grove Press, 1995).
Giap, Nguyên Võ, *People's War, People's Army* (Seattle: University Press of the Pacific, 2001 reprint of 1961 original).
Goodson, Barry, *Cap Mot: The Story of a Marine Special Forces Unit in Vietnam, 1968-1969.* (Denton: University of North Texas Press, 1997).
Grinter, Lawrence and Peter Dunn, *The American War in Vietnam* (Westport: Greenwood Press, 1987).
Guevara, Ernesto, *Guerrilla Warfare* (Hawthorne, CA: BN Publishing, 2007).
Hearden, Patrick (ed.), *Vietnam: Four American Perspectives* (West Lafayette: Purdue University Press, 1990).
Henderson, Charles, *Marshalling the Faithful* (New York, NY: Berkley Books, 1993).
Hennessy, Michael, *Strategy in Vietnam: The Marines and Revolutionary Warfare in I Corps, 1965-1972* (New York, NY: Praeger, 1997).
Herring, George (ed.), *The Pentagon Papers: Abridged Version* (New York, NY: McGraw-Hill, 1993).
Hunt, Richard, *Pacification: The American Struggle for Vietnam's Hearts and Minds* (Boulder: Westview, 1995).
Jamieson, Neil, *Understanding Vietnam* (Berkeley: University of California Press, 1993).
Jones, Charles, *Boys of '67* (Mechanicsburg: Stackpole Books, 2006).
Kaiser, David, *American Tragedy* (Cambridge: Belknap Press of Harvard University Press, 2000).
Karnow, Stanley, *Vietnam: a History* (London: Pimlico, 1994).
Kilcullen, David, *Counterinsurgency* (New York, NY: Oxford University Press, USA, 2010).
Kinnard, Douglas, *The War Managers* (New York, NY: Da Capo Press, 1991).
Kitson, Frank, *Bunch of Five* (London, UK: Faber and Faber, 1977).
Kolko, Gabriel, *Anatomy of a War* (New York, NY: New Press, 1994).
Krepinevich, Andrew, *The Army and Vietnam* (Baltimore: Johns Hopkins University Press, 1988).
Krulak, Victor, *First to Fight* (Annapolis: Naval Institute Press, 1984).
Lee, Alex, *Utter's Battalion* (New York, NY: Ballantine Books, 2000).
Lehrack, Otto, *No Shining Armor* (Lawrence: University Press of Kansas, 1992).
Lehrack, Otto, *The First Battle* (New York, NY: Ballantine Books, 2006).
Lind, Michael, *Vietnam, the Necessary War* (New York, NY: Free Press, 1999).
MacDonald, Peter, *Giap the Victor in Vietnam* (New York, NY: Warner Books, 1994).
McMahon, Robert, *Major Problems in the History of the Vietnam War* (Boston: Houghton Mifflin, 2003).
McMaster, H.R., *Dereliction of Duty: Lyndon Johnson, Robert McNamara, the Joint Chiefs of Staff, and the Lies that led to Vietnam* (New York, NY: Harper Perennial, 1998).
McNamara, Robert, *In Retrospect: The Tragedy and Lessons of Vietnam* (New York, NY: Times Books, 1995).

Marr, David, *Vietnam 1945: The Quest for Power* (Berkley, CA: University of California Press, 1997).

Marston, Daniel and Carter Malkasian (eds.), *Counterinsurgency in Modern Warfare* (Oxford: Osprey, 2008).

Miller, John, *The Co-Vans* (Annapolis: Naval Institute Press, 2000).

Millett, Allan, *Semper Fidelis (*New York, NY: Free Press, 1991).

Milne, David, *America's Rasputin: Walt Rostow and the Vietnam War* (New York, NY: Hill and Wang, 2008).

Mumford, Andrew, *The Counterinsurgency Myth: The British Experience of Irregular Warfare* (Abingdon, Oxon: Routledge, 2012).

Murphy, Edward, *Semper Fi Vietnam* (Novato: Presidio, 1997).

Nagl, John, *Learning to Eat Soup with a Knife: Counterinsurgency Lessons from Malaya and Vietnam* (Chicago: University of Chicago Press, 2005).

Palmer, Bruce, *The 25-Year War* (New York, NY: Da Capo Press, 1990).

Palmer, Dave, *Summons of the Trumpet* (Novato: Presidio Press, 1995).

Paret, Peter and John Shy, *Guerrillas in the 1960s* (London: Pall Mall Press, 1962).

Parker, Captain William, *US Marine Corps Civil Affairs in Vietnam, April 1966 to April 1967* (Washington, DC: Historical Division, HQ US Marine Corps, March 1970).

Peterson, Michael, *The Combined Action Platoons: The US Marines' Other War in Vietnam* (New York, NY: Praeger, 1989).

Pike, Douglas, *PAVN* (New York, NY: Da Capo Press, 1991).

Pike, Douglas, *Viet Cong: The Organization and Techniques of the National Liberation Front in South Vietnam* (Cambridge, MA: MIT Press, 1966).

Podhoretz, Norman, *Why We Were in Vietnam* (New York, NY: Simon and Schuster, 1983).

Porter, Gareth, *Vietnam, a History in Documents* (New York, NY: New American Library, 1981).

Race, Jeffrey, *War Comes to Long An* (Berkeley: University of California Press, 1973).

Record, Jeffrey, *The Wrong War* (Annapolis: Naval Institute Press, 1998).

Schaffer, Ronald (ed.), *Small Wars Manual* (Manhattan: Sunflower University Press, 1996 reprint of 1940 original).

Sharp, Ulysses, *Strategy for Defeat* (Novato: Presidio Press, 1986).

Sheehan, Neil, *Bright, Shining Lie: John Paul Vann and America in Vietnam* (New York, NY: Picador, 1990).

Shore, Captain Moyers, *The Battle for Khe Sanh* (Washington, DC: Historical Branch, G-3 Division, HQ US Marine Corps, March 1969).

Shulimson, Jack and Major Charles Johnson, *US Marines in Vietnam: The Landing and the Buildup: 1965* (Washington, DC: History and Museums Division, US Marine Corps, 1978).

Shulimson, Jack, *The US Marines in Vietnam: An Expanding War 1966* (Washington, DC: History and Museums Division, HQ United States Marine Corps, 1982).

Shulimson, Jack, Lt. Col. Leonard Blaisol, Charles Smith and Capt. David Dawson, *US Marines in Vietnam: The Defining Year 1968* (Washington, DC: History and Museums Division, US Marine Corps, 1997).

Sorley, Lewis, *A Better War* (Orlando, FL: Harcourt, 2000).

Spector, Ronald, *After Tet* (New York, NY: Vintage Books, 1994).

Stolfi, Captain Russell *US Marine Corps Civic Action Effort in Vietnam, March 1965 to March 1966* (Washington, DC: Historical Branch, G-3 Division, HQ US Marine Corps, March 1968).

Summers, Colonel Harry, *On Strategy: A Critical Analysis of the Vietnam War* (Novato, CA: Presidio Press, 1982).

Swinton, Major General E.D. (writing as Lieutenant Backsight Forethought), *The Defence of Duffer's Drift* (London: William Clowes & Sons, 1904).

Tanham, George, *Communist Revolutionary Warfare: The Vietminh in Indochina* (London: Methuen, 1962).

Telfer, Major Gary, Lt. Colonel Lane Rogers and V. Keith Fleming, *US Marines in Vietnam: Fighting the North Vietnamese: 1967* (Washington, DC: History and Museums Division, HQ USMC, 1984).

Thompson, Sir Robert, *Defeating Communist Insurgency* (St Petersburg, FL: Hailer Publishing, Florida, 2005 reprint of 1966 edition).

Thompson, Sir Robert, *No Exit From Vietnam* (New York, NY: David McKay, 1970).

Thompson, Sir Robert, *Make for the Hills* (London: L. Cooper, 1989).

Trinquier, Roger, *Modern Warfare: a French View of Counterinsurgency* (New York, NY: Praeger Security International Paperback, 2006 reprint of 1964 edition).

Truong, Nhu, *A Vietcong Memoir* (New York, NY: Vintage Books, 1986).

Tse Tung, Mao, 'On Protracted War', from the *Selected Works of Mao Tse-tung Vol. 2* (Foreign Languages Press, Peking 1967) <http://www.marx2mao.com/Mao/PW38.html#s1>

Tse Tung, Mao, 'Problems of Strategy in Guerrilla War against Japan', from the *Selected Works of Mao Tse-tung* Vol.2 (Foreign Languages Press, Peking 1967). <http://www.marx2mao.com/Mao/PSGW38.html>

Valeriano, Napolean and Charles T.R. Bohannan, *Counter-Guerrilla Operations: the Philippine Experience* (New York, NY: Praeger Security International Paperback, 2006 reprint of 1962 edition).

Walt, General Lewis, *Strange War, Strange Strategy* (New York, NY: Funk & Wagnall's, 1970).

West, Francis, *The Village* (New York, NY: Pocket Books, 2003).

Westmoreland, General William C., *A Soldier Reports* (New York, NY: Da Capo Press, 1989).

Willbanks, James, *The Tet Offensive* (New York, NY: Columbia University Press, 2007).

Woodruff, Mark, *Unheralded Victory: Who Won the Vietnam War* (London: HarperCollins, 2000).

Woods, E. Thomas, and Donald Gregg, *Vietnam Declassified* (Lexington: The University Press of Kentucky, 2009).

Woods, Randall, *LBJ: Architect of American Ambition* (New York, NY: Free Press, 2006).

Articles and Papers

Marine Corps Gazette, "Silver Lance Ends; Mission Accomplished", (April 1965).

Time, "The Generals Smith", (Sep 18, 1944) <http://www.time.com/time/magazine/article/0,9171,796737,00.html>

Time, "The War: A Marine's Protest", (28 July 1968) <http://www.time.com/time/magazine/article/0,9171,841317-1,00.html>

Ang Cheng Guan, 'Decision-Making Leading to the Tet Offensive – The Communist Perspective', *Journal of Contemporary History*, Vol. 33, No. 3 (July 1998), pp. 341-353.

- 'Khe Sanh from the Perspective of the North Vietnamese', *War in History*, Vol. 8, No 1, (2001), pp.87-98.

Birtle, Andrew, "PROVN, Westmoreland, and the Historians: A Reappraisal", *The Journal of Military History*, 72 (October 2008), pp. 1217-1247.

Brush, Peter, "Perspectives -- Khe Sanh Could Have Been Another Dien Bien Phu if the NVA Had Cut Off the Marines' Water Supply" *Vietnam*, (August 1997), pp.58-60.

Clutterbuck, Richard, "Jungle Courier", *Marine Corps Gazette*, (June 1964), pp. 32-36;

- "Why Chi Keong Surrendered", *Marine Corps Gazette* (July 1964), pp.32-36;

- "An Anti-Communist Agent in Malaya", *Marine Corps Gazette* (August 1964), pp. 32-35.

Connable, Major Ben. "Culture Warriors: Marine Corps Organisational Culture and Adaptation to Cultural Terrain", *Small Wars Journal* website, (7 Feb 2008). <http://smallwarsjournal.com/mag/docs-temp/4-connable.pdf>

Fall, Bernard, "Street Without Joy", *Marine Corps Gazette* (January 1962), pp. 32-42.

- "Vo Nguyen Giap - Man and Myth", *Marine Corps Gazette* (August 1963), pp. 34-37.

Gentile, Gian, 'Misreading the Surge Threatens US Army's Conventional Capabilities', *World Politics Review*, 4 March 2009 <https://www.worldpoliticsreview.com/articles/1715/misreading-the-surge-threatens-u-s-armys-conventional-capabilities>

Hazelton, Jacqueline L., 'The "Hearts and Minds" Fallacy: Violence, Coercion, and Success in Counterinsurgency', *International Security*, 42:1 (Summer 2017), pp. 80-113.

Heinl, Lieutenant Colonel Robert D. "Small Wars – Vanishing Art?", *Marine Corps Gazette*,

Johnston, David E., *Doing What You Know: The United States and 250 Years of Irregular Warfare* (Washington, DC: Centre for Strategic and Budgetary Analysis, 2017).

Leinster, Colin. "The Two Wars of General Walt", *Life Magazine* (26 May 1967), pp. 77-84.

Liddell Hart, Basil. "Guerrilla War: Factors and Reflections", *Marine Corps Gazette*, (December 1962), pp. 22-27.

Moranto, Robert and Paula S. Tuchman, “Knowing the Rational Peasant; The Creation of Rival Incentive Structures in Vietnam” in *Journal of Peace Research*, Vol 29, No. 3 (August 1993), pp.249-264.

Paret, Peter, and John Shy, “Guerrilla War and US Military Policy”, *Marine Corps Gazette* (January 1962), pp.24-32.

Porter, D. Gareth ‘The 1968 “Hue Massacre”’, article in the *Indochina Chronicle*, No 33 (June 24, 1974), pp.2-13.

Robichaud, Colonel Clifford. “Silver Lance”, *Marine Corps Gazette* (July 1965), pp. 44-47.

Index

Index of People

Abrams, General Creighton 118, 128, 133
Ang Cheng Guan 121, 124, 130, 153

Bickel, Keith 10, 46, 49, 138, 149

Corson, William 77, 107
Cushman, General John H. 13, 117–119, 127–128, 145

Davidson, General Phillip 38, 49, 88, 114, 120, 129, 133, 136–137

Edson, Major General Merrill 'Red Mike' 45, 130
Eisenhower, President Dwight 9, 39

Galula, David 8, 15, 22–23, 27, 29–33, 36–38, 67, 100, 149
Giap, General Vo Nguyen, 14–15, 17–20, 52, 120, 131, 150, 153
Greene, General Wallace M. 13–15, 48, 55–57, 59–61, 63–64, 83, 116, 144–145

Ho Chi Minh 15, 17, 20, 121

Johnson, President Lyndon 13, 55–57, 59–60, 86, 91, 96, 116, 124, 148

Karch, Brigadier General Frederick J. 62, 65, 69–70
Kennedy, President John F. 22, 42, 47
Khrushchev, Nikita 21, 42
Kitson, Frank 33, 139
Komer, Robert 13, 99
Krepinevich, Andrew 39, 42–43, 78, 80, 83
Krulak, Major General Victor 10–11, 13, 22, 26, 29, 43–44, 49, 51–54, 58, 62–63, 69, 71–72, 78, 82–85, 89–90, 99, 110, 112–114, 118–119, 125–130, 139–142, 145, 147, 150

Ky, Prime Minister Nguyen Cao 86, 91–92, 94, 96

Lansdale, Edward 21, 33
LeMay, General Curtis 55–56
Lodge, Ambassador Henry Cabot 76, 86

Mao Zedong (Mao Tse Tung) 14–17, 42, 52, 149, 152
McMaster, H.R. 56, 60–61
McNamara, Robert 9, 26, 29, 42, 53, 56, 86, 88–89, 112–113, 147–148, 150
Mumford, Andrew 12, 38

Nagl, Colonel John 11, 32, 45, 111, 139–140, 151
Nguyen Van Man, Dr 92–93
Nixon, President Richard 13, 37, 136

Peterson, Michael 76, 78, 104, 107–108
Puller, Lieutenant General Lewis 'Chesty' 45, 138

Rostow, Walt 42, 151
Rusk, Dean 86, 148

Schaffer, Ronald 44, 46–47, 138
Sharp, Admiral Ulysses 53, 63–64, 86–87, 145, 151
Shoup, General David 43, 74
Shy, John 52, 151, 154
Stolfi, Captain Russell 67, 73, 102

Tanham, George 20, 33
Taylor, General Maxwell 28, 42, 55, 57, 60, 64, 66, 148–149
Thi, General Nguyen Chanh 62, 68–70, 91–93
Thompson, Sir Robert 15, 21–24, 27–33, 35–38, 53, 66–67, 76, 84, 100, 114, 139, 152
Trinquier, Roger 15, 22–23, 32–33, 37, 152

Walt, Major General Lewis 'Lew' 10, 12–13, 42, 44–45, 47, 54, 65–68, 72–74, 76–79, 81–82, 92–95, 99, 110, 113, 125, 138–140, 146, 148, 151–153
Westmoreland, General William 10–11, 35, 48, 56, 58–60, 62–66, 69, 72–73, 80, 82–83, 85–86, 88–89, 93, 97, 99, 111–114, 116–120, 124–130, 133, 140, 145, 148–149, 152–153
Wheeler, General Earle 60, 86, 126

Index of Places

I Corps Tactical Zone (ICTZ) 55, 64, 68, 71, 75, 78, 80, 90, 101, 103, 105, 109, 117–121, 123, 128–129, 132, 136, 145

Algeria 8, 15, 21–23, 29, 34–35, 37–38, 50, 66–67, 111, 149

California 17, 40, 54, 150–151
Cambodia 19, 55, 57, 73, 80, 114
Caribbean 10, 44–45, 47, 51–52, 139
Central Highlands 57, 80, 83
China 15–16, 37, 39, 42, 56
Chu Lai 9, 71–72, 79, 81, 100, 106, 125, 134, 142

Da Nang 9, 54–60, 62, 65, 67, 69–74, 78, 81, 92–94, 96, 99–100, 105–106, 114, 116–117, 119, 123–124, 130–134, 136, 140, 142–143, 146, 148
Demilitarised Zone 8, 88
Dien Bien Phu 19, 29, 32, 124, 127–128, 130, 153
DMZ 8, 54, 88, 99, 109, 112–114, 117–118, 125, 127, 129, 132, 135–136, 140
Dominican Republic 44, 46, 138

El Salvador 12, 139

Gulf of Tonkin 9, 32, 54

Haiti 44–46, 138
Hanoi 17, 21, 56, 86, 89, 121
Ho Chi Minh Trail 19, 73, 80
Hue 71, 81, 88, 92–94, 96, 100, 112, 120, 124, 128, 130–134, 136, 154

Indochina 8, 15, 20–22, 29, 32–34, 37, 50, 53, 62, 66–67, 152, 154
Iraq 11–12, 24, 27, 149

Japan 16–17, 40, 54, 152

Khe Sanh 13, 111, 113–115, 123–133, 140–141, 151, 153
Korea 39–40, 42, 46, 55, 99

Laos 19, 36, 55, 57, 73, 87, 112, 125–126, 132, 142
Latin America 44, 61, 139
Le My 71–72

Madagascar 8, 149
Malaya 11–12, 15–16, 21–24, 27–28, 31–34, 36–38, 40, 46, 50, 52–53, 66–67, 110–111, 139, 151, 153

Nicaragua 12, 43–46
North Korea 42
North Vietnam (NVN) / Democratic Republic of Vietnam (DRV) 8–9, 17, 19–21, 37, 55–58, 60, 80, 84, 87–88, 91, 95, 112–114, 117, 121, 124–127, 130, 132–134, 136
Northern Ireland 33, 36

Pacific 15, 40, 61, 126, 150
Peking 17, 42, 56, 152
Philippines 21, 33–34, 37, 40, 46, 67
Phu Bai 9, 69–72, 76, 81, 100, 106, 117, 120, 134, 142
Pleiku 9, 57

Quang Nam 69–70, 105
Quang Ngai 100, 121, 133
Quang Tri 82, 100, 114, 129, 132–133, 135, 145
Qui Nhon 9, 57

Saigon 28, 42, 59–61, 66, 77–78, 80, 82, 92–96, 100, 121, 130, 148
South Vietnam (SVN) / Republic of Vietnam (RVN) 8–9, 19–23, 28, 38, 53, 55–57, 59–60, 64–66, 68–69, 72–74, 84, 86–88, 90–91, 109, 112, 114, 117, 120–121, 125–126, 129, 132, 135–136, 140, 148–149, 151
Southeast Asia 9, 21–22, 42, 53–54, 57, 83, 88, 144, 149
Soviet Union 37, 39, 42

Thailand 31, 36
Thua Thien 69, 82

United States 8–13, 16–17, 39–41, 43, 47–48, 50, 56–57, 59–60, 62, 65, 73–75, 86, 88, 94–95, 116, 120, 138, 141, 143, 146–148, 151, 153

Washington, DC 11–13, 16, 27, 43, 47–48, 50, 53–56, 58–60, 62, 64, 67, 71, 75, 81–82, 86–87, 91–92, 94, 96, 100, 110, 115–116, 126, 128, 141, 144, 146–148, 151–153

Index of General & Miscellaneous Terms

1st Cavalry Division 80, 117, 129
1st Marine Air Wing (1st MAW) 54, 119
1st Marine Division 9, 40, 66, 82, 99, 116
2nd NVA Division 100, 123–124, 134
324B NVA Division 112, 114, 132
3rd Marine Division 9, 40, 54–55, 65–67, 71–72, 74–77, 116–117, 128–129, 143, 146
9th Marine Expeditionary Brigade (9th MEB) 9, 54–55, 59, 61, 65, 69, 72. See also III Marine Amphibious Force
9th Marine Regiment 65, 78
I Corps 55, 64–66, 69, 71, 75, 80, 83–84, 89–95, 99, 109, 121, 135, 144, 146, 150
III Marine Amphibious Force (III MAF) 9–10, 13, 24–25, 32, 47, 49, 59, 62–75, 77–82, 85–86, 89, 94–101, 103–114, 116–121, 123–129, 131–133, 135–136, 140–146, 148

Army of the Republic of Vietnam (ARVN), see South Vietnamese Army

Banana Wars (1898-1934) 44, 58, 110

Civil Operations and Revolutionary Development Support (CORDS) 13, 77, 99–100
Cold War 39, 42
Combined Action Platoons (CAPS) 44, 50, 74, 76–78, 84, 99–100, 102, 104, 106–108, 116, 120, 123, 134, 137, 139–140, 150–151
Commander, US Military Assistance Command Vietnam (COMUSMACV) 10, 63–66, 71, 81, 126, 142, 148
County Fair 99, 101–103

Demilitarised Zone (DMZ) 54, 99, 109, 112–114, 117–118, 125, 127, 129, 132, 135–136, 140

First Indochina War (1946-54) 8, 15, 21, 37
Fleet Marine Force Manual (FMFM) 21 47–49, 52, 67, 147
Fleet Marine Force Pacific 10, 22, 51, 53–54, 59, 63, 143

Geneva Accords 8, 19
Golden Fleece 50, 74, 78–79, 99, 140

Hogaboom Board 40–41, 58, 141
Hoi Chanhs 103–104
Honolulu conference 88–91, 97

Joint Chiefs of Staff (JCS) 10, 13, 22, 28, 40, 51, 53, 55–57, 59, 60, 64, 66, 87, 124, 126, 144, 148, 150
Joint Co-Ordinating Council (JCC) 74–75, 77, 99–100, 135, 139

Kit Carson Scouts 103–104
Korean War (1950-53) 10, 16, 43

Malayan Emergency (1948-60) 22, 36
Marine Corps Gazette 15, 40–41, 45–47, 51–52, 138, 140–141, 146, 153–154
Military Assistance Command Vietnam (MACV) 10, 56, 62–63

New Look Policy 39–40
North Vietnamese Army (NVA) / People's Army of Vietnam (PAVN) 9, 18–20, 24–25, 32, 38, 49, 54, 59, 68, 73, 80–83, 86–88, 95–101, 104, 106, 108–109, 111–115, 123–126, 128–136, 140, 151, 153

Operation Golden Fleece (1966) 78–79, 140
Operation Hastings (1966) 109, 112, 114
Operation Rolling Thunder (1965-68) 9, 57
OPPLAN 37-64 55–56, 146

People's Army of Vietnam (PAVN), see North Vietnamese Army
Popular Force 76, 94, 104–105

RAND Corporation 16, 22–23, 33–35, 37, 141,

147, 149
RAND Symposium 34, 36, 38
Republic of Vietnam Armed Forces (RVNAF) 59, 62, 64, 71, 90, 104

Second World War (1939-45) 12, 16–17, 40, 43–44, 46
Small Wars Manual 44–49, 67–68, 138, 151
South Vietnamese Army/Army of the Republic of Vietnam (ARVN) 9, 35, 56, 67, 71, 73, 75, 80, 91, 93–94, 96, 99, 102, 104, 112, 117, 122, 124, 128–129, 131–134, 136
Strategic hamlets 22, 27, 29–30, 102
Struggle Movement 93–96

Tet Offensive (1968) 13–14, 103, 115–117, 120–124, 126, 129–136, 141, 149, 152–153

US Air Force 119, 129
US Army 9–13, 21, 23, 37, 39–40, 42–43, 46–48, 57, 64, 83, 93, 99, 105, 109–110, 114–119, 123, 125, 129, 139, 141, 153

Viet Cong (VC) 8, 10, 15, 19–21, 23–24, 28, 32–33, 56–59, 65, 68, 70, 73, 74, 78–79, 81, 83–84, 89–91, 94–96, 101–105, 108, 110, 115, 136, 140
Viet Cong Main Force 19–20, 78, 81, 88–90, 100–101, 113, 136
Viet Minh 17, 19–20, 33